THE MYSTERY OF THINGS

The Mystery of Things is a philosophical reflection on the paradox of the psychoanalytical process, which objectifies psychic life through the deep subjectivity of its two engaged participants, a mysterious encounter which Christopher Bollas examines in creative and illuminating new ways.

The method of enquiry at the heart of psychoanalysis – the patient's free association, the analyst's evenly suspended attentiveness – runs contrary to everything that we are taught is the logical, rational, 'scientific' way to acquire knowledge. Yet it is only through using such an apparently illogical and subversive method that the patient's psychic truth can be articulated, a breakthrough not only in the treatment of pathological structures of thought and character, but a revolution in the Western mind's access to its unthought forms of knowledge.

In his inimitable and highly readable style, Christopher Bollas focuses on the wider implications of this form of knowing. Using clinical studies, he concentrates on the dilemma of bringing this method to those patients for whom the mind is long since an enemy of the self, and writing on creativity he shows how psychoanalysis offers new-found forms for personal liberation.

The Mystery of Things will appeal to students, professionals and the lay reader alike.

Christopher Bollas is a psychoanalyst in private practice in London. He is the author of *Shadow of the Object* (1987), *Forces of Destiny* (1989), *Being a Character* (1992), *Cracking Up* (1995) and *The New Informants: Betrayal of Confidentiality in Psychoanalysis and Psychotherapy* with David Sundelson (1995).

THE MYSTERY OF THINGS

Christopher Bollas

London and New York

First published 1999
by Routledge
11 New Fetter Lane, London EC4P 4EE

Simultaneously published in the USA and Canada
by Routledge
29 West 35th Street, New York, NY 10001

Routledge is an imprint of the Taylor & Francis Group

Typeset in Times by Routledge
Printed and bound in Great Britain by
Biddles Ltd, Guildford and King's Lynn

British Library Cataloguing in Publication Data
A catalogue record for this book is available from the British Library

Library of Congress Cataloging in Publication Data
Bollas, Christopher
The mystery of things / Christopher Bollas
p. cm
Includes bibliographical references and index.
1. Psychoanalysis. 2. Free association (Psychology).
3. Self. 4. Psychotherapy–Case studies. I. Title.
BF175.B57   1999
150.19'5–DC21. 98-53607

ISBN 0–415–21231–6 (hbk)
ISBN 0–415–21232–4 (pbk)

FOR LARS BEJERHOLM

...so we'll live,

And pray, and sing, and tell old tales, and laugh

At gilded butterflies, and hear poor rogues

Talk of court news; and we'll talk with them too –

Who loses and who wins, who's in, who's out –

And take upon's the mystery of things

As if we were God's spies...

(*King Lear*, Act V, Scene 3)

CONTENTS

CONTENTS

ACKNOWLEDGEMENTS

'Occasional madness of the psychoanalyst' was published under the title 'Regression in the countertransference' in *Master Clinicians on Treating the Regressed Patient*, edited by Boyer and Giovacchini (Jason Aronson). 'The place of the psychoanalyst' was published in *Psychoanalysis and Development*, edited by Ammaniti and Stern (New York University Press). 'Mental interference' was published in *The Mind Object*, edited by Corrigan and Gordon (Jason Aronson). 'Borderline desire' was published in the *International Forum of Psychoanalysis* (1996). 'Figures and their functions' was published in the *Psychoanalytic Quarterly* (1996). 'Wording and telling sexuality' was published in the *International Journal of Psychoanalysis* (1997). 'Origins of the therapeutic alliance' was delivered to the English Speaking Congress and published by the Congress in 1989 and then by the *International Forum of Psychoanalysis* in 1998. Permission from the above publishers to include these essays is much appreciated. Lines from THE CANTOS OF EZRA POUND by Ezra Pound. Copyright ©1934, 48 by Ezra Pound. Reprinted by permission of New Directions Publishing Corp. for the US and Canada, and Faber and Faber Ltd for the British Commonwealth.

INTRODUCTION

Freud's invention of the psychoanalytical method has radically transformed Western epistemology. In order to know what we think we are requested to relinquish the understandable demand to be scrupulous and objective – in contemporary terms to be scientific – and abandon ourselves to the apparently loose enterprise of speaking whatever crosses our mind. To Western minds, cultivated in a patriarchal order that privileges mental adventures so long as they are mediated by custodians of consciousness, the free associative method seems not simply lax but subversive. What does it mean to seek an understanding of our inner life by abandoning ourselves to talk, talk, talk, and more talk?

The location of analysis – often a room in the analyst's home, or a living-room setting in an office building – is unlike the corporate, scientific, theological, or academic enterprises. And to lie down in the presence of an other? In most European settings, the analysand reclines on a bed, head on a pillow while the interlocutor sits out of sight, in comparative silence, urging the patient to say whatever happens to cross his mind at that moment. This seems more like a counterculture, perhaps deriving authority from the world and work of women – especially mothers – who are more than accustomed to taking the other into care, into a silence with many voices speaking through forms of unconscious communication.

As I shall argue, neither Freud nor the psychoanalytical movement that followed found this discovery an easy one. Like all of us, Freud needed certainties and he spared little time in telling us (in his twenty-three volumes) what motivated man and why. But his method was also to be his foil. For in requesting this kind of talk Freud released us all to be continuously mysterious to ourselves and others. The free associating analysand loses himself in speech, often saying something like 'I can't understand why I am talking about this, because I had fully intended before the session began to talk about something else'. As the narrative moves in puzzling ways, patients become informatively incoherent and they learn that the analyst wants them to speak passing ideas occurring in the back of the mind, caught up as they are in the logic of a narrative about something quite unrelated. 'But if I tell you what I am thinking, I won't make sense' is an understandable cry, yet in time they may come to appreciate this remarkable and strange freedom to speak in fragments, each telling a small cameo of a different order of thought.

The therapeutic genius of this method is that it quite naturally breaks down the paralysing authority of any symptom or pathological structure. For example, imagine a person caught up in a delusion that years ago he was infected by a friend's cologne, and convinced that this was the moment when he lost his passion for reading Rilke and was forced to read Pound whom he cannot bear. Anyone caught up in a delusion is incarcerated in a fixed idea and even if they accept from time to time that it is crazy, it remains an unmovable structure. Until, that is, the deluded person is asked to free associate. 'What comes to mind when you think of "cologne"?' is not simply a question: it is a key that will open a passageway to many unrelated ideas bound in the delusion. Asking questions begins to break down the structure of a delusion. Indeed, the deluded person can feel this, and commonly enough will resist the threat. 'What has this question to do with anything?' he might ask. Of course the analyst does not know. Which is exactly the point. The question and the method with which it participates break open certainties, delusional, or…psychoanalytic.

Analysts have the somewhat thankless task of supporting a process that undermines the intellectual sanctity of analytically acquired truths. So analysts have tended to push free association to one side as they have moved towards a greater assertion of their own findings. This is regrettable if understandable, as patients are hard enough to comprehend as it is, without having to employ a method that fosters profound mystery.

The first six chapters of the book include essays that focus on the nature and effects of the free associative process that is at the heart of the psychoanalytic method.

Chapters 7 to 12 comprise clinical studies of madness, especially the self's alienation from mind. Whether we are talking about an obsessional person who must follow bizarre dictates before being free to get on with daytime life, a depressive patient whose mind punishes the self remorselessly, or a schizoid person who seems curiously impelled to act out scripts offered up by the mind, madness finds its theatre in psychoanalysis as nowhere else. To some extent, the patient's mental illness is incarcerating and thus organising so the analyst's interpretive work will have essential limits, but mental illnesses – or perhaps more accurately character complexes – are also rather wonderful, if painful, mysteries. To work one's way through the maze of such complexities to reach an understanding of why the self is arrested by its lived experience is deeply fascinating and profoundly meaningful. We may wonder if one of the purposes of mental disturbance is to promote thought, forcing the self into self awareness.

Mental illness or psychological suffering brings people to analysis and, ironically enough, makes this work compelling to both participants. Although I shall use terms like 'pathologic structure' to discuss forms of illness, these ailments are more like curiosities of character that impose repeated patterns of thought and action upon the self and the other. They are restricted forms of being, but they may also be strange distillations of the experience of living, frozen cameos of a self's experience of being, presented as enigmas. The interpretive work of analysis, then, is not simply an engagement with the self's pathology or mental illness, but with any self's distilled experience of its own enigmatic formation, calling out for interpretation.

Perhaps people need to have 'a problem', one that is frequently at the forefront of the mind. It may be a symptom or a character anomaly, but it may also be a vexatious question like 'shall I marry Jim or Bernie?' or 'should I move to the country or the seaside?' or 'should I give up life as a musician and become a psychotherapist?' Everyone seems to have one set of such problems that refuse to go away, or if they do, another set happily takes its place. We may think of these seemingly ordinary problems as mysterious not because they defy solution but because they are the dilemmas selected by any self out of the quotidian, ordinary problems which we seem to need to live by.

Writing about psychoanalytical work is as challenging as trying to describe a symphony or a painting, yet what we find from these explorations is at times wonderful, full of mystery, so I write for lay readers as well as for the psychoanalysts, because what we discover in this work should be of much wider interest. In Chapters 13–16 I discuss several of the more mysterious features of self: what we mean by embodiment and how wording and telling brings sexuality into discourse. No doubt, by association, the chapter on creativity extends this question; what forms do we choose to transform the self?

Readers of my earlier works will find a continuation and further elaboration of certain ideas, particularly the concept of human idiom, or that peculiar form of being called 'self' which seeks lived experience to realise its own particular aesthetic intelligence. 'Character is that which reveals personal choice, the kinds of thing a man chooses or rejects when that is not obvious' writes Aristotle in the *Poetics*. Our idiom reveals itself through these choices and, as Winnicott argued, through the way we make use of the objects of life. A form of desire, this choosing is the expression of any self's destiny, the aim of which is to realise one's own form of being through experience. We sense this drive to present and to represent our self as if it were an intelligent life force, and it is from this inner sense of destiny that we unconsciously create our belief in divinity.

The chapter on creativity and psychoanalysis examines how art objects are distillations of a self, or form objects that momentarily objectify the aesthetic effect of being a self.

Finally, however, something runs through us that cannot be gathered into representation, either that of illness or art. 'Fortunate he who's made the voyage of Odysseus' writes Seferis in 'Reflections on a Foreign Line of Verse', 'Fortunate if on setting out he's felt the rigging of a love strong in his body, spreading there like veins where the blood throbs'. Because if so it yields:

> A love of indissoluble rhythm, unconquerable like music
> and endless
> because it was born when we were born and when we die
> whether it dies too neither we know nor does anyone else.

Something of a mystery to the very end.

1

ORIGINS OF THE THERAPEUTIC ALLIANCE

Understandably people on the verge of psychoanalysis are anxious about such an undertaking, but it is striking that they take to it in a remarkably natural way. Why? On what basis do they agree to this curious division of function, they as free associating speaker, the analyst as 'evenly suspended' listener?

Perhaps the concept of the therapeutic alliance recognises an essential partition within the analysand: an intense, anguished, dreamy, illogical and sometimes child-like part, and another, not completely absorbed by such intense private realities, an observer cooperating with the analyst, countering such intense states with delay, with insight, and often enough with understanding.

The analysand seems to understand that analysis works if he submits to a process which holds him as he free associates. Giving up narrative control to become a certain sort of subject within a process guided by the intelligence of the other may be unconsciously familiar, as the foetus has been inside the mother, the infant inside a world largely managed by the mother, and the child all the while inside the logic of family structure. The partitioning of self in the analytic process, when one gives up focalised consciousness to become part of a psychic evolution derived from more than one consciousness, is a division which each person knows, though to varying extents.

Even if we disagree over whether a foetus has a sense of being inside a womb, or when and how an infant perceives the mother, perhaps we can agree that at some point infants have a sense of some external organising intelligence (for the foetus it would be the spirit of the biological work of the uterus) to which they are allied, which they are inside, but about which they have limited knowledge. Allowing for the infant's subjective capability, for his capacity to render his experience of place in that psychic area available to him, we may assume that he knows he is part of an intelligence beyond his thinking and yet it is essential to his physical and psychic well-being, if not survival.

In other words, infants know that they are inside a human process, which Winnicott termed a holding environment, that contains them, and the alterations sponsored in the infant's psychosomatic states by this other contributes to the sense of this being a transformational situation: one that recurrently alters self experience.

Alongside the mother is the father's transforming presence, and eventually the child recognises that he is inside a very particular family with its ways of being and relating. The Oedipal stage is, in many respects, the discovery that one's fate is to be inside a complex, consisting of the family and an internal world of one's own making.

Hence the analysand will unconsciously perceive the treatment alliance as a derivative of earlier alliances that goes back to the formation of being: to a foetal sense of being inside a uterine intelligence, and to the increased sense in infancy that one is inside a container that is alive, psychic (in the sense of unconsciously determinative) and consequential. To varying degrees this experience of being inside a process to which one contributes will be transferred to the clinical space as the patient reconstructs his experience of being contained by the body and psyche of the other.

Thus people ally with the process of analysis, not simply with the person of the analyst. The two alliances are not the same. If the patient attends regularly, lies on the couch, free associates and expresses himself in the transference, he is allied to the analytic procedure. How a particular patient uses this process will depend on his earlier psychic alliances with containers such as the womb, the mother, the father and the mind itself. Naturally how the analysand uses or relates to the person of the analyst (differentiated from the process in which both are participants) is of enormous significance, particularly when juxtaposed to the use of the alliance. If he uses the analytical process to eliminate the analyst's interpretations, for example, or abandons participation in the analytic method and relates more to the person of the analyst, he is conveying a great deal about his previous alliances.

Indeed a part of any therapeutic alliance is the mutual recognition and use by patient and analyst of the analytical process which precedes, holds and will outlive any specific analytical couple, and which is implicitly present as a third object. It cannot, of course, go without saying that the psychoanalyst – for innumerable reasons – can lose his alliance with the third object such as when he dispenses with requests for free association, or abandons the essential ballast of silence to make interpretations.

Analyst and analysand are part of something which in a certain sense guides them in a most paradoxical way. To work together they must seemingly abandon one another. The patient must abandon his normal social behaviour and lose himself in a method which becomes a new means of self expression. The analyst must abandon his wish to be helpful, decline the patient's requests for immediate therapeutic remedy, and immerse himself in a receptive attitude, open to the patient's unconscious communications, if he is to receive his analysand's internal world.

Both participants know that each becomes a temporarily lessened consciousness, and analysable patients are often very aware that their analyst's interpretations come from that place of essential psychic devolution where the analyst lives while listening to and being in-formed by the other. Recognition of the particular nature of the analyst's comments – emerging into speech from evenly hovering attentiveness – further consolidates each contributor's role in the alliance to the method. The patient appreciates the analyst's alliance to a method that must be prior to the analyst's experiential relations to the patient (transferential and countertransferential). The analysand knows that each must enter the process in order to form any alliance that will eventually prove therapeutic.

It is no accident that Freud took the dream as the cornerstone of psychoanalysis, where the person splits into two basic psychic structures: the 'simple self' who is the experiential subject inside the dream; and the organising intelligence that creates the dream environment and gives it meaning. This mirrors the split of foetal and infant life, of a simple self immersed inside a complex intelligence, a structure which becomes part of the nature of intrapsychic life. Nor should it elude our notice that the simple self's experience of the cosmology-creating work of the unconscious ego psychically substantiates the conviction that we live inside a mysterious intelligence.

When we wake from a dream, we reflect on it and understand something of it with that complex self which is able to consider its many parts while the simple participant self is too caught up in (or 'enlisted by') the ego's theatre to observe.

In analysis the person is deconstructed by projections, diverging self experiences, shifting moods and free associations, becoming a comparatively simple participant who does not know, joined by the analyst who also devolves self consciousness to the free movement of thought, the better to be informed of his patient's psychic effect. Patients know that they and their analysts use the analytical process to maximise the registrations of psychic life, licensed by periodic loss of the ambitions of consciousness.

In the dream a simple self is repeatedly inside a highly complex theatre of eventful thoughts and allegorical personages, which constitutes an intrapsychic warrant for the treatment alliance. As each analysand has just been inside a process of projective renderings of his complexity into words, images, events and feelings – walked through them as the simple experiencing self in the dream – now when he enters the analytical space to freely realise this complexity through the gaps of meaning latent to the chains of signifiers, the iconic hieroglyphs of visual images, the allegory of persons composed, the mnemic function of persons resurrected from the past, he seems to create another space and another purpose for dream life.

When Freud divided the analytical couple in two – the one to free associate and report dreams, the other to evenly hover and then interpret – he cannily exploited an ordinary partition between subjective and objective states of mind, oscillating between more or less deeply subjective renderings of reality and more or less objective reflections upon prior subjective states. Often lost in thought, perhaps inside a daydream, or just perambulating through preconscious senses of part ideas, part memories, part instinctual representations, we emerge to think more clearly, incisively and even systematically before we return to more subjective states of self. This recurring oscillation between two mental positions (subjective/objective) is essential to process life's episodes and one's contextual state of affairs. Recognition of this need contributes to the analysand's unconscious realisation and use of the analytical relation which places intrapsychic life into interpersonal space so that the analyst could eventually affect the nature of the patient's psychic structure.

This oscillation between the self immersed in its complexity (associations and projections) and a more reflective self subsequently objectifying those states (dissociations and reflections) is also the structure of inner speech: split as we are between the speaker (the I) and the addressed (the you). We often employ this rhetorical split in order to mediate between unconscious derivatives and perceptions proper. When the analysand speaks freely he does so not just to an historic object from the transference, but also to the rhetorical other: the you who never replies. (Only the I speaks in inner speech.) The analyst's silence allies with the rhetorical you of intrapsychic discourse, and contributes to unconscious recognition of the nature of the analytical partnership.

There are fateful alliances between the self in the dream and the dreamer, between the I and the you of internal speech, and between the I and the world of reported objects, that serve as structural precedents for the psychoanalytic relationship. In order to think psychic reality, one of the characters in the split must be the simple self abandoning focus to the other part(ner). The working alliance recognises the need for episodic lessened consciousness in the interests of increased unconscious representations (in dreams, daydreams, perambulatory ideas, creative processes) as well as the need for equally recurring moments of reflective observation, scrutiny and analysis. This essential internal contract, an ordinary feature of mental life, is the division of labour constructed by the separate roles of analyst (reflective, observant, scrutinising, analysing) and of patient (dreaming, daydreaming, free associating, ideationally perambulating).

The subject is summoned to think about his life because he is confronted by its mystery. From *mysterium*, originally a 'supernatural thing', or also in Latin a *mysterium*, a secret rite, mystery now means 'something unexplained, unknown' or 'any thing or event that remains so secret or obscure as to excite curiosity'. An infant lives inside a world substantially beyond comprehension and most deeply mysterious, and partly because of its novelty (which Daniel Stern stresses) it invites what Melanie Klein

8

emphasised, the 'epistemophilic instinct': a drive to know. This drive is an essential part of one's encounter with the mysteries of life, from the ordinary recurring mystery show of dreams, to the secret of the internal world, to the enigmas of the universe and of the physical world that inspires scientific curiosity and work. Theological explanation of this world of ours, and our place in it, is an essential endeavour to think about the complexities of life, but its premature vision, sustained now by anaemic faith, testifies to the strain of trying to know more than one does.

Patients and analysts enter into an alliance that aims to examine and change pathological mental contents through the analyst's interpretive work and containing function and in so doing to alter psychic structure itself. Some, having significantly benefited from this process, institute a type of negative therapeutic reaction which seems to destroy the alliance. One patient, for example, echoed every word I uttered in a session. Many attempt to turn the tables, demanding to know what the analyst 'really thinks', not what he says he thinks.

There is something ordinary – indeed perhaps rather essential – about this challenge to the alliance. Living as the comparative simple selves of consciousness, in our mother's system of care, our family's complex, our dreams, our polyphonic sequentials of self experience, the you that receives the I's discourses, there is a natural curiosity to know what drives the entirety. The infant and dreamer: 'Where is this all coming from?' The self at experience: 'What organises and generates all these different experiencings I am having?' 'How can I turn this wheel that turns my life, / Create another hand to move this hand / Not moved by me, who am not the mover' writes Edwin Muir in 'The Wheel'. But who shall ever be there to answer such questions, even though Faust is the tale of one who requested just that?

Then one day, in Western civilisation, the psychoanalyst appeared, upholder and guardian of a process that evoked some of the mysteries of human life. Did he know that the structure of the analytical process could evoke the transfer of so many different if interconnected alliances: of foetus inside womb, infant inside maternal world, child inside the Law of the Father, child inside family complexity, self inside the dream, addressee inside the textures of the I's discourses? Did he know the extent and range of what he elicited by creation of the analytical space?

Because of the uncannily evocative effect of the psychoanalytic structure, many analysands, inside a mystery play, seek the secret of its intelligence, like the infant seeking knowledge of the mother's unconscious, the dreamer the other who dreams him, the self the *ur* source of self experiencing. A form of noumenal transference, the subject insists upon breaking through the derivatives to find the real or the thing in itself, just as Captain Ahab insisted on finding the actual white whale which he felt surely would be like breaking through 'the pasteboard masks of all outward presentiments'. It is this which destroys the intrapsychic working alliance that operates through an illusion that the world we imagine is the real one, even as we nourish the forces of psychic reality that continually transform it. Rather than transferring a mental content to the psychic person of the analyst, the noumenal transference bears an epistemophilic demand to the presumed intelligence informing the analytic process. From this demand answers about the true nature of reality are meant to emerge, a reversal of negative capability: a wilful insistence of evidence for belief.

The analysand who challenges the working alliance may express a noumenal transference as he challenges illusion in order to see the real: the real analyst, the real intelligence assumed to be there somewhere guiding the movements of the analysis. Analysis of the destructive, paranoid and primal scene derivatives may not suffice, as the extent to which this action characterises the destruction of any working alliance necessitates a recognition of what the analysand actually seeks.

Analysands are shocked to find their analyst in the street, a surprise deriving from the feeling that he has just glimpsed the analyst as he really is, functioning in his real world. However pleasing such an encounter, it is always on the verge of the traumatic as the analyst, now in the real, seems to erupt in the field of culturally endowed objects.

To come towards the end of an analysis – just as one approaches the end of life – knowing much more about oneself, possessed of new and valued visions, but still feeling that life is deeply mysterious, can be hard. Do analysands break the alliance to ask who really runs this show? The fact that no one may, that it just is, and that we just are, may drive many to disprove the processive cure of analysis by aiming to see through the person of the analyst.

On the other hand, analysands have been in the presence of the 'other as process', formed and transformed by the analyst's silences, perceptions, imaginings, constructions, interpretations, and vocal engagements, all reflecting an unconscious formal response to the movement of the patient's character as it uses (and shapes) the analyst. These two juxtaposed aesthetics shape and know one another as moving idioms of effect.

The patient will therefore feel that he has encountered the real as the analyst, immanent to the analyst as an intelligence of form, and that his own unconscious has engaged this intelligence. Unconscious to unconscious, a noumenal–noumenal encounter, a meeting of two immaterial logics engaging one another. To this inner logic guiding us we have always used our highest signifier; it is from this experience that we construct a theory of God from which we originate. And the intelligence inside us – internally guiding us – seems to connect with a similar 'soul to soul' meeting in the other. It is a paradoxical meeting. So deep and yet so impossible to describe.

Winnicott wrote of an area of 'essential aloneness', a part of the inevitable and necessary solitude of any one self. Such aloneness was not equivalent to isolation or loneliness, indeed, it was generative, precisely because its existence was underwritten by the presence of the other. Hence one could be alone in the presence of the other, a complex statement to be read in many ways. This capacity to be with one's self, unintruded upon by the need to relate, also designates the arrival of the capacity to *be* one's self irrespective of, and in difference with, the very presence of the other.

When Freud encouraged his patients to freely associate in the presence of the analyst and not be bullied by an inner notion of what was or was not worthwhile material, he too was making an exceptionally complex statement: he was urging the person to speak irrespective of the presence of inner censorship, but simultaneously acknowledging that the capacity to do so also depended on the patient's ability to forget the anticipated judgements of the other. To speak the patient had to forget the other's presence, but ironically, such a negative capacity brought about the very arrival of a speaker in the thick of solitude.

Psychoanalysts have not adequately written about the profound but deeply generative aloneness of the psychoanalyst, his patient...and the psychoanalysis. I know that I cannot describe the place where I work, even though the terms 'evenly suspended attentiveness' or 'reverie' or the 'analytic attitude' are fortunately there as signifiers which I can use, but do they really designate psychical life in this place?

Psychoanalysis takes place between two people yet feels as if it lives within the deepest recesses of my private life.

This may be another way of discussing the unconscious, but if so, I wish to address this fact personally. For every encounter with a patient sends me deeply into myself, to an area of essential aloneness processed by voiceless laws of dense mental complexity.

As I shall discuss in the next chapter, the analyst and his patient are in a curiously autobiographical state, moving between two histories, one privileged (the patient) and the other recessed (the analyst), in the interests of creating generative absence, so that the patient may create himself out of two 'materials': his own movement in language and his unknown journey in the material of the analyst's passing ideas.

The place where we live. Alone and yet...in the presence of the other.

Guided by a temporality that is both immediate and yet bears the past, that is both infinitely polysemous and yet bound by the limits of consciousness and culture, that cannot be shared with the other, even though it needs the other's presence to thrive, the participants 'enter' analysis.

Alone yet active, this thick inner networking carries on regardless. It cathects objects, signifies them, mobilises psychic intensities, demands and gets dreams, and bears the subject through the objects presented from day to day. In the consulting room, less stimulating than ordinary life, and yet more deeply prescient to this inner world, the analysand finds himself living an illusion: that here, at last, he is able to speak from this inner place. Here at last he is able to give voice to this densely moving complexity. The analyst shares that illusion.

But an illusion, not a delusion. How deeply moving an irony it is that both know that analysis does not really provide the place of representation of such deep inner sharing, and yet each believes it to be so. There is such a wonderfully radical defiance of the possible in a psychoanalysis; indeed, a defiance that has more than once earned it comparison with the theatre. But surely this defiance allows both participants a deep developing sense that they are coming closer and closer to truths that inform life.

Even when we specify a very particular aspect of the clinical situation it is still impossible to speak for the unconscious. For all our discussion of the here and now transference, is it really possible to describe the immediate? It is so tempting to say that because it is happening in our presence – rather than in the past and somewhere else – that therefore we can know it. But perhaps this very luxury of presence proves on further consideration to be such a paradox. Blanchot writes that the vexing problem of the immediate is that it always eludes representation even if it informs all moments.

> The immediate is a presence to which one cannot be present, but from which one cannot separate; or again, it is what escapes by the very fact that there is no escaping it: the *ungraspable that one cannot let go of.*
>
> (1993: 45)

The movement of the present moment is not part of a process of intelligent collecting of experience even if it may be an outcome. Rather it is 'the infinite shifting of dispersal, a non-dialectical movement where contrariety has nothing to do with opposition or reconciliation, and where the *other* never comes back to the same' (46).

Thus we do not know our experience of the present even as it is part of our intelligent movement through life. 'What is obscure in this movement', writes Blanchot, 'is what it discloses: what is always dis-closed without having had to disclose itself, and has always in advance reduced all movement of concealing or self-concealing to a mode of the manifest' (46). The immediate is the impossible (to describe) and becomes objectified as that which is outside our knowing but receiving special status.

We must, says Blanchot, recognise 'in impossibility our most human belonging to immediate human life' (47). Communicating this human experience is not possible; speech both attempts to cross that intrinsic divide between self and other and reaffirms the fundamental difference between any two people.

It is our task, Blanchot says, 'To *name* the possible, to *respond* to the impossible, [to] respond to this speech that surpasses my hearing, to respond to it without having really understood it, and to respond to it in repeating it, in making it speak' (65).

There is a 'strangeness' between people. An 'interruption escaping all measure' (68), an infinite separation, that is the outcome of that difference between any two persons. I cannot know the other, claims Blanchot. Indeed the other in his ultimate unknowability – I cannot know his inner self experience – constitutes a psychic presence in all our lives, which Blanchot terms 'the neutral'. The Other, or the He, is the 'Third Person' and yet not a person as it brings the 'neutral into play' (71).

'*The neutral relation, a relation without relation*' (73) [italics mine] brings man in all his strangeness to himself, and constitutes the 'unknown in its infinite distance' (77).

When Freud created neutrality did he implicitly recognise in it the immediate presence of the unknowable? Was the patient's speech, then, to be part of the ultimate realisation that communication recognised the impossibility of itself, insofar as speech both conveys mental content and yet does not?

We may further wonder if the creation of neutrality bears the curious truth of the impossibility of transferring the self analytic experience to the self–other relation. Turning to contemporary interest in the field of the interpersonal, we would have to find a place for neutrality as a representation of an essential feature of all human relations: that the other is beyond hearing and knowing – speakable to but impossible to hear from. Neutrality is, then, an indispensable part of the psychoanalysis. Too interpersonal a relation, one that socialised neutrality and displaced it, would refuse this truth.

While not denying the interpersonal element or the comforting contexts of living inside an interpretation, the patient feels that the analyst too acknowledges the indisputable fact that the other is ultimately beyond knowing. That which operates alongside and yet outside the pair, in the solitary privacy of these separate individuals. Psychoanalysis does not fail to represent this separate movement, one that lives between the lines, and has always recognised it as the character of the unconscious. To be found in Freud, much as Lacan indicated, is a subject who speaks to no one, not even to himself; indeed, where to speak is to be spoken through, interrupted by this unconscious that slips us up as it expresses unconscious psychic reality.

The silence of the analyst, a particular form of listening, privileging the word as the means of the subject's movement, addresses that side of a psychoanalysis alongside and outside the countertransference: it is a movement that operates regardless of what the analyst thinks or feels. Caught up in an intense imaginary theatre with his patient, the clinician may be well on his way to organising an important story, all the while moved by factors mediated by the imaginary.

Free association, for example, is independent of a relation to the analyst, even when it alludes to it, and even though it exists only meaningfully within proximity to an attentive other. The link between signifiers and the constellations of signifieds, however, operates according to its own networks, outside the imaginary fields that it nonetheless evokes. As I shall discuss in Chapter 5 the psychoanalyst's inner subjective response is always counter-pointed by this inner movement of the objective: the march of signifiers that dispenses psychic truths irrespective of human relations.

Important features of psychoanalysis are beyond the interpersonal. We cannot know the other or the meaning of the immediate, but these pressing facts of life are given honorary place in a psychoanalysis through a certain presentation of their natures: the immediate has given an impact in and through the interplays of free association, and analytic reverie and the unknowability of any other is sustained by the function of the neutral.

Rudely inconsiderate of feelings, personal relations, and theatres of the mind, the symbolic function of language simply speaks regardless. It does not care about the countertransference.

Is psychoanalysis a dialogue? A conversation? An intersubjective occasion? Is it a one body psychology or a two body psychology? Where is it to be found? There are dialogues. It can be interpersonal. In some respects it is also intersubjective. And of course both participants are always intrapsychics. Transference always occurs as does countertransference and they are rather enamoured of one another. Every above-named element is present. It is all of those things, but in the end, none of them.

It is the site of a mystery that will not vanish through the appropriative aims of categorical nomination.

2

THE PLACE OF THE PSYCHOANALYST

It may have been St. Augustine who first used a theological form to create a new psychological relation. Prompted by his spiritual crisis, he reflected in the *Confessions* on his internal world in a unique way, as both subject determining the enquiry and the object of his investigation. His introspection was, of course, licensed by the Christian model of conflict, between the forces of Christ and anti-Christ, but the literary form derived from his practice was, as Abrams maintains, the 'first sustained history of an inner life' (1971: 83).

Men had always looked to themselves in one way or another. St. Augustine did not invent introspection, but he created a voice that influenced all subsequent autobiographical endeavours.

Certainly Montaigne in his *Essays* and Pascal in his *Pensées* reflect something of an autobiographical stance in their essays, but it is really in the seventeenth-century Puritan diary, such as that by Michael Wigglesworth, that self examination achieved a new depth, although typically these confessions are driven by a desire to reveal the self to a shrewd deity not fooled by bad faith. Like so many Puritan writers, Wigglesworth tore his soul from its small-minded habitations to confess to his God every nook and cranny of evil's doings.

Unlike St. Augustine, the Puritan's self-disclosure was driven by unconscious efforts to fool God into voting the believer into the world of the elect and therefore to an afterlife. Puritans faced the clearly unhappy task of disclosing devious personality features hoping confession would win grace, even though this was meant to be an arbitrary and predetermined choice of the God.

With Rousseau, the urge to inform on others virtually overwhelmed his enterprise, yet he also confessed his own sins and his work has the hallmark of autobiography. The first writing of this specific literary form, however, belongs to W.P. Scargill, whose book *The Autobiography of a Dissenting Minister* was published in 1834 (Olney 1980: 5). The word 'autobiography' was invented at the end of the eighteenth century when 'three Greek elements meaning "self – life – writing" ' were brought together: an act that subsumed confessions, diaries, and memoirs.

In 'The Prelude' Wordsworth constructed a poetic form that not only reflected the self as a figure of action and event that moved through history, but evoked that self in an act of recollective meditation. 'The Prelude' is subtitled 'Growth of a Poet's Mind; An Autobiographical Poem'. 'Oh THERE is blessing in this gentle breeze / A visitant that while it fans my cheek/ Doth seem half-conscious of the joy it brings / From the green fields, and from yon azure sky.' He conjures the refreshing arrival of childhood memories. 'I breathe again!' he writes. 'Trances of thought and mountings of the mind / Come fast upon me' he thrills as the movement of imagery imposes itself, displacing his 'own unnatural self' that seems the outcome of a false self ascribed to the 'heavy weight of many a weary day / Not mine, and such as were not made for me' (1959: Book One, lines 1–25).

There is romance here. And liberty. Freed by memory to transport the self into prior states of being, Wordsworth takes autobiography a stage further, reincarnating former selves through an act of mind called poetry.

Ninety years later Freud pushed autobiography to a new place through self analysis, an act never attempted in such rigorous terms before. 'I am gripped and pulled through ancient times in quick association of thoughts', he wrote to Fliess on 27 October 1897, in terms not dissimilar to Wordsworth's.

Like Wordsworth, Freud invented a particular form to push the autobiographical idiom to new limits through rigorous analysis of the dream and associations to it. Not only the past came rushing to him, but repressed sexual urges, rivalries and losses. His drumming raised the ghosts of Sigmund from the tombs of repression to a haunting presence before his very eyes.

What Freud did through the dialogue of his autoanalysis, however, is really quite curious, though by now well known. He enriched the psychoanalytical situation. Now the patient was to be the tormented inhabitant of such recollections, leaving Freud as the cool, dispassionate, deconstructor of their meanings. 'My moods changed like the landscapes seen by a traveller from a train', he wrote to Fliess, describing his self analysis. Some years later, when telling his analysands how to free associate, he asked them to imagine they were riding a train through a landscape of the mind and to report what they observed.

Prior to this, in the circuit of self analysis, the train (the unconscious) and its passenger (consciousness) were both in Freud. If his train took him to new landscapes then he would try to report them in phenomenological detail that metapsychologically would certainly have to assign to this landscape its status as the visual representation of the train's desire.

As long as he was both train and passenger he could in the best of times join the psychic representation (the landscape) with an inner movement that his egotrain took, thus linking his urges, his affects, his thing presentations and his word presentations. But the moment he broke up the train service, he divided up affects, ideas, words and images in a particular way, something he was (perhaps correctly) to see in his obsessional patients who did the same.

The gain of Freud's contributions to the evolution of autobiography was lost by splitting it up to form psychoanalysis – a failure from which we have, ironically enough, been the beneficiaries. This is not an occasion for apology, however, since Freud tried to share that autobiographical discovery with the other. Consciously or not he may well have relied upon Fliess as a transference figure, implicitly acknowledging the possibility of being the subject engaged in the process speaking to a dispassionate other who would, as it were, hear of it. That may have been the origin of the psychoanalytical division of labour. But if so, then Freud also recognised, again perhaps unknowingly, that the auditory other (a Fliess) was a bit of a dummy, hardly instrumental at an empathic interpretive level in the comprehension of Freud's trains of thought.

So did Fliess' position form the basis of a naive listener, who from afar made his occasional interpretations? And although Freud's place as train driver, passenger and witness was absent in the presentations to Fliess, did Freud give up this particular axis of the mental, emotional and memorial, to a distant, remote and rather psychically removed person when he passed on this function to the psychoanalyst who would listen to the patient? In other words, did Freud pass on Fliess to the analytical community as a model of the analyst who 'practises' dissociated detachment, while retaining for himself the memoirs of the heart of the matter?

Certainly by 1923 Ferenczi and Rank were alarmed by the type of technicians emerging in psychoanalysis who would practise this art from a position of extreme detachment. At the same time Freud was moving from a certain conquistadorial enthusiasm to a growing pessimism about the therapeutic effectiveness of psychoanalysis, in sharp contrast to the years 1897–99, when through his self analysis he drew true personal and visceral inspiration.

Is it not possible then that his pessimism stemmed in part from a personal sacrifice as he gave himself (his self analysis) to mankind, so that others might benefit from the sacramental Host, to be found in the ritual practice of psychoanalysis? Was the excessively silent analyst a death in Freud, slain by the creation of psychoanalysis? Not, as discussed in Chapter 1, the presence of the neutral, but when extremely imposed, the morbid mood of the killed? Well, who knows.

The point is, Freud disowned a very particular form of representation, drawn from a long history in Western culture, but unique to himself. He could speak to himself but at the same time the voice that replied constantly undermined the rationalist enquirer who found the premises of his prior resolutions ultimately usurped by a new series of unconscious expressions. We may certainly ask about the nature of the original Freudian analysis, referring now to that circuit of ideas that moved in his self analysis. To pose this question is daunting and mildly insulting to that integrity of effort undertaken by Freud, but ask it in a limited way I shall.

To begin with he lived in a personal context: the near death of his father, his complex relation with Fliess, and an increasing delibidinalised relation to a woman whom he loves. From this reality come his dreams, which take him to the world of his former and present selves, and all disturbed by his present context: back to his childhood, to scenes of contemporary professional life, to Rome, city of imagined but thwarted desires. As always, the dream performs its ahistorical mixture function, bringing disparate memories into one place. It is left to the awakened dreamer to determine its value as a source of self questioning, but Freud allowed the dream this place, and over time he both licensed its voice and added his own associations, bringing his reasoned effort to make sense of it all.

The sheer power of this self evocation is fearsome, the autobiographical venture taken to its limits. Fliess, though a 'classical analyst' minimalist who did not interpret, stood in for the helpful other, but the capacity to live in the place of such continuous self evocation was too much to bear. The task was then split: the patient would bear the dream and Freud, from a considerable distance, would listen and interpret. He was no Fliess of course. But his occupation of Fliess' place was now transferred to the practising analyst. For over a century this split has been maintained in the practice of psychoanalysis and even though the division of analytical labour has been an essential step, it has nonetheless been a flight from the stringencies of self analysis. Indeed, Freud's increasingly dispassionate invocation to the patient to be the object of a surgical calm suggests that by 1926 he had moved a very long way from this impassioned participation in the power of the unconscious to unseat the sanest of minds. As I shall discuss in Chapter 6, however, this was hardly a dispassionate engagement since the partnership between patient and analyst centred on their unconscious effect on each other.

Nonetheless a unique splitting of the autobiographical, or the self analytical act, was achieved by Freud's insistence that the bearer of memory, instinct, pain and trauma, be the patient; leaving the analyst free to think about these matters from an unbiased, emotionally unmoved place. But as time would tell, the patient's transference intentions seemed to be aimed at forcing this dispassionate observer into a less than objective place, and slightly back to the heart of the patient's inner turmoil. Initially this appeared as a form of transference love, which may well have been the analysand's effort to love this excessively distant figure back into involvement. Freud viewed it as a resistance to his split-off function, but we may wonder if it was the patient's effort to undo this split, to force the analyst back into a union of minds, affects and associations that Freud abandoned with his renunciation of self analysis.

The psychoanalytical literature is replete with articles which argue that the patient's courtly love bears an aggressive demand that the analyst not only feel the analysand's love, but, even if he will not return it, will suffer it. By now, however, the patient had become the object of Freud's intensive study, out of which he constructed his metapsychology and clinical theory. The Freudian blank page became a third object in the analytical situation, one to which Freud (1985: 274) increasingly would refer himself for dispassionate life. His curiosity, his wish to know what was true, had taken him like Faust into troubled waters, a reason perhaps why he quoted Goethe in the 27 October 1897 letter:

And the shades of loved ones appear;
With them, like an old, half-forgotten myth,
First love and friendship

Self analysis had taken him to a place of 'fright and discord', he wrote, 'Many a sad secret of life is here followed back to its first roots; many a pride and privilege are made aware of their humble origins'. He knew what it is like to occupy the place of the analysand: 'All of what I experience with my patients, as a third [person] I find again here'.

To achieve the classical place of dispassionate living and scientific study is respite indeed from the place of pain and suffering. As I have suggested, however, Freud never really allowed himself to study the true implications of a patient's transference precisely because he had disowned the experience of psychic pain that any emotional participant (including the psychoanalyst) feels in the analytical location. Transference was at first a resistance to the semi-autonomous function of psychoanalysis. Later, it was the force of a repetition of early childhood scenes which were placed onto the figure of the doctor, scenes which were fairly coherent and could be reconstructed and referred back to childhood.

In any event, evenly suspended attentiveness, neutrality and benign remove have become the standards of analytical presence in the analytical situation. Indeed, it is fair to say that such positions are essential to the psychoanalytical process which partly rests on the analysand's freedom to speak without fear of the clinician encroaching on this privilege with his own prejudices, passing points of view, or wild interpretations.

There are moments in the analysis of most individuals, however, that call upon a different analytical disposition – when the patient speaks to the analyst through the moods, images, self states and ideas that are called up in the analyst. This countertransference is an effect of transference actions on the patient's part, which, amongst other things, causes distress to the analyst, an issue explored in greater depth in Chapter 12. In the early years of psychoanalysis, countertransference was seen as an obstacle that interfered with evenly hovering attentiveness, so it had to be either privately self analysed or overcome (presumably by invocation of a powerful psychoanalytical super ego) so that the analyst could resume his special place. In time the movement of feelings, ideas, and self states evoked by patients came to be regarded as a valuable source of information conveyed by the analysand.

The analyst views himself as a kind of host for different parts of the patient; some unwanted, some valued, projectively identified into the analyst. If he entertains a censorious view of the analysand, he might show how a patient puts harsh disapproving parts of himself into the analyst, as they are too difficult to bear in the self alone. If we imagine a patient describing, without self reproach, his promiscuous relations with lovers who are then cast aside, the analyst might feel reproach; the analytical task then might be to point out to the patient how hard it must be to contain reproachful feelings.

With the introduction of this concept of the relation between transference and countertransference an important if hazardous move was accomplished in the psychoanalytical theory of representation. Hitherto unconscious representations were to be found in the movement of signifiers that bore through word representations the logic of unconscious ideas. Crucial words would contain inscriptions of events that wrote themselves into the symbolic order. For example, a patient has a rat phobia and seeks analysis to recuperate her from this near debilitating fear of this loathsome object. The analyst discovers that the patient first experienced this fear as a child, lying in bed at night listening to the sounds of rats scurrying about in the attic. Later, when discovering the interesting if puzzling behaviour of her mother, she described her as 'erratic', perhaps inscribing in the word 'rat' a fear of the mother's behaviour.

Unconscious representations were also to be found in the ego's move to negotiate its relations to the id and the superego, so, by watching the ego's state (its impulses, its despairs, its rigidities, etc.) the analyst could speak to it as a beleaguered hero on a pilgrim's progress towards adaptation, thus modestly helping this figure to follow the paths of sane judgement toward the good enough life of which he or she was capable.

Psychoanalysts also regarded affects, defence constellations, actings out, repetitions, and linguistic idioms as further forms of the unconscious, each well considered within the psychoanalytical literature. The theory of the patient's transference communication and its corresponding effect upon the psychoanalyst was a radical new view of human representation. Freud's revolutionary discovery of free association was followed half a century later by Kleinian studies of projection, that people pass parts of themselves into objects; first into objects of the internal world (such as an employer standing for the bossy parts of the personality, or admiration of a nurse holding the caring parts of the self), and second into other people (such as repeated delinquencies which will bring about a boss in the other, or expressions of disability which will elicit the nurse in the other). Patients transfer these parts of their personalities into mental objects and others, and it is this latter capability (and the recipient's unconscious reception of the role) that has been so profoundly illustrated and extended in the writings of Rosenfeld, Bion, Segal, Joseph and others.

This theory is, of course, not entirely original. The Old Testament describes how God spoke inside the body and mind of the other, who would have a special capacity to hear from this most effective voice. The hallucinating hysterics of the Middle Ages heard the voice of the devil in their ears and by the nineteenth century salons were appearing where imposing female spiritualists acted as mediums for the voice of the departed. But Kleinian theory provides the first real understanding of this transference and promises a profound rethinking of what takes place between people.

Let us return to Freud.

I have argued that his self analysis, built around dreams usually sponsored by events from the day before, constituted a unique and important step in the autobiographical form and a slight move beyond Wordsworth, because Freud's sexual strivings, murderous impulses and selfish preoccupations were presenting themselves to him in a shocking but intriguing manner. Through free association he knew he had found a new form for being spoken to by the self, therein advancing the course of human understanding.

However, by splitting this discovery into a two-person relation (which benefited the neurotic) Freud no longer fully valued what Hannah Arendt terms 'the two-in-one dialogue' (1958: 185). In psychoanalysis, what happened to that internal dialogue that seemed both to evoke prior selves and urges and to emotionally inform the interpreting subject with the full range of essential information crucial to a good interpretation? By converting the two-in-one into one-in-two, Freud seemed to divest psychoanalysis of its very soul.

Revival of interest in the countertransference is such an important part of the psychoanalytic movement because it restores the heart of the matter: the analyst who receives the transferences willingly, and who quietly notes the many moods, self states, wild ideas and credible theories that occur inside him, gradually comes to the place of two-in-one – the shared 'psyche' – where the analyst will feel the pain of joy, experience the confusion of fast-moving ideas or the doldrums of mental inertness.

Much has been written about the necessity of a theoretical (in theory, but not in practice) blank screen upon which the patient projects, or of an evenly suspended attentiveness valued precisely because transference acts punctuate themselves by disturbing this evenness. The classical attitude is a crucial basis for analytical listening. Gradually, however, the analyst feels himself mentally occupied by the patient's associations, moved to different self states by transference actions, sculpting the patient's internal objects out of the material of the analyst's subjectivity. As I shall discuss in detail in Chapter 12, a patient who acted out repeatedly got me to worrying that all the misdeeds committed at the hospital were his fault. As he was talking about how his mother was always intruding into his space with her worries about him, I could use these two sets of data (his report and my inner state) to say that I thought he was unconsciously aiming to bring out in me the worrying mother whom he now enjoyed teasing and controlling by his actings out. Another patient, who began the analysis as a very engaging reflective participant soon had a love affair which preoccupied all of his energy so that self reflection ceased in the analysis. I first felt angry at this loss of analytical rapport and work and then, over time, I felt rather eradicated. Over a few months he told me that as a small child his mother deserted him by passing him to the nanny, this total withdrawal leaving him feeling deadened and full of hate toward her. Using his narrative account of his life history and my countertransference I could now point out how his actings out showed me what it was like to have an alive beginning followed by a sudden abrupt absence and a determined refusal to remain alive to a relationship.

Such moments are not an everyday part of an analysis; indeed, they are more like epiphanies which emerge out of a kind of two-in-one moment, when both patient and analyst are seemingly speaking and experiencing the same phenomenon. These episodes are notable, however, because the patient is usually narrating life events or historical scenes in a dispassionate way while the psychoanalyst is feeling them, often in a most intensive manner. What a curious reversal of the classical model built as it is around the patient's passion and the analyst's dispassion!

Nonetheless, such moments constitute important psychic occasions when the analyst brings to the analytical encounter – and therefore back to the patient's psyche – split-off portions of the analysand's scenes or objects.

But what about the long periods in between these epiphanies?

Freud's self analysis, like Wordsworth's evocative relivings, and St. Augustine's reflective rememberings, is an act of intelligence, living in a place of constantly used, hence familiar, solitude. I refer to our inevitable relation to ourself – in a two-in-one dialogue – when an unrepresentable inner speech condenses the unspeakable.

So we may sympathise with Freud's attempts to represent this inner happening, and we can see how the dream, with its somewhat neat story content, lent itself to representations while the opera of inner speech is so beyond telling. But we must also extend our compassion to the working psychoanalyst, who toils in a place exceptionally similar to that occupied by Freud once he undertook to hear his voices speak.

When I meet a new patient I encounter a stranger. Usually I know nothing of them. In the seconds following my first shake of his or her hand I nonetheless have my first 'impression'. It is there inside me, a representation of this person who stands before me. To spare us the exhaustive list of evidential registrations (i.e., dress, facial expression, gait, etc.) I will simply say that each person has his or her idiom and that it begins to impress me right from the beginning. Time passes, new impressions arrive: patients tell me where they grew up, impressing me with the landscapes of their childhood; they describe friends and enemies, parents and siblings, relatives and strangers who had impressed them; they tell me of their everyday life, events at work, or at home, or at a cultural event. Waves of impressions, like some intelligent sea, work on the material terrain of my subjectivity.

As analysands present fragments of their life history, endless cameo shots of the mother, the father, brothers and sisters, episodes from their present-day life, dream after dream after dream, layers of subtle silence upon layers of silence, a condensation of these stories, pictures and abstractions builds up inside me to form a very particular moving composition.

Just as Freud attempted to analyse his dreams, to liberate himself from psychic pain and find sufficient truth around which to live, I think at certain points interpretations form to survive this action, to transform the pain of countertransference. However, my custom is to sustain receptive silence that facilitates new impressions as sometimes the analyst's work is accomplished in the solitude of this engaging struggle.

I think back to a particularly distressed patient who had a remarkable narrative ability. He could and did describe his father's personality in painstaking detail. Pursuant to my analytical obligation I struggled internally to see this father as a metaphor of unwanted parts of my patient. When I interpreted this, linking it to my view of his transference to myself, I felt marginally relieved. But the accounts of the father's incredible small-mindedness continued, in contrast to my patient, who shared with me some strange relief in thinking of his descriptions as a metaphor of his own internal world. It was as if we were both asserting the omniscience of projection despite the force of a reality well beyond our control. The memories continued. One night I dreamed of my patient's father. He corresponded to my theory of him as a good man, abused by my patient, then in the closing frames of the dream I saw what looked like a wrinkle under his chin, a crease, which upon further inspection I knew to be a mask. When I saw my patient the next day, my attitude toward his father had changed. I no longer attempted to see the father as a projection, and I just listened and mulled over my patient's memories. These recollections took me into the family home and to their kitchen with its small cooker and a refrigerator barely able to contain a daily meal, to the sombre living room with its gas fire to warm the place at specified hours, to the tool room where the father worked to fix objects in the house, allowing the son to watch but never to touch the objects.

This is not meant to be a case illustration, but is given to represent some sense of what it is like to live as a psychoanalyst, to inhabit a patient's world, to be carried by his narrations into his life.

A patient tells me a dream in which he travels by bus to the seaside. He glimpses the blue sea and is momentarily elated, but is lost in a crowd of people. He walks along a hillside and a bottle rolls down the embankment, it breaks, and fragments of glass puncture his skin. He has been in analysis for five years and as he tells me this dream I am there as a participant. I ride the bus. I glimpse the sea. I feel the annoyance of the crowd, but when the bottle rolls down the hill, although I 'see' it, I associate: 'just as he is about to reach the sea (i.e. to see) he loses his bottle (English slang for the loss of courage)'. The patient as is customary is silent, awaiting the chain of ideas that emerge. I am carried back in my mind to a dream he reported some four years before, when he walked down a boat slip near a childhood holiday resort and saw the sea that graced his childhood: a sea of simplicity. The patient's associations are to his recent journey abroad, its crowded city, and to an abscess on his leg. He is quiet. I ask, 'and the bottle?' He replies 'nothing really, only a sense of it breaking up'. 'To lose one's bottle?' 'You mean, my courage?' A long pause. I say:

> it brings to my mind your recent journey across the sea where I think you have high hopes of business success. The sea is wonderful because it has no obstacles on it; you can see as far as you like, but you must deal with the crowds of businessmen before you can reach such a place and I think you are afraid you will lose the courage necessary to cope.

The correctness or not of this interpretation is immaterial here. Each of my patient's dreams becomes my dream. They arise in me, each time a novelty even though conveyed in unmistakable fictive form, and so I am, in some slight respect, in the place of the dreamer who is dreamt by it. The telling of it moves me from place to place, through adventures, to the bizarre, and each step of the way it evokes associations within me. Occasionally it is the affective register when my inner life is caught up in an evolving emotional experience, sometimes the visual order is so compelling that I simply travel on an internal train through inner landscapes. At times the density of plotting pushes me back to a more literary remove as I concentrate intensely, aiming to remember the characters, their actions, and the strange twists of events. Sometimes word presentations emerge from the imagery as sub-title formations, resting there until joined by other signifiers speaking in the symbolic order. Wandering back to dreams evoked by present dreams, I wonder why the dreamer returns to the same landscape.

In a way, I am escorted by my patient from the social surfaces of life to the moving depths of his dream, presenting familiar cinema (his father or mother) transporting me through the subtly graded time zones of his past, as I attend his school with him, play on the cricket field, join in his erotic experiences, bear the breakdown of his marriage.

Each session, a fifty-minute evocation, somewhere between dream and reality, yet distinctively characteristic: each patient's idiom directs me to new places, calling me to my 'other' lives.

It is no small measure of the accomplishment of these dreams and their memories that patient and analyst walk in the past, giving it life once more, however briefly. An act, against the passage of time. 'Time done is dark as are sleep's thickets: / Dark is the past: none waking walk there' (MacLeish in 'Conquistador'); yet, analyst and patient create a form of dreaming that briefly and poignantly illuminates the darkness.

Our comments are a minute fraction of our total experience, for in this place of solitude and surprise we sit in 'The Freud Chair', day in and day out, our quiet condition of our work and theories. In the Wordsworthian sense we travel a sometimes 'pleasant loitering journey' but one often densely exacting of our self exploration: 'When, as becomes a man who would prepare / For such an arduous work, I through myself / Make rigorous inquisition' (1959: line 145). The place we occupy as analysts, like that of poets, is an evocative one, when memories seem to come to us with urgent claims. When I recall patients' dreams, former sessions, or imagine the mother or father, I feel I am called to a place of intense work and responsibility.

> Dust as we are, the immortal spirit grows
> Like harmony in music; there is a dark
> Inscrutible workmanship that reconciles
> Discordant elements, makes them cling together
> In one society
> (Wordsworth 1959, lines 340–5)

With my patients, in this solitary Chair, I travel through categories (affects, thing presentations, word presentations, somatic states) and through time spans in the analysand's life. With the ego bringing us to intensely meaningful condensations of the discordant elements of a life, associations which come to mind (or body) are often those of 'fright and discord' though there are also days when, like Freud, I 'drag myself about dejected because I have understood nothing of the dream, of the fantasy, of the mood of the day' (1985: 274).

Carved by Melanie Klein and W. Fairbairn, this British Chair is warmed to familiarity by Winnicott, when I am subtly moulded into being other than myself, moved into an unwanted part of my patient's mind that I now feel to be my mind, or into feeling myself the particular mother of my patient coming now into being, not simply listening to stories about them.

These occupations, places inhabited by the self, are the seats of the psychoanalyst who, in the quiet of his room, is engaged in an often intense, self analytical enterprise. The outcome may be simply sustained silence, or an association, or an interpretation, but such analytical acts are mere derivatives of an intense internal process of being moved, shaken, bewildered, bored to near narcoleptic inertness, puzzled by the word: in short, I am in that first Freudian place, self analysis.

If we think that our patients are ignorant of our personal struggle we not only do them a disservice, we discredit our understanding of the unconscious. But I find that, except for the occasional enquiry (e.g. 'What are you thinking?'), my patients leave me to my psychoanalytical chair and the task of analysing myself as I live through, am evoked by, and inhabited by their childhoods and their personal idioms. They will only rarely know where I have been, and so it should be: my gift, as is any psychoanalyst's, is my silence which supports the verbal priority of the analysand, and also ensures the boundary of my own privacy essential to the task of holding the patient and myself through this long process.

We shall know our patient's stories and discover in our selves the emergent shape of part of the patient's mind, perhaps itself the transfer of a part of the mother or the father. It is possible to think and eventually to represent these knowings. As discussed in the previous chapter, however, there is another type of knowing, the work of 'in-formation', as one person's particular character affects the other as an idiom of presentation. So there is the knowledge of content and I can describe what my patient said when he told me about his dream. I cannot, however, describe the idiom or style of presentation. You would have to have been there to have experienced it yourself. For this knowledge is mostly unthinkable and unrepresentable.

Psychoanalysts are often criticised for saying that you can only know what psychoanalysis is by experiencing it. But is this simply a means of avoiding explanations and a pretext for getting people into an analysis? Critics certainly think so.

But the analyst is confronted by the same categorical problem facing a person, who, having just heard a symphony, is asked by a friend what it sounds like. As it cannot be described, the enquirer is encouraged to listen to it. It is a matter of listening to the form of a work, immersing oneself in the immanent logic of transformation determined by the particular aesthetic idiom of the form in question.

When Freud invented the analytical space, he fashioned a relation that elicited this formal knowledge which although impossible to know in consciousness and thus to relate, is nonetheless the core of human communications.

So, I cannot tell you what I have known from my patient as a self. I can tell you his story. I can discuss his illness. Who he is, or who he was, however, is the unforgettable movement of life itself, in its various forms an extenuating composition of being, deeply effective but mysterious beyond words.

3

THE NECESSARY
DESTRUCTIONS OF
PSYCHOANALYSIS

Customarily people come to psychoanalysis because they are suffering. Bringing a dominating fear, such as a dread of riding in cars; telling a sexual obsession practised to their dismay, such as fetishism; feeling denuded by consistent deficiencies, such as retreat from intimacy; hearing voices. They arrive because illness sends them.

The analyst is called by illness to seek its truth and though patients will often complain about the slowness of analytical work, or protest about interpretations that feel persecutory, they authorise the search. This quest is not without irony, for just as illness forecloses unconscious freedom, the analyst's quest to understand pathology narrows the capacity to appreciate other aspects of his patient. Interpretive work on a complex shadows its structure (like illness, it is a form of repetition) and were this to be the sole characteristic of psychoanalysis, the situation would become the grotesque, with the illness and the interpretation competing for pathologic prize.

The psychoanalytic process, however, sustains generative forms of destruction that break disturbances of thought and character. In very differing ways the method of free association and the act of interpretation are forces of destruction that decentre the analysand's psychic hegemony and the repeated sensibleness of the analyst's interpretive grasp.

Free association, for example, breaks up mental knots, just as it destroys the dream text. By deconstructing its parts into psychological divisions, each a turning point in a movement through differing memories and desires, it fragments the analyst's interpretations. As I shall discuss in Chapter 6, it subverts the authority of both participants and this is the way it should be.

This destruction is the joint work of the death instinct, breaking up links in order to reduce excitation, and the life instinct, creating new combinations of thought. If the thrill of consciousness is to create fresh unities and momentarily bind the unconscious in narrative, then the breaking of the texts of consciousness, by a work that endlessly displaces it, defeats that pleasure by a kind of fragmentation. After all, how far can consciousness go in its effort to comprehend the unconscious? Not so very far after all, particularly when both analyst and patient so often find thrills of understanding destroyed by new material, which sends them both packing, the one to free associative breakage, the other to evenly suspended attentiveness.

The dissemination of thought is destructive. Each psychic intensity is formed as the result of the movement of prior lines of thought conjoined by the evocative power of the object only to be dissolved by the force of displacement, condensation, substitution and symbolisation as constituent elements launch new lines of thought.

Freud believed these fractures were acts of intelligence, protecting consciousness from unacceptable ideas, breaking them up and presenting them in displaced forms. There is ample evidence in Freud's writing, however, to suggest this was wishful thinking. Obviously some mental contents do go through the work of the unconscious to emerge into consciousness in scattered and altered form serving hidden wishes, but the majority of psychic intensities do not find housing in such witness protection plans, instead they become new entities, in turn fragmented to become new formations, an endless chain of mental productivities that procreate in that intercourse between any particular line of unconscious deployment and the surprising action of the object.

If idiom is the self's intelligence as form, being as the shaping of reality, then does it not impose on mental objects the hegemony of its desire? How do free associations disseminate idiom if this is a form imposing itself on or through life? Indeed, dissemination identifies the logical dispersal of the contents of the dream, of the memory, of the narrative of life. How does this logic square with the aesthetic of form?

From the beginning of life one's idiom is rather like a vision-in-waiting, a preconception, as Bion would say, of things to come, which takes shape over time. Idiom seeks objects because they materialise form which realises itself as it shapes these contents of a life. This is a deep pleasure. It is a manifestation of the drive to present the peculiarity of one's being, a form which suggests itself as a visionary movement through the object world. As Eliot puts it in *Burnt Norton*, 'desire itself is movement'.

The disseminations of a single mental context – a dream, memory, story – release latent (and future) contents, creating lines of meaning, but the act of dispersal is an expression of unconscious work, indicating that the ego knows that to sustain the elaboration of a self's idiom – to make one's music out of life – it must break up hegemonies of content to re-form them, to reshape them into new and differing compositions of meaning. It is the function of a principle that life can only be formed in the birth of new ideas and although new contents (stories, memories, texts) are created, the principle of one's being a form destines the self to destroy the sanctity of any found idea.

What drives this movement? Not derived from any individual libidinal instinct or group of instincts, this urge is realised through cumulative instinctual gratification, which authorises the subsequently independent desire to represent. If it originates in instinctual life, it emerges from the limited ambition of any group of instincts, as it finds in the structure of the instinct, the pleasure of representation that now directs larger ambitions: to fulfil the self's investments – past, present and future.

The unconscious begins as a feeble organisation of stimuli moving gradually into a limited mental structure that develops into the most complex order imaginable. It grows not only as it thinks, its constitution lives in the network of the thought, and each day brings new thoughts that further develop this network. The work of dissemination – the releasing of any content into its derivatives – sends a meaning unto meanings, serving the drive of any self to extend its interests. This aesthetic interest, form as desire, seeks itself in the future, sensing that its idiom will be realised again and again.

Freud tried to designate a new kind of urge in *Beyond The Pleasure Principle*, something which he could sense was in the order of a compulsion to repeat, and to which he assigned new instincts: those of life and those of death. The life instincts were the phylogenetic repetitions: the compulsion to combine. The death instincts were an inborn tendency to return the organism to its pre-animate existence – to achieve a constancy that would be death. He nearly grasped the pleasure beyond the fulfilment of the wish, the joy of being subverted by the displacement of the wishing subject, continuously relocated by the free-moving discoveries of the self's encounter with the object world. Each is an essential element of the triad seeking truth.

The child builds a castle (the edifice of consciousness and coherence) and then loves to destroy it in one swift blow. Creation then obliteration. 'The end of something has a satisfaction. / When the structures go, light / comes through / To begin again' (Charles Olson, 'La Torre'). The destruction signifies the creative side of riddance, opening up new internal space, available for the re-imagining of reality, unburdened by the accomplishment of a particular wish. Bion inscribed this necessity into psychoanalysis when he wrote of the analyst's need to be without memory and desire, a plea for pleasure beyond the ordinary, bliss that comes with the destruction of prior wishes and memories. Winnicott's concept of the true self identifies that side of destructiveness which is creative, which annihilates the true identity of the object, in order to create something new. The burdens of perception can be lifted by the power of imagination. Liberation comes through destruction.

Free association uses the mental objects of consciousness in almost exactly the same way as the true self uses the object. The unconscious process of bursting the compaction of condensation employs aspects of consciousness to ruthless intent: to elaborate the desires created in the psychic intensity. Moving forward through the dissemination of such intensities releasing the latent codes of idiom's desire, objects are found and used as articulating pathways of the self's evolution.

Could celebration of the force of dissemination become an argument against the value of interpretation?

Good interpretations develop from long periods of evenly suspended attentiveness, delivered when the analyst feels the patient can virtually speak the interpretation himself. In some respects, they are derived from and reflect condensation. But precisely because an interpretation is an over-determined act, built upon the imbrications of the patient's many narratives, dreams and actions in the transference, once delivered it breaks up under the disseminating force of its truthful constituents. Elaborating one or another of the truths contained in the interpretation, the patient alters it when they talk it. This process of interpretation – where the material is gathered, coheres into a narrative in the analyst's mind and is delivered, followed by its dissemination through free association – not only mirrors Freud's theory of the total dream process (day events, night dream, next day associations) but reflects the basic structure of freedom of thought itself. Meandering through the material of our day, inspired to coherent moments of special meaning, destroyed by the freedom of thought – it is a pleasure to create, a thrill to destroy.

Human idiom weaves its way through the fabric of life, fashioning its 'knitwork', realised through the endless creation of patterns peculiar to itself. Mental conflict, as R.D. Laing argued, creates knots that can be untied through the labour of interpretation, but most interpretations lose unconscious contents not germane to the hegemony of the interpretation. These lost contents are destroyed by the priorities of the analysand's knots and the analyst's interpretation of them.

My analyst's interpretations almost always made sense. They pointed to a journey that I could already see myself taking as I was carried away. But I could also see how each was slightly wrong; I felt the loss of what had been abandoned on the journey of interpretation, or what was going on in the silent backwaters of my being. One day my analyst, sensing that I was not in full accord with his comment (although I had seen its sense and relevance) said he thought I was not entirely in agreement, and I instantly corrected some of what he said. I did not think much about this again, although I am sure it was a telling moment, for some years later, when working with one particular analysand, I said 'perhaps you would put it slightly differently' and he immediately corrected me. I realised how important it was to be more systematic in this regard.

By seeking correction the analyst gives pleasurable place to destruction as the patient destroys varied words, images, or 'senses' within the interpretation that fulfil the need for understanding, a desire driven by the pleasure of self representation.

Even as patient and analyst create hermeneutic unities they are immediately dispersed by the very associations they inspire. There seems to be a universal unconscious movement that generates self experiences: from unconscious collectings to conscious manifest texts, to free associative deconstructions. As the analyst breaks down the analysand's comments, in that silent chamber of thought that is his privilege, and as the analysand breaks down the analyst's communications, both learn how to work unconsciously upon one another. Both are lost to the intrinsic work of the unconscious, moved by psychically intense moments becoming latent thoughts, providing a psychical gravity that momentarily centres being until a clear idea arrives, representative of the latent thoughts, a transitory moment, in turn fractured by its new arrivals.

In addition to the special destructiveness of unconscious mental processes and the invitation to the analysand to correct, and thereby destroy, the analyst's wording, certain interpretations are designed to break the patient's pathology of mental structure.

It is hard for psychoanalysts to write about the destructive side of their interpretive work, in which they intercede to bust up a patient's well rationalised or pathologically taught narrative. Yet when the analyst gives the patient a substantially different view of his material, he destroys his narrative cohesion and self image. The patient may struggle against such difference and when patient and analyst are in dispute with one another, each of necessity breaks the other's narration as these anti-narratives are designed to disperse the hegemony of consciousness.

However well delivered, this is an act of aggression, as the analyst knows before he speaks that what he says will disrupt the patient, often causing psychic pain. This does not deter him. The patient eventually recognises this determination and appreciates its aggression, which meets his resistance or his need to become ill in the service of presenting his illness. The analyst's aggression is a force of sorts, best acknowledged for what it is and certainly felt as such by the patient.

Psychoanalysis, however, is shy of its essential destructiveness. Freud was more honest than most, as his interpretive didacticism is clearly present in his analytical deconstructions of his patient's unconscious truths as he saw them. Klein's vision is unquestionably a powerfully imposed truth, one fortunate enough to carry enough grains, for her difference to have launched her analysands on important journeys of the unconscious. Winnicott, for all his talk about the holding environment, was often exceptionally tough in his statements to his analysands, but the real difficulty analysts have in knowing quite how to write their confrontational manner into their accounts can be seen in the more unfortunate attempts: Masud Khan's *When Spring Comes* presents the most obvious example.

Let us now consider some generative examples of interpretation-as-destruction.

A young man tells of his intense love and affection for his mother, whom he looks after dutifully, unlike his father, whom he sees as an insensitive brute. Time passes and a moment occurs when I say that he seems to be

31

enjoying a triumph over his father as he proves himself a superior companion for the mother. Prior to this comment, indeed for twenty years, he has held himself in exceptionally high self-esteem. Praised by many people for his selfless affections towards his mother and his courage in standing up to his father, now, in one single blow, his house of cards falls down. Stunned by the comment, he restates his history, certain that I have missed something. Again and again he tells me of his father's brutality, but to his own consternation discovers that his dream reports confirm the interpretation: he harvests his father's insensitivity. His self idealised characterisation destroyed, he is thrown into turmoil, and eventually into considerable psychic change, by a single interpretive point of view that 'broke' him.

A very proper, word-perfect woman comes for analysis. She commemorates many sessions to a lament as she portrays the people in her life as losers, although she has distant acquaintances who are having a meaningful and luxurious life. She sees herself as long suffering and yet pregnant with her own wonderful child self that only needs *real* understanding, love and intelligence to bring it forth gloriously into the world. However, in the sessions the only times when she leaps from otherwise careful narrative delivery into spontaneity is when I announce a change of session, or when I have made an error of interpretation. 'What?!' she chimes, followed by a long silence. 'Oh!' she exclaims. Another long silence. These moments seem to delight her, but the exuberance is on the side of the gleeful censor whose joy is in finding error in the other. I tell her that it is difficult to put into words what I wish to say, as it does not derive from the narrative material, but from her way of being and of relating: 'You say your existence is lifeless, and your sessions are laments which fill this room with despair, yet you take delight in something I say – such as announcing a change of session – that allows you to disapprove of me with relish.' Although she had often discussed how she took revenge on people, this comment was deeply disturbing. Thrown into anguish, she could feel a bizarre idealised self dissolving in the acid of her own hatred, now leaving her not knowing quite who she was.

A manic depressive patient talks non-stop. I have to interrupt him in order to speak. He had told me that his own mind was like an endless source of nourishment, and I was to use his comment many times, when breaking in upon him. 'George, I am breaking in.' He would often raise his voice and try to talk over me and I would up the ante. 'George, you are trying to yell me out of this room, but I'm not going to go away', sometimes followed by 'Can you stop, or can't you stop?', or some such abrupt comment on my part which usually led to an intensely furious pit stop, as he waited impatiently for me to say what I thought. These moments were, therefore, very important, as in a matter of seconds, he could be off and racing. 'George, you are sucking off your own mind-breast, smacking your lips with your wonderful ideas', or some such comment. Whatever his reply – and sometimes it would be in anger, often in deep sadness, occasionally in tears, and now and then in deep almost restful silence – the manic dimension to the session would *be broken*. The aim of interpretation here was not simply to convey meaning – which it did – but to break his pathology, which it also did.

Breaking is essential to interpretive work that cracks up pathologic cohesions and drives the analysand's subsequent associations – tinged by hurt, anger or anxiety – into disseminating lines of thought that reveal underlying convictions, and yet immediately launch the patient into an unconsciously creative dispersion of the prior preoccupation of thought or behaviour.

One part of us is dedicated to the search for our truths, and in such quests we narrow our interests, despatching certain disseminations to oblivion, ignoring a great deal, following our intuitive sense of the right paths toward a limited aim. We bind unconscious contents into a complex that may be an interpretation, or the originating idea behind a work of art, or a 'psychic genera'[1] – ideas gathering into an unconscious nucleus that upon completion launches new perspectives on life. The search for truth is a form of passion. 'The profoundest of all sensualities / is the sense of truth /and the next deepest sensual experience / is the sense of justice', writes Lawrence in 'The Deepest Sensuality'.

Yet no sooner are such cohesions formed, than they break under the force of inspiration that conjured them in the first place and, in turn, become major factors in the generation of new articulations of the self. Cohesions are meaningless without a disseminative effect; disseminations would be empty evacuations of the subject's idiom were it not for our cultivation of areas of specific interest that serve the search for meaning.

As the work of dissemination releases contents to their future combinations of meaning, derived from the experience to come, form seeks its future. If today I tell myself a story of my past, it will crack up under the force of its constituent truths, the vectors of which serve as potentials waiting for the arrival of further material from future evocative objects of life experience to form yet new stories...and so the process continues.

We create meaning.

And then meaning finds us.

Genera and dissemination, dream and association, cohesion and fragmentation, express a fundamental movement between different but mutually essential forms of desire: the one toward a deeply unconscious abandoned freedom of expression, the other toward the desire to know. Dissemination generates material. Cohesion brings about truths. Dissemination subverts authority. Cohesion makes sense of chaos. Dissemination elaborates the singular idiom of each of us through an infinite potential declension. Cohesion finds what is common to our idiom and organises the self into themes. Dissemination implicitly suggests the impossibility of its aim ever leading to a narrated unity.

These forces, to cohere and to disband, express different types of desire. Dissemination is the desire of form in being, articulating the self's idiom by scattering interests into multiple places. The search for meaning (or truth) expresses the epistemophilic instinct, the urge to discover and to know. Dissemination incessantly points to the fact that human life is increasingly complex, de-centred by the meaningful becoming meaningless. On a thousand disparate journeys amongst meanings, the self does not congregate such divergences into transcendent significance. Cohesion implies a life full of meaning, but these strange opposites share an odd conclusion: the meaningful is meaningless, the meaningless is meaningful.

Freud's mentality set this stage. Passionate to discover his patients' truths his method displaced their arrivals; yet the search for meaning and the destruction of any found truth by the force of dissemination are not just essential companions: one without the other is meaningless. The work of an analysis operates between this binary opposition. Faced with vast areas of material, a part of the analyst is comparatively free of mind to respond, yet another part of him searches for the organising nuclei of psychic truths. A single word, a phrase, an image, or the memory of a previous session will feel weighty with meaning. As time passes a small psychic chamber fills up with these denser objects and suddenly in a moment's illumination the analyst sees why they join; out of this genera an interpretation arises. A passionate and a pleasurable act, no sooner is it spoken than the patient's unconscious breaks it down, cracking it open, deriving psychic nourishment from its different dimensions. This is the force of truth itself as such genera feed the desire for knowledge just as they displace the knower from his findings. This pairing is at the core of analytical work, one predicated on a form of destruction that breaks unities in order to develop further truths.

If psychoanalysis causes pain to its participants and is destructive of respective hegemonies of consciousness, it always finds pleasure in such destructiveness as they give birth to new realisations that will all too soon be divested of truth's apparent finality, as sub-truths drive forward to unforeseen destinies. An immediate feature of the free associative method, this force of mental life is enlisted by the psychoanalyst's mentality, such that the conducting of analysis utilises the aggressions intrinsic to intelligent growth of mind.

4

FIGURES AND THEIR
FUNCTIONS

At the very heart of psychoanalytic practice resides a stunning opposition of aims. The patient presumably comes for analysis because of psychic ailments which invite concentrated attention and interpretive hard work on the part of each participant, yet both are meant to abandon intentions that logically arise from the assumed task and give themselves over to the free association of ideas. Will is immediately defeated. The wish for knowledge must not interfere with a method that defers heightened consciousness in favour of a dreamier frame of mind, encouraging the free movement of images, ideas, pregnant words, slips of the tongue, emotional states and developing relational positions.

Freud never had an easy time with this. He clearly advocated the patient's right of free association, knowing full well that it was only through such unpremeditated speaking that psychic truth asserted itself. But he also believed he possessed universal truths, such as the Oedipus complex and other ubiquitous organising structures that bound the network of associations. He wanted to find his truths in the material, yet he never won the day against his own method. It is still possible to see where the analysand's introduction of unexpected ideas and unconscious complexes took him by surprise and dislodged one of his theories.

The record of his treatment of the Rat Man, for example, illustrates how he sometimes collaborated with patients. Telling the patient that his omnipotence dated to the first death in his family, 'that of Katherine – about which he had three memories', he found that the Rat Man 'corrected and enlarged the first of these'. Or again: 'While I was discussing the possible reasons for his feeling guilty of her death, he took up another point which was also important because here again he had not previously recalled his omnipotence idea' (1909: 300).

He enjoys announcing truth – 'He was astonished when I explained that his masturbation was responsible for...' – but he also relishes the unexpected:

> He told me the whole dream, but understands nothing about it; on the other hand he gave me a few associations to WLK. My idea that

this meant a W.C. not confirmed; but with W ['vay'] he associated a song sung by his sister '*In meinem Herzen sitzt ein grosses Weh*' [also pronounced 'vay'].

(1909: 294)

Freud does not know what will happen next and when the Rat Man discloses fantasies about Freud's daughter, the analyst can barely suppress his delight at being led into new terrain by the patient's unconscious.

As with all his writings, Freud is forever full of summary discoveries and truths just waiting for their right to universal placement; yet, he still takes pleasure in the capacity of the unconscious to upset certainty. Session after session establishes the ambiguities of any psychic life, not least those occasioned by the analyst's own unconscious responses to the material. Listening to the Rat Man's account of early losses, Freud tells us that he had not mentioned three memories from a previous session, in part because he was not certain if the third memory – of the patient's father bending over a weeping mother – was the Rat Man's memory or that of another patient: 'My uncertainty and forgetfulness on these last two points seem to be intimately connected' and '(They were forgotten owing to complexes of my own)' (1909: 264), including those movements of his own unconscious life that arise in work with any patient. We see here something of the self-analysing Freud of the dream book: the provider of material in a dense articulation of packed unconscious interests (the dream), the self who unravels this gift through free association and the self who searches for points of convergence in the material.

Did he realise that he had discovered the non-dialectical relation between several ways of knowing? The dream condenses into imagery a thousand differing strands of thought which have arisen in light of events of the dream day. Author of a script which bears considerable knowledge, the patient does not comprehend his own creation; and although psychoanalysis offers a way to know something of this dream, it introduces a different means of knowing. Free association informs through destruction of a conscious wish to give the dream immediate meaning, and through destruction of the dream itself, as its text is cracked open and dispersed by free speech. A third type of knowing is gained through interpretation, when the analyst searches amongst the debris for a tissue of thought that reveals the trail of a wish or an unconscious interest.

However, none of these forms of knowing are displaced by any of the other forms. If the knowing that is the dream is destroyed by the logic of free association, the truth to be found through the forming of any dream is never eradicated by free speaking. If an interpretation brings together several themes latent in the network of associations, it does not displace the truth evoked by dissemination.

The dreamer, the associater, the interpreter, each render lived experience in differing ways and makes his own truth. Each of these ways of knowing is vital to the function of the human personality. We need to make dreams and disseminate them, just as we need to form interpretations. Even though Freud privileged the analyst's interpretation of meaning, his fascination with dream contents and the matrix of unconscious material and his fidelity to the process of free association meant that at no point in his writings did his belief in his interpretive truths ever displace a method that would always undermine him.

These ways of knowing reflect the three different psychic positions in the Oedipal triangle. And just as the Oedipal complex involves three distinctive yet overlapping persons – the mother, the child, the father – so these processes derive from the members of this triangle. As Freud indicated, to make the dream is to think like an infant again: in intense hallucinatory imagery that conjures a reality. To recline next to a quiet yet present other, evokes the half-dreamy state of a free associative being – infant and mother engaged in differing states of solitude and relatedness. When the analysand reflects on his communications and provides an interpretation he always bears the name of the father: the outsider who breaks the unhindered movement of desire and defence.

The psychoanalytical way of knowing reflects the analysand's prior ways of knowing: the infant's pure hallucination of his reality, his participation in the mother's way of knowing, his encounters with the father. Each is an essential element of the triad seeking truth.

As the patient makes his dream, breaks it up through free speech, and searches amongst the remains for fragments of meaning, he keeps alive the interactive yet intermittent exchange of three mentalities: the infant's, the mother's, and the father's. With three types of comprehending and rendering existence fully available, each analysand is put through the paces of these constitutive orders. Being an infant, becoming a child, taking in the mother, introjecting the father are the constituting tasks of a childhood. Rather than emphasise the person of the mother or the father as objects to be internalised, I prefer to speak of them as bearing *orders*: sets of functions which engage and process the infant.

The self that is alone yet in the presence of the other (the dreamer), the self that is unknowingly involved in uttering contents to a reverential other (the infant and the mother together), the self that comes to account for and accept responsibility for knowing the internal world through penetrating insights (the child and the father) are an essential *family* of authors. No single one of these authors will establish an ultimate truth; indeed, as time passes, each form of knowledge finds itself in a family of truth seekers and narrators.

By placing certain attributes under the name of the father (e.g. interpretation) or mother (e.g. reverie), I am not saying that the father is incapable of reverie or that the mother is not without her own form of interpretation. It would be interesting to explore the concepts of the maternal and paternal orders – the kind of reverie that derives from the paternal process, for example. That would suggest that there is a clear distinction between the two orders: I think it is preferable for individual psychoanalysts to determine for themselves whether functions belong under the name of one figure or another. Finally, it is important to bear in mind that these orders are not descriptions of how all mothers or fathers behave, but of processes associated with and usually conducted by the mother or the father, who assume differing forms of significance for the developing infant and child. Behaviourally, the mother will perform paternal functions and the father will operate the maternal order.

If one of the three members of the triad discussed above becomes too influential, or, if one function is eliminated completely, then full knowing is not possible.

Any emphasis on one of the three constituents to the subtle exclusion of the others automatically undermines the structure of knowledge derived from psychoanalysis. Yet an exhaustive review of psychoanalytical writings would indicate a surprising number of essays in which authors favoured one or another of these three structures of knowing. Winnicott, for example, emphasised the dreamy free associative state of the patient in which he offered 'uninterpretation', clearly elbowing out the function of interpretation. Kleinian writing consistently stresses the interpretive work of the analyst and admonishes analysts for emphasising the function of holding and the generative work of silence. The group of analysts who surrounded each of these writers doubtless did so for internal political reasons: the Kleinians over-emphasised the internal world because the Winnicotteans over-emphasised the holding environment. The result was polarisation and a distorted, less complete view of psychoanalysis.

These debates are not without irony. The Kleinians focus much of their theory on the first year of life and privilege the mother's body, yet they also advocate a highly active interpretive stance surely conducted in the name of the father ('As my account shows', wrote Melanie Klein in the preface to her account of the analysis of ten-year-old Richard, 'I could *penetrate* into very deep layers of the mind...' (1961: 13) [italics mine]). The Lacanians, many of whom barely conceal their contempt for the British emphasis on holding, are curiously maternal: the patient is free to speak with only rare interruption and even then the analyst's speech is allusive, elliptical, and porous.

It is more than a matter of curiosity that while many psychoanalytical schools of thought are built around single persons, they break the Oedipal triangle of unconscious structures operating in a psychoanalysis and kick out either the mother or the father. Thus we have embarrassing Oedipal debates in psychoanalysis – interpretation versus holding, or nature versus nurture, or internal world versus external world – which inevitably favour one Oedipal object over another. For example, read 'mother' versus 'father' in the title 'holding' versus 'interpretation'. Psychoanalytical conferences or essays often operate around Oedipal divisions of this kind. Indeed, entire regions or cities of the world appear to have marginalised one parent and appropriated the other. Thus the breasts seem to have become the intellectual property of the British to be found in London, while the phallus resides in Paris as the intellectual property of the Lacanians. Psychoanalytic groups continue to appropriate treasured parts of one or another parent's bodies – breast, penis, womb – or to appropriate attributes in an Oedipal manner. To caricature this a bit: 'We can tell you about envy and destruction'; 'We know about empathy'; 'We have potential space in our house'; 'We have language and the name of the father!'

When reading clinical material, those who favour the maternal order often suggest looking to the 'pre-Oedipal' elements by which they mean (amongst other things) looking deeper and therefore closer to the truth. Proponents of the paternal order, on the other hand, stress the Oedipal, suggesting that focus on the pre-Oedipal evades the problematics of sexuality. To look at the Oedipal is to face the true challenge of the enigmatic. Depending on their Oedipal positions many analysts assert a more intimate knowledge of the truth, which can be understood as a special claim to be the more favoured child of psychoanalysis: the one closest to the mother or closest to the father of true knowledge.

As we witness important parts of human life being singled out to become flag-bearers of entire psychoanalytical movements – i.e. *self* psychology, *intersubjective* theory, *relational* theory – the absence of a stampede to grab other essential parts of the total picture is somewhat surprising. One could envision movements springing up in the name of desire, or meaning, or…how about authenticity? Authentic psychoanalysis. Each of these appropriations tends to put off those who are outside the more narrow political group surrounding them, perhaps because it is unintentionally offensive to feel that one group assumes it knows about the relational, another the instincts, another the body, another the self. A psychoanalyst from another territory may be invited to speak before a group whose identity has been formed around a single word or set of privately coveted parts of the body of psychoanalysis. Should he, in his talk, use an unconsciously patented word, his hosts will be profoundly irritated – either because he has failed to cite the new parents of this 'born again' word or, worse still, because he has failed to use words or concepts in a way which pays homage to the host clan. This is less intellectual development than it is intellectual totemism.

Not infrequently a visiting psychoanalyst is asked an apparently simple question, but members of the host institution know that it is a 'coded' message. It contains key words around which a sub-clan has formed and in this moment becomes an iconic gesture. It may contain a word used by one of the society's analysts in a book or a paper and is something of a local offering to a well respected individual. Needless to say, however, these cryptic communications are often not appreciated by the visitor and unwitting offence is given.

Psychoanalysts who are outsiders to these causes[1] often either take up rather irrational dislikes of the signifying terms of the above groups, thus opposing an exceptionally important idea intrinsic to the development of psychoanalytical theory, or, they are left to plead a kind of forlorn plurality, appearing to favour an 'anything and everything is fine' attitude. It is not a matter of restoring a 'one happy family' inclusion of ideas but of deterring the politically-driven dismantling of the body of psychoanalytical theory. This body could only be eclectic if it was in pieces to begin with, but not if there were a set of models (held by Freud and the early group of analysts) that has since been cannibalised by his analytical children. The primal horde of brothers who devour the body of the father is an inadequate account of the origins of humankind, but at times it is all too apt a myth for the nature of the psychoanalytical movement.

Is one simply jesting in pointing out the partition of the body, the psyche, and the other, or, as I believe, is there some important truth to be found in a battle that takes place between groups across the globe, as first years battle with fifth years, as mothers and infants battle with fathers and children, as the phallus battles with the breast, as the foetus tries to take the cake?

The breaking up of the Oedipal structure essential to a full analytical freedom is no laughing matter, however, and it is worth considering why we may be in this unfortunate situation. I take the view that psychoanalysis needs to objectify and resolve its own Oedipus complex – defined here as the killing off by one group of the other group's affiliation with one parent – in order for that knowing I described above to take place. Jung, for example, embodied qualities that Freud both admired and feared. He enacted the maternal and feminine (as did Winnicott later) which Freud found faintingly fetching, but also wished to keep outside his affiliation to the father. Ridding himself of Jung also expelled consideration of other matters which he found irksome such as aesthetics, philosophy, music, which may have felt like the wish(y) wash(y) world of maternal knowledge. To this day, too many Freudian analysts marginalise Jung whom they find flaky, impressionistic, otherworldly, or lacking in rigour, apparently unaware of the contempt expressed towards the maternal order that saturates much of Jung's work.

Psychoanalysis continues to struggle with and against its Oedipal dilemma. Klein, Lacan, Kohut, Winnicott, Bion, the great thinkers of psychoanalysis, have each favoured one parental member of the triangle over another. Like Freud, each unconsciously opposed full and cognisant inclusion of all three members of the Oedipal family. Intriguingly, the discipline that founded the concept of the Oedipus complex and that prides itself on insight into its unconscious appearances has yet to objectify the anti-Oedipal dimensions of its own formations.

This politicism of psychoanalytical ways of knowing has inevitably affected the different forms of authority in the consulting room. On closer inspection there would seem to be a long-standing split of the Oedipal couple. Although there is widespread disagreement in the analytical world between many groups it is possible to see how this world is divided between those analysts who apparently remain fundamentally quiet and say relatively little and those analysts who are interactive and regard the relationship as dialogical. Thus classical analysts in the United States and France, who imagine their patients' inner worlds differently, nonetheless see the analyst's silence and paucity of comment as an essential factor in clinical work. While interpersonal psychoanalysts and Kleinians would make very different comments to their patients, they both regard the analytical relation as interactive and believe their task is to interpret what the patient is doing to the analyst moment to moment. Naturally there are shades of difference, inevitable grey areas where analysts operate in domains where hard and fast rules of technique seem to be of little value.

We may wonder quite why this fundamental difference has occurred. What does it mean if analysts of different schools of thought nonetheless divide over such a fundamental approach to their task?

It may come as no surprise that these differing attitudes toward the fundamental object relation of a psychoanalysis pivot around whether the analyst chooses to affiliate with the mother's or the father's way of being. The other who is quiet, waits, privileges the movement of the barely articulate, appreciates the nuance of developing meaning, and comments in an allusive or elliptical manner, contributing to the flow of life existing between the two: is 'in' the maternal order. The interpretive other who brings his patient to thoughtful account for what he is doing 'right now': is 'in' the paternal order.

When we think of the figure of authority in these analyses we may turn around Paula Heimann's question (1956) about the patient's transference – who is speaking to whom and why now – and ask of the analyst 'who is this speaker, to whom is he speaking, and why?' This is not easy to answer and one must avoid the temptation to oversimplify. The Kleinian enacts the interpretive presence of the father while fundamentally orienting the patient to the mother's body. European classical analysts would object to the idea that they speak with the voice of the mother, as in making an interpretation they see such a comment as often the introduction of a third element, brought into the analytical couple by the insight of the father. But placed between the maternal voice of the analyst – the 'ummming' being who listens and receives – and the infant or child playing his desire in the transference and through free association the analyst operates in the maternal order. Thus there are subtle and important differences when we ask who the analyst is when speaking and justice cannot be done to them here.

Important theoretical differences between analysts may partly derive from 'the order' of their speech. Kohut and Kernberg, for example, have different views of the narcissistic personality. In a sense, Kohut works more from the maternal order and is occasionally simplistically seen as cosseting. Kernberg, on the other hand, writes from the paternal order and is sometimes unfairly seen as too confronting. Surely the solution is not to pick sides, nor to attempt a false synthesis of their differences. Each position is valid so far as it goes and represents an important perspective. I think most psychoanalysts would find that they worked differently with narcissistic analysands, sometimes more in the manner of Kohut and other times more in the manner of Kernberg.[2]

One way or another, then, fundamentally different analytical positions either speak in the name of the mother or the father, but simultaneously enact the attitude of the opposite parent. In this respect it could be said that both members of the parental couple are present in the conducting of an analysis although one partner is forced into a silent role. To my way of thinking this is an unfortunate outcome in the evolution of a psychoanalysis. We may wonder, for example, why a typical series of sessions could not naturally be a mixture of these two positions, with the analyst sometimes quiet for long spells of time, implicitly supporting the generative development of internal associations (in the patient and in himself) and other times talkative, as he brings both himself and his patient into a more 'objective' place. The associative place would be operating within the maternal order, the interpretive within the paternal order, and the patient's participation in both worlds would constitute a structural use of the parental couple.

Functioning within both positions is essential to *full* analysis. The analysand needs to use the elements of the maternal order that support dreamy and sentient production of unconscious material. Provision of the maternal process facilitates that unconscious freedom that analysts conceptualise as part of the primary process. At the same time, however, the patient's psychic life requires the creative interventions of the paternal order.

Winnicott might well have disagreed with this. He wrote that a psychoanalyst's interpretation was like the shining object (the spatula) presented to an infant (1971: 67). Certainly the experience of receiving something 'from the outside' – beyond the bounds of immediate self experience – has precedent in an unseen part of the mother bringing something from the outside world into the intimate relation to the child. At the same time, however, Winnicott and many other analysts have argued that this outside object links the mother's function with the father's presence, as he is the ultimate arbiter of the outside and associated in the unconscious with he who is outside the dreamy world, waiting with a different frame of mind and different expectations. Thus the shining object that comes from elsewhere, introduced through the hands of the mother, already points in another direction – toward the father. In turn, the father's processional identity that resides in his particular way of being and relating, in the self as a process, bears elements of the maternal order. So when the child encounters him he can feel elements of the maternal order within the father's personality.

Many of the analyst's comments are more associative than interpretive. Interpretation brings many elements together and is an implicit act of confrontation. The analysand is expected to recognise this and make use of this object. Failure to do so, or dismissal of the interpretation, will often be regarded as a resistance and bring the analyst back to why the comment was deflected. More associative remarks, however, bear less expectation and demand and sustain the stream of consciousness essential to unconscious collaboration between patient and analyst.

Viewed this way, a typical series of sessions would be authored by three different orders – the infantile or childish, the maternal, and the paternal – as the patient oscillates between periods of silence which facilitate dense internal experiencing,[3] periods of talking that open up such inner experience through free speech that disseminates the self in an infinite series of directions,[4] and moments of reflective concentration when analyst and patient collect meaning from the prior time.

All three ways of knowing are experienced in differing ways by the two participants. The analyst also has infant-like experiences in his daydreams and those mental contents that emerge while lost in thought. The patient emerges from free association and suddenly sees something unseen before: he may interrupt the analyst's reverie to make an objectifying comment.[5]

The image (dream or dense inner experience) arriving in the still centre of being (at night or in a day reverie), its break-up through free utterance, its facilitation by a sentiently welcoming other who desires and shares this swing from quiet to intense experience, its interruption by an other who comes from the outside (and yet is part of our own way of thinking all along), all these movements are ways of knowing that are true to all life but brought together uniquely in a psychoanalysis. This *is* the Oedipal structure of a psychoanalysis. These participants, ghosts of at least three human others, live on as functions. Each is a different type of authority. Who is to say that the dream or the image or the psychic intensity or the affect is to be privileged over all else? To do so would be to cosset the infant and worship him yet again. Who is to say that the reverentially sentient receptive order, the world pregnant with meanings yet to come, is the sacred author of knowledge? To do so would be to worship the Madonna of silence and being. Who is to say that until the duty-bound part of the mind brings the self to account through interpretive grasp of the truth, that all the above may be nice but is meaningless?

These three forms of authorising knowledge and ways of entertaining the truth are as essential to a full analysis as the presence of the mother, the father, and the child are essential to the true realisation of the Oedipal family. It is well known, but worth restating, that Sophocles' *Oedipus Rex* is not the tale of an Oedipus complex, but the story of a family that did not happen. The Oedipal family that the loving Oedipus desired constitutes a creatively destructive child, a receptive other taking in the child and playing with him, and the outsider who is to become part of the inside: the father who is always there and ultimately to be included as the bearer of laws and prohibitions that are essential to thinking and establishing one's being in a social world.

One of the most important tasks of a psychoanalysis is the deconstructive working through of symptoms, pathological structures, and character ailments, but what else is it that a psychoanalysis accomplishes? Psychoanalysts would describe the development of a psychoanalytic attitude[6] as an important outcome of a psychoanalysis; they might, like Lacan, say that it is time to stop an analysis when the patient can tell the analyst about himself, or, like Kohut, they might point to the momentum of the patient's 'health potential' (1984: 44). These views are, to my way of thinking, very important. Indeed it is arguable that the psychic changes illustrated above are only accomplished if the patient can discover the analytic attitude. It requires the capacity to operate according to the three elements of authoring and knowing: a celebration of the dreamer, the infant, the child, the producer of vivid ideas; a capacity to receive life and to bear a not knowing about what is taking place even though a profound mulling over and playing is the medium of such reception; and finally, a search for the truth that calls for judgement. The analysand at the end of an analysis is a dreamer who values his dreams, receptive to the essentials of a lost-in-thought elaboration of dreams and vivid ideas,[7] and intermittently given to insights that bear the unmistakable feel of a truth about the self.

For a psychoanalysis to live up to itself the analyst must be sensitive to the need in each patient of these different forms of knowing. The patient must be a true author of their sessions, as they produce and recollect dreams, narrate vivid moments from the day before, and bear the contents of their own unconscious life. The analyst must sustain the maternal order by comprehending and utilising the essentials of analytical quiet and reverie, a vital presence that receptively introjects the analysand's contents and is essential to the constant flow of unconscious communicating that is always beyond words alone. Finally he must use the function of the father. He is not there simply to celebrate the analysand's capacity, nor is he there only as a holding environment. To provide the third way of knowing he must interrupt the flow of associations with well thought out interpretations that bear psychic change within them.[8]

A psychoanalytical session is an inevitable regression to the early orders of existence not because the analyst acts like a mother or a father, nor even because the patient acts as an infant or child, but because the psychic structures that typify these orders and constitute the very core of mental functioning are amplified in a psychoanalysis. Dreaming and recalling the dream, freely speaking with little sense of the direction of thought, articulating one's inner life through fragments of speech that are incomprehensible metonyms of the denser and thicker world of self experience: these features of analysis call up the maternal order. Then, one self still inside this order, a different frame of mind ensues that is more focal, more intense, more accountable, penetrating into the network of material to find a core truth. Now the patient is inside the paternal order. In a session he may oscillate between these two orders but no position annihilates its opposite. The free associating analysand is still in part affiliated with the law of the father and when the stream of consciousness naturally converges toward a sentient point the patient turns to his paternal functioning to discern what he knows.[9]

Is there an opposition between these two differing ways of thinking and being? A battle of the sexes? In the best sense, yes. The maternal and paternal order are engaged opposites, each essential to the child's evolution. The analysand will succeed only to the extent that the maternal and paternal order combine him. Patients of course have difficulty in tolerating the one or the other and psychoanalysts will make clinical adjustments. A narcissistic patient may find the paternal order too persecuting and the analyst may wisely opt for a long time to be more maternal, slowly introducing the father. An obsessive compulsive personality may feel a deep contempt for the loose world of maternal processes and seek only the lucid hard objects of the father's world. The analyst will take his time introducing the patient to the deconstructive invitation to silence and self abandonment.

The types of authority and knowledge in a psychoanalysis could certainly have been cast in different terms than those I have selected. Writing about a maternal order or a paternal order can feel somewhat archaic and clumsy, perhaps too arbitrary and typecast. Surely *the* mother and *the* father are not to be so clearly defined. We know that both share qualities of the opposite sex. Am I not allegorising where abstract terms would do us better? This may be so. But I prefer the strength of these terms. The maternal and the paternal in us, a combination of differing persons and their functions, appeals to me because I believe our constitutions derive from our inherited form and its transformation not only by two unique but distinct persons with particular attributes but by two persons who have come to embody quite different ways of being and thinking. We can talk about who the mother is and who the father is and talk and talk: it is an endless conversation. Do the terms 'primary process' and 'secondary process' have that life to them? I think not. Nor do the functions these terms designate bear their own histories, while if we think of the mother and the father we simultaneously evoke our own precise histories with these persons and their structures: shared in common between all people. So we are immediately part of our personal history and a universal order, as all of us have *our* mother and *our* father and yet each of us participates in psychic orders that are properly listed under the name of the mother and the name of the father.

Under the regressive move of a psychoanalysis the three participants of the Oedipal triangle are revived, not only in the specular sense, but more importantly in their structural relation to one another. Perhaps Freud's construction of the psychoanalytic process was simply an Oedipal enactment, but if so, it is surely a deployment in the clinical theatre of the most essential parts of us. An adult self is an outcome of these functions, capable of generating inspired ideas that derive from the insulated regions of any self yet able to fully use the complex range of processes introduced by the mother and able to use those functions held in the name of the father. A mix. The adult in analysis knows instinctively how to regress and what parts of the roles on offer to make use of in this profoundly deep revision of one's self.

The political movement that is psychoanalysis – distinguished here from the clinical practice that also bears this name – too often cannibalises parts of the body, elements of the self, dimensions of the other and constructs a group around the part object. It is disconcerting that an important motivation in the psychoanalytical movement is murder of one parent or the other; at the core easily seen in the bifurcation of practice around silence or speech. The failure to combine the parental processes in psychoanalytical practice means that patients are all too often having to live within either a space that is overly maternal or a space that is overly paternal. Efforts to resolve this division are regarded as pluralistically watering down a more pure approach, which may well be a purity based on expulsion of an undesirable object. The Oedipal violence that generates too much of the psychoanalytical movement has inspired a 'part object theory': taking a part of the overall theory of meaning available in psychoanalytical theory and founding either a school or body of thought around that particular part object and then treating it as a sufficient ground of knowledge – more a form of intellectual cloning than it is a true development of theory, with supporters standing in for critical examination, sheer numbers ultimately determining the validity of the theory and its perpetrators.

For the maternal order and the paternal order to be reproductive processes generating a full analysis, psychoanalysis will need to critically examine the movement's violence against this pair. To give birth to truly creative formulations of theory as it relates to practice, the movement will have to appreciate the combined virtues of what derives from the mother and father as a couple. Otherwise our intellections will continue in their matricidal and patricidal ways and psychoanalytical theory will continue as a single-parent family.

5

ONE, TWO...SEVEN

In 'The factor of number in individual and group dynamics' (1950) John Rickman wrote that 'if we were to divide the kinds of psycho-dynamics according to the number of particles or bodies or persons concerned, we could speak of one- and two-body psychologies'. He adds that 'a three-body psychology' would deal with 'all of the derivatives of the Oedipus complex' (166) and further that a 'multi-body psychology' would 'deal with the psychological forces operative when several or many individuals are together' (167). Rickman and his colleague Bion were conducting groups and their division of self and human relations into types of bodies derived in part from their need to conceptualise the source, aim and object of differing dynamics in the group.

Rickman argued that each of the above bodies had its own region of psychological space, something that Michael Balint extended in *The Basic Fault* when he stated that there were 'three areas of the mind'. The first is 'the area of creation' and is characterised by the number 1: 'there is no outside object involved, consequently there is no object-relationship and no transference' (1968: 29). We know little about this part of the mind as 'the subject is on his own and his main concern is to produce something out of himself' (24). It may or may not be an object, Balint says, and it is the mental space through which an individual is creative. The number 2 designates the 'area of the basic fault', two people are involved, but in a more primitive area than 'that obtaining between two adults'. Balint used the term 'fault' because patients considered themselves defective, not, he thought, a structural conflict of the mind – that would be area 3 – but a failure in the self's engagement of the other, reflecting a breakdown in the infant–mother coupling.

Marion Milner (1952) did not enter the numbers game as such, but her paper 'The role of illusion in symbol formation' suggests that the area of illusion, through which the symbol signifies the joined work of self and other, functions as a third object: not the creation of the one, but the work of two. Winnicott subsequently acknowledged the significance of this paper (1971: 44) in the formation of his theory of culture. Asking the question

47

'where do we live?' he said we live neither in an inner world nor an outer world, neither a world driven by inheritance nor one by the environment. Instead, we find ourselves in 'the third area' which 'is a product of the *experiences of the individual person* (baby, child, adolescent, adult) in the environment that obtains'. Typically Winnicott neutralises, if not resolves, one of the thought complexes of psychoanalysis by stating that eventually we are the outcome of the instinctual and the environmental, the works of one and two, now mingled to constitute a third area. He has moved the world of psycho-dynamics to a space where 'there is a kind of variability...that is different in quality from the variables that belong to the phenomenon of inner personal psychic reality and to external or shared reality'. The range and capabilities of this area will depend on 'the summation of actual experiences' (125).

From this we may momentarily assume that 'one person' refers to the work of the individual in solitude and 'two person' refers to the communications between self and other. Three-person psychology would seem to be more complex. Not surprisingly three becomes a crowd of different notions of the third: the Oedipal area for Rickman and Balint, the area of illusion for Milner, and the 'intermediate' area for Winnicott. Rickman suggests a fourth space – the multitude or group – and we can, as I shall discuss later, suggest 'higher' numbers.

There is much interest in contemporary psychoanalysis in the infant–mother interaction but Freud did not take the observed relation to be the fundamental object of psychoanalytic enquiry, and some analysts, such as Andre Green (1996), regard the observable actual scene as a misplacing of the psychoanalytic attention. There is another, unobservable scene, through which we appear as selves: the internal theatre that intensifies through the absence of the other – not the figure of the interacting self filmed by infant observers but the internal world constructed by the infant's desire. Furthermore, as Winnicott put it, it is often the world 'of sleep and the deep dreaming that is at the core of the personality' (1971: 128) rather than the world of wakeful alert perception. (Still another scene is language where we speak the self through chains of signifiers, encoded by the private context of lived experience.)

Freud discovered a new way to view the inner world. By sitting with the analysand out of sight, out of touch and relatively speechless, he minimised the actuality of developed otherness, but by inviting free associations he indicated the presence of a deeply attentive other. When represented, the patient's internal objects often bore clear resemblance to actual others – but dreams alone created composite figures not only made up of several people, but part people who were themselves signifiers of diverse places, times, events, and non-interpersonal problematics. Once again the human figure was used as a representational device for the presentation of complex ideas not inevitably conceptualising the interpersonal. (The unconscious comprehension that the form of human relations is often used for non-relational purposes is frequently realised in the paranoid fantasy of the human race being occupied by aliens who intend to take it over by falsely adopting human form. Arguably, this take-over occurs whenever we dream, when ideas colonise our self and our others for their own purposes.)

The materialisation of psychic states in the figure of a self or object representation is illusory as a person or part person is used to present multiple elements. On the fringes of the dream is its abstract expressionist vision, sometimes entering the dream space itself to Picasso potentially recognisable figures into bizarre figurations, and always briefly visible in the slash editings from one intelligible dream sequence to its next frame. These are the rare sightings of the dream process revealing itself, at the momentary expense of the conventional figures of everyday life.

The realisation of internal object relations, of elements functioning through the dynamic play of presentations in the two-person enactments of the transference, is also illusory, as the theatre psychoanalysis manifests the always absent immaterial processes of psychic life through the comforting presences of a self with its other.

The classical model's theories of evenly suspended attentiveness and neutrality were never intended to imitate interpersonal reality, but rather, to portray the intrapsychic through the projective possibilities of the interpersonal where the object's reply is of the self's own making. The structure of two allowed the internal figures and dynamics of one to speak.

As we know, however, it was not long before Freud noted that a patient's transference was a form of thinking. The presence of the analyst evoked needs, interests, anxieties and desires directed towards his otherness and with the passing of time psychoanalysts realised countertransference was another medium for the expression of unconscious ideas.

This brings us to a watershed of sorts.

There are two rather different types of transference and two rather different forms of countertransference. We can think of one as the 'classical' mode of functioning, transferring internal objects onto the screen of the analyst, and countertransference composed of that moving complex of ideas occurring during his state of evenly suspended attentiveness. Freud termed this 'the untroubled transference', to which we add the untroubled countertransference, the moment when the analyst 'means to catch the drift of the patient's unconscious with his own unconscious' (1923: 239). Not fundamentally the figuration of people, these passing mental objects are personified instincts, affects, fantasies and memories: the interpersonal conscripted as psychic allegory.

The other transference, however, is an unconscious action upon the person of the analyst, using his embodied subjectivity to realise some unconscious idea. The analyst feels himself employed not simply as a screen, but as an other called into a role relation, intended to act thoughts, not think them. We are now in the relational mode of functioning.

Analysts of the English Independent group (see especially, Rycroft 1986, Khan 1974, Klauber 1987 and Wright 1991) write about the functions of illusion in the analytical setting, such as the illusion that whatever crosses the analyst's mind while in the presence of the patient, expresses the patient's being. This illusion allows for maximum consideration of the patient's psychic life, especially as the psychoanalyst's countertransference is understood as the patient's voice.

But is this not a distortion of the truth? As the analyst's subjectivity is a vital constituent in this communication, how can it be taken as the patient's presence?

Because, the English argue, through this illusion the analyst heightens his subjective realisation of the patient. Assuming that what crosses his mind in the evenly suspended state is created by the patient's communications – a licence issued by the suspension of the complete truth – allows for unhindered thought. Freud said that the 'course of free association produced a plentiful store of ideas' (1924: 196), to which we could add that the analyst's associations do that as well, and the classical mode of listening employs a deep subjectivity.

We remind ourselves that the material used by any other to affect our self must be our own subjectivity. It is the clay out of which the other is shaped.

This illusion not only creates a wealth of ideas, it also enhances objectivity. Why? Because with the patient's imaginings, following one after another, a plenitude of ideas is created, often contradictory, all soon to be the ephemera of the free associative, as idea is changed by next idea, in turn changed by next idea, in a steady stream of the subjective.

It is the mutability of this stream that modifies our view of any one or another of its single elements. Work within this area of a self is full of paradox. For example, by not only accepting but welcoming one's subjective elaborations of a patient's presence and discourse, the analyst is clearly at ease with his unconscious participation in the analysis, yet paradoxically, the plethora of associations diminishes the effect of any single subjective response. Furthermore, images, words and feelings often contradict one another – the subjective is impressive as the movement of differences – and upon reflection the analyst can objectify his or her own prior states of mind precisely because the work of difference highlights the variables of thought.

This is not to say that the psychoanalyst is objective while in this frame of mind, but it is of interest that they produce more objects of thought through heightened subjectivity, and, in this very important respect, ally themselves with the process of objectification. Classical analytical training supports a less subjective frame of mind. In the course of the analysand's free associations they will move from one topic to the next in an unpremeditated chain of associations. It is an important part of the psychoanalyst's work to note the exact order of these associations and to ascertain whether the logic of the chain of ideas reveals a hidden line of thought. If so, it will be their task to indicate to the analysand what has been on their mind.

These two frames of mind operate in different temporal orders. The deeply subjective imagining of one's patient is the unthought-out movement of ideas from moment to moment, a dense feeling of thoughts, that does not know itself for what it is. The retrospective identification of the analysand's free associations can only occur when one looks back on what the patient has been talking about in the session.

Paradoxically, most efforts to objectify the moment in speech would shut down the work of subjectivity and its objective yield. An effort to speak mutuality, through for example the ongoing disclosure of one's cognised 'subjective response', would so stylise the intersubjective as to deprive it of its function, allowing a subjectivity to create itself out of the other's psychic life. But such creativity is not akin to reciprocal effect or symmetrical rendering: what one self does with the other's effect will eventually become a deep elaboration lost on both participants, as finally it enters the unconscious to be changed forever.

Where is self disclosure to be found? Where is any person's subjectivity? Revealed that is? In what they say *about* themselves? Or *in* the saying, especially when not talking about themselves?

And so, where does the intersubjective operate in the analytical pair? In what the analyst discloses of themselves? Or even in what they presume to know of themselves? Or in what the patient knows or discloses of themselves? Or, thinking of the analyst, does the intersubjective work through the unconscious perception of the patient, of the selection and focus on one image or word, on the extenuation in the analyst's mind of a particular feeling in response to what the patient says, in the decision to speak up about something, and not something else, in the way it is worded and the tone of voice in which it is articulated? And if this is where it operates then how can it possibly be reported? Would it not be too unconscious, except when pathology repeated something so much it forced itself on the analyst? But otherwise, isn't the intersubjective outside the field of the subject's consciousness...that is, if it is truly intersubjective?

The injunction that analysts should report their 'personal response' or 'personal contribution', their conscious sense of the total local meaning of one moment to the next, is possible, but only in the most shallow sense. Unfortunately, routine reporting of one's 'personal' response to a patient's material, or the gracious egalitarian sharing of one's own historical contribution to the problematics of the analytical encounter, or reporting these details in peer group meetings or in one's writings, unwittingly evacuates the work of subjectivity in the name of being personal.

Back to the function of illusion.

When an actor, let us say Ralph Fiennes, plays Hamlet, he must get into a state of mind where he believes he is Hamlet. And just as we, watching this play, must entertain the illusion that we are watching Hamlet and not, in fact, Fiennes, so too the psychoanalyst must believe that what crosses their mind is occasioned by the patient and not by the analyst. They will appreciate the patient more and they will learn more. When a supervisee interrupts themselves to explain how their response to their patient derives from their own past, perhaps recounting something of their early relations or their psychic structure, they unwittingly abort their patient's transference in the name of equality. They have failed to see that all along, their narrative (i.e. the case report) is the unconscious expression of their countertransference and the supervisor will consciously or unconsciously feel the supervisee's representation of the patient. Further, countertransference experiencing – if it is to be true to the unconscious – is fundamentally unknowable and efforts to identify it and to indicate what comes from one's own sensibility as opposed to the patient, bears the strain of the rationalised.

But if countertransference is fundamentally unknowable then what use is it and how does it bear on the two-person psychology? Is it not simply one's own processing of another person, so deeply subjective as to be beyond conscious exploitation for therapeutic aims?

The vast majority of analytical writings on the topic do not describe the countertransference as such (which is an unconscious process) but rather its failures, which usually create distress in the analyst and force something into consciousness. They describe an interaction derived from a patient's pathological structure, that has moved the analyst into a recurring mental state, which he or she may match with the transference and eventually make into an interpretation. Indeed, this discovery has been of considerable importance in the history of psychoanalysis as many of these pathologies are derived from disturbed self–other relations in childhood and the analyst can use his position to objectify aspects of that history.

One-person psychology, then, appears to recognise the work of the self in relative isolation – quintessentially in the dream, but also in daydreams, unconscious fantasies, passing mental fragments, affects, instinctual derivatives and so forth. Two-person psychology however receives the work of the self in relation to the other. One-person psychology recognises the centrality of the libidinal body as the erotogenic signifier of the self's desire, while two-person psychology recognises a different body: the interactive conveyer of meaning and response to the presence of the other. Intriguingly, one and two interanimate in the state of sexual attraction, when one finds another of particular libidinal interest. This moment is quintessentially dependent upon two factors: an unconscious preconception in the self of the sexually attractive other, and the appearance in reality of someone who transforms that preconception into a realisation, to use Bion's thinking for a moment. It would be meaningless without the driving that is instinctual life, but it would be impossible without the arrival of the other who fits the bill. This is a moment when two very powerful objects, Freud's instinctual object and the integrity of the other, interpenetrate.

Meetings between the two objects cultivate erotic knowledge, that knowing that arrives when lovers instinctively comprehend one another's erogeneity surrendering to a timing, a touching, a pressure, a hesitation, a...that comes from this knowing. This knowledge is laid down through maternal touch of the infant's body and met by the infant's instinctual readiness.

As I have said, neither of these two psychologies could ever be separated entirely from the other. Winnicott's theory of the capacity to be alone is useful in considering their coexistence. He saw in the small child at play in the presence of the mother, a coexistence of one- and two-person psychology. The child is alone in his own subjectivity, but the presence of the other is vital authorisation for this departure from interpersonalisation towards deep inner experiencing and its partial materialisation through play. Sometimes he will turn to the mother and use her as a medium for self expression, in which case what looks like two-person mutuality is more like one person using the other as an extension of the self's expressive vocabulary. But at other times the child will turn to the mother as integral object, seeking her out for her difference and her response. Arguably each is a pleasure fulfilling differing desires.

This is practice in being one-of-two, as a former two-in-one.

And do we not find that in a single session the analyst moves back and forth between these two different areas? Is it not vitally important for him to know when he is being used as an object of thought for the elaboration of the analysand's state of mind and when he is being coerced as an other, aimed into the interpersonal? Does the former state not call for quiet sustaining the right of thought itself? Bearing in mind that when he is used for the projection of an internal object – in the interest of psychic elaboration – that as the screen for an internal object he contains a condensation of many psychic elements and these elements could not, and should not, be sorted out through the remedial work of the analyst welcoming it into the relational field. This would be a category error, would it not? The error here would be akin to mistaking the dream space for actuality, wrongly assuming that the dream can be worked through if the dream objects speak back to the dreamer about his own experience of being dreamed.

Alternatively, psychoanalysts have learned in recent decades that sustaining the silent screen for the analysand who is urgently constructing a conflicted self or disturbed other through the transference, is to misconstrue the patient's effort. Such would not be a mere act of projective elaboration, but a request for interpretive understanding of what is being shaped through the relational.

I shall use a brief clinical vignette to highlight something of what I mean.

A patient in the middle of a long analysis begins the hour, in silence. He says nothing for about five minutes. He then tells me that as he was driving to the session he passed by Bush House and while he did his mood changed. He had been thinking about a writing project earlier in the day, then had thought about his wife who was enduring some difficult physical pains, and had viewed his session as something where he might be relieved of certain anxieties, but when he passed Bush House his mood changed. He was silent for about a minute and I knew from work with him that he was losing himself in further inner associations, so I remained quiet, although I had my own associations both to this place and to its presence in the hour. He then free associated to the name 'Bush' and later to 'House', which created a complex but interesting network of mental contents that thickened the hour. I thought I saw a thread running through them, in which he seemed to be saying 'I am bushed with life in my house'.

For the first thirty-five minutes of this hour I think he used me fundamentally as the realisation of a listening part of the self delegated to me. A transference interpretation crossed my mind – I thought of saying that he seemed to lose his sense of purpose on the way to talk to me – but this was not a serious idea and would have been an interruption of his free associations. Then I felt a change of speech in the patient, from let us say the classical mode to the relational one, and it was out of this context that I shifted in myself and gathered some of my prior associations into consciousness where they sat for about five minutes before I said that I thought he experienced me as 'bushed' – i.e. tired of him – and thus disinterested in working further with him. This occurred when his associations diminished and a silence seemed heavy, during which I imagined that he might be turning now to familiar and rather tiresome weekly if not daily complaints. I was aware of feeling fatigued and looked at my clock to see how much time remained. He said that he didn't know how long it would take him to discover what his feelings meant that day, and clearly he too was aware of the ending of the session. But it was my state of mind that contributed to my decision to say that I thought he might be struggling with an anxiety that I was tired of him. To be sure, this was a refrain in the analysis, so my thought did not come out of the blue, but in fact derived from the history of our collaboration. And it was true enough on this occasion to bring relief when spoken: he went on to add that now he remembered some ten minutes after passing Bush House, while turning a corner in his car, an image of me as 'Father Time', which had amused him, but also worried him as he was not sure how he could tell me this, and further, he wondered how old I was, and whether I was in the sort of physical health that I should be.

I believe that my interpretation evoked prior thoughts having to do with the two-person relation and these are important. But simply because we do not know what he was thinking in his silences, nor what was on my mind in my own associative life, we must not assume that what takes place in the one-person area is of less significance. The word 'Bush' for example, proved in subsequent sessions to have wide and divergent meanings, both for the patient and for myself, which not only outlived my parochial use of it from the countertransference, but also eventually proved to be independent of transference and countertransference.

In any given session, then, the patient oscillates. Sometimes he speaks to the analyst as an internal object with which he is communing – not addressing him, but speaking in the presence of an other that serves as the human screen for mental life itself. At other times he both acts upon and talks to the analyst, and the analyst feels his otherness called into interpersonal engagement. Sessions mirror life in this way, don't they? We know the difference, don't we, between ourselves lost in thought – often in the presence of the other – and ourselves intently engaged in dialogue with the other.

By a one-person psychology, then, I think we mean to refer to all those thoughts and feelings that fundamentally derive from the dream works of a self. By a two-person psychology I think we refer to all those ideas and feelings that derive from the work of two engaged subjectivities. Clinically, 'one person' refers to that potentially infinite dissemination of unconscious derivatives released through free association, an unbinding movement that Laplanche terms the 'anti-hermeneutic' element of psychoanalysis. Clinically, 'two person' alludes to the mutually organising effect that two may exert upon each participant, a binding through mutual effect and the sense made of it.

Nonetheless, these terms are somewhat misleading, especially if we ask where the two person exists. In some mutually constructed interpersonal mental area, equidistant from the participants? Of course not. For after all, the two shall always be registered in the one, often fitting neatly into the interpersonal paradigm that has derived from the history of self–other relations, and that lives on as 'internal dialogue' between a speaker/imaginer and its others. Winnicott's third area is the creation of two, but each will interpret and use it differently. In the end, all relations between two people are collapsed into the labile immateriality of the individual psyche.

It was this world that Freud took to be the object of psychoanalysis.

Let me illustrate this problem by examining a typical moment in any group psychotherapy, but which also happens in a less obvious though no less important way in any individual treatment. A group has been discussing several themes, such as the fear that several of its members are striving to form a sexual pair, or the wish to have a leader who is more accepting of aggression, or the anxiety that one member of the group is being scapegoated because she is visibly irked by the way the group is going today. Differing members of the group struggle with one another to clarify what they truly feel and think. Some of these discussions are successful. For example, one member thought that another member had dismissed her out of contempt, but the other replied that this was not true, as he found her

55

attractive, yet as she did not sit next to him that day he was hurt and did not know how to react to her. So one member had an internal object relation corrected by the actual other who was there to negotiate on his behalf. But as the session wound to a close the group was palpably anxious. Of the many differing sources of this anxiety one is always invariant. Each member of the group unconsciously knows that as the differing members leave one another as actual others, they are now fated to become an internal object inside these others where one's self is no longer negotiable. For even if this internal object relation to be is derived from the self–other actuality of the group members, soon it will be distorted not only by small *Nachträglichkeiten* (or after thinkings), worked in the unconscious by subsequent experiences and what is evoked, but by the character of psychic life which will, amongst other things, link one person with another, and another, forming a condensed internal object, or link a part of an interaction with one person and join it with another person's comments. In time, selves in their experience of actual others dissolve in the solution of the primary process.

And yet our unconscious, that strange object of our endopsychic aware-ness, and puzzle to consciousness, is substantially derived from what Laplanche terms the 'enigmatic signifier' (1992: 21): the mother's uncon-scious which seduces us into psychic life. She conveys, as Lichtenstein argued, 'imprints', 'an identity upon the human child' (1961: 78). And for Pontalis, the dream 'as an object in the analysis, refers to the maternal body' (1981: 29). Thus the very zone of the deconstructed – what we term the primary process – derives in the very first place out of a relation.

Does this not now 'worry' the distinction we seek to make through a separation of the world of one and the world of two? Two seems to be an intrinsic part of one, both in its formation, and subsequently in its psychic structure, organised as it is around the illusion of an internal dialogue. And yet, the unconscious as mother is an other that not only operates as the ungraspable, but as deconstructor of the conventional aspirations of the relational world. Even as two people unconsciously communicate with one another, they find in the unconscious of the other, a principle of mispercep-tive recreation (of oneself) that belies the notion of such communication as mutual or partnering.

Still, in order to discuss the relative worlds of the one and the two, some will accept these terms for all their limitations, as they serve a heuristic purpose.

And within the spirit of illusion, we return to Rickman who points to the Oedipus complex as a third space and to an unnamed but implicit fourth object that would be the group. The Oedipal includes that mental object that is one's family, an object that is not the outcome of any one person or indeed any two persons, but is the work of at least three. We might think of it as a culture saturated with implicit unconscious rules of engagement determined by the interacting personalities. Or, we might say that it is a mentality in which one lives and from which one derives certain basic assumptions about being and relating. As an internal object it would be composed of all those rules and the mentality that it gives rise to might be rather palpable in consciousness. When I think of certain friends' families, a certain feel of what it was like to take part in their life comes to mind, as does the feel of my own family.

But when the child goes off to school he more fully encounters a fifth object, beyond the self, the self and mother, the self and family. While there are now rules of engagement, there are also breakdowns in the function of convention that group theory argues is psychotic. There is, then, a fifth object within us that registers and gives mental place to our experience of life beyond our family, but life in a society of others.

We might add the number 'six' to refer to what we may think of as the 'universal order' – those assumptions, principles, and laws of our civilisation that render us part of a group that is not immediate and which may be negated or suspended by contemporary culture, but to which we belong very deeply and to which we refer ourselves often, consciously and unconsciously. Thus those incarcerated during the Holocaust felt they were suspended in a world that had negated the values of the Judaeo-Christian world, but this negation only highlighted the existence and importance of those values to which we subscribe.

'Six' still refers to human culture, to what we are joined to, even if society does not bear it. Further, concepts such as love, knowledge, truth and beauty, are part of this universal order and are often less easily defined, much less usable as cultural objects by any society.

The number 'seven' might refer then to objects relatively beyond the limits of the thinking we call culture – to the presence of objects mentally ungraspable, such as the universe, or infinity, or the structure of the unconscious. It would also be a designation of death or oblivion, or the thingness of an object that is always beyond perception, that signifies the limits of vision. It was Lacan who re-emphasised the concept of the real to mark this plane of one's existence. We see evidence everywhere, don't we, of our death to be, from momentary blindness, to losses of consciousness, to unknown sleeps during assumed wakeful life.

Certain objects move between these numbered orders. Transitions between registers of experience are created, none more so than through the word 'God' which is both immanent to each order and therefore transcendent.

One-person and two-person psychology have places then in a kind of modern cosmology of what Milner terms 'overlapping circles' (1977: 279), to which we would add further numbers designating other domains of mental life, all of which in differing ways are experienced and registered in a psychoanalysis by our patients but some of which still elude our conceptual ambitions. Each number refers to a different state of mind and to a different psychic constellation, although, as each is a part of our mental life there are types of relation between each of these differing orders.

These orders are thought by any individual self alone, even if he or she has collaborated many times over with many different others and even as each recalls the work of prior generations. As overlapping circles of influence they also serve as metaphors of what is meant by the depth and thickness of an individual self. Bearing the layers and their intrasubjective networks, at any moment in time, a self is a dense striation of orders, overworked by the elements of psychic life.

In the midst of writing this chapter, I asked Marion Milner a question that I knew she had considered in differing ways throughout her life.

AUTHOR: I am trying to describe that part of a two-person relation where one (or both) are engaged with one another, in some way, but are not fundamentally being 'inter'subjective, when their respective inner experiences are thick and deep and not 'mutual'. What type of relation is this?

MARION MILNER: You mean, when the self uses the other as a medium like a painter a canvas?

AUTHOR: Yes, that's it.

Of course, if the canvas could speak, what would *it* say?

6

THE GOALS OF
PSYCHOANALYSIS?

An early morning patient talks about his growing realisation that his long-vilified business associate is a stand-in for aspects of himself that he hates. The next patient, two years in analysis, twitches in silence, thrashing about, complaining that he does not know what to talk about. What is the point of lying in silence, he wonders, if neither of us has an agenda for him? I remain silent. The next patient, a schizophrenic woman in her second analysis, is just now allowing herself to recollect her childhood which she does in a kind of Proustian narrative, moving from room to room, person to person, and event to event, in a meticulous if somewhat cautious manner. She is followed by a brilliant former philanderer who has sexualised all his relations in order to evacuate others along with extinguished instincts, now in the third month of a depressive breakdown. After tea an anorexic adolescent arrives in a manic mood, determined to convince me that her body is of no consequence and a hindrance to the transcendent beauty of disincarnated thought.

As my day continues I experience the distinct being of each and every one of my patients. The complex of this registration – or countertransference – marks each as different; I am affected in mind and body by the 'impressions' they make on me. From month to month, week to week, session to session, and from segment of hour to segment of hour, certain tasks arise in my mind, which I set about to accomplish. The schizophrenic analysand, for example, was involved in an important retrieval of her early life and of a self arriving out of recollection, and for days this change in her disposition was met by a kind of supportive silence on my part. Then it seemed to me that she changed her aim. Overly meticulous recollections seemed to dissipate the emotional experience of remembering through excess detail, so I commented on this.

The anorectic began the hour in a manic mood and I felt immediately that I would have to bring her relation to her body into the field of mental vision, and my manner of working was informed by this goal, but once she was more incarnated, my disposition changed and I simply listened to her.

Would it be possible to write a type of notebook recording the changing goals of working with a patient, one reflecting the complexity of psychoanalysis?

These goals, however, would also have to include the vicissitudes of the analyst's unconscious aspirations, some of which would be less than clear. For example, with the philanderer I was aware of hoping that his discovery of true affection for a recent female acquaintance would result in his experiencing true loss when he jettisoned her. And when he experienced something of this loss I was pleased that it had come to this. I was pleased too when my anorectic patient gained weight and resumed her academic career with some success.

These feelings indicate all kinds of wishes for my patients, some understandable, others unfortunate. The development of these countertransferences is inevitable, some are analysable, and they form an important part of the treatment of any patient. As a group of goals, however, they verge on partly answering the question of why one becomes an analyst in the first place: to help people in distress, to contact parts of oneself through the other, to repair a damaged object, to.... Each analyst could only ever partly answer this question through his own personal analysis.

Further, what we know of the countertransference is remarkably meagre in light of its composition; as we shall only ever be able to think through the structure of the patient's pathology when it repeatedly shapes our inner life with the rather dreadful force of the redundant. Otherwise, our response will be deeply subjective and complex. We shall always distinguish in our unconscious the precise idiom of any individual patient's impression upon us, but this is more a matter of form than of content, known through the odd experience of being deeply affected by the way a patient exists through us, even when he says little of significance to us. This knowledge will be forever unthought even as it is known, simply because we do not have the means of thinking it. Marion Milner (personal communication, 1997) believes that at this level the analyst's goal is often to serve as a 'medium' for the patient. We could think of the analyst as being composed by the patient much the way a writer composes a novel, or a painter a painting, or a musician a score.

The goals of the analyst in psychoanalytical work with any person are subject to numerous psychic vicissitudes, inevitably part of the unconscious communication that we call transference and countertransference, but are these goals the same as those of analysis?

Were we to turn from the individual psychoanalyst establishing tasks in work with each of his particular patients to groups of analysts we would discover another set of goals. These are hatched, developed, marketed, and sometimes imperialistically supported by the so-called schools of psychoanalysis. Here we can see a wide-ranging difference between psychoanalysts, in terms of their stated goals. Klein (1932), for example, writes: 'In regard to the adult the function of psycho-analysis is clear. It is to correct the unsuccessful course which his psychological development has taken' (1961: 279). Analysts of other schools would not see the goal of psychoanalysis as 'course correction', with successful analysis of the paranoid schizoid condition allowing the patient to enter the depressive position.

Indeed analysts of differing schools select particular areas of interest, which then tend to dominate their theoretical writings and group relations for periods of time. For example, while there is comparatively little emphasis in British psychoanalysis on the notational observation of the instantiation of the patient's unconscious through slips, free associations and the flow of signifiers, it is an important part of the Lacanian technique.

There is a surprising variation in the stated goals of psychoanalysts from the differing schools. A Kleinian might say that the aim is to return projectively identified parts of the self to the individual, a Kohutian that it is to alter pathological self–object relations and replace them with generative self–object relations, an ego psychologist that it means enlarging the conflict-free sphere of the ego, and a Lacanian that it is to bring the patient into a position to comprehend the truth of his desire. Each of these aims refers to a complex theoretical system and to clinical practice waiting in the wings.

When we consider the goals of analysis, are we not referring to the differing aims of 'schooled' analysts? And if so, where does that leave us? It would seem to put us in a curious location. A careful examination of the difference between schools might reveal that virtually all that is held in common amongst analysts is the room with a couch. Furthermore, consideration of the psychology of analytical schools that become movements would, I believe, reveal an extremism of thought, partly because movements of this kind need to canalise their focus and partly because schools that become movements often engage in the kind of warfare which affects the mentality of its participants. On a more positive note, this narrowed focus can also yield deeper insight as seen in the Kleinian understanding of psychotic object relations or the Lacanians' grasp of the subject's articulation through the signifier. But the overall psychoanalytical movement – composed of all the differing schools and movements – is a jagged affair and hardly an advertisement for enlightened intellectual development.[1] If we put aside this rivalrous quest for power, and destructive opposition, the effect of such movements on thinking and the development of psychoanalytical thought, what we observe, in my view, are extreme positions taken in the name of instincts, object relations, language, affects, true self living, empathy, or the transference. But as each of these interests is a vital part of the entire picture of any one self and work with any one person there is a kind of recurring mad scramble to recover one or another of these areas that has been put in the margins by the canalising effects of any one of the groups acting in the name of a part of the self.

Is it possible to consider the goals of psychoanalysis independently of the goals set by any of the schools which have become movements? And if each movement is inevitably extremist, then are we not goal-directed in extreme ways? Would a young person seeking a 'complete' analysis have to visit different countries during the course of a lifetime, and go through a course of differing analyses, each of which elucidated according to its speciality some part of the total self – the self's internal object relations, interpersonal responsiveness, linguistic markings, affective requirements, integrating adaptiveness, and so forth?

To some extent this chapter could conclude here. Perhaps it should. For if we now ask of ourselves, what other goal or goals of analysis there could be – other than those of any of the differing schools – what possible answer do we have? We could only find an answer if we regarded the schools as necessary concentrations that have substantially developed a particular area of consideration – relation to the object, arrival of the signifier, transference, spontaneity in being – but the movements as partly destructive of the very accomplishments of any school's concentration, because a part object theory is promoted as a whole object realisation.

Is there or was there ever something in psychoanalysis that seemed to be *its* goal, before ego psychology, object relations, self psychology, Lacanian theory or relational theory got hold of it and redefined it? Accepting the advances achieved in the name of these revisions, was there anything that not only cannot be revised, but which in its essentials was the quintessence of the psychoanalytic enterprise?

Could we ask the muse psychoanalysis, what is your goal?

I do not think this muse would say, as Klein did, that the goal of psychoanalysis was to correct the course of psychological development. Nor do I think the muse would isolate one of the elements of a self – be it its object relations, language, relational skills, nature of its being, or affective architecture – and privilege it. I do not think she would suggest improvement anywhere. The wish to alleviate suffering, to correct destructive processes, to heal symptoms, may be goals of the individual psychoanalyst, but they do not constitute a particular psychoanalytic goal, that is, an aspiration that only psychoanalysis can bring into existence.

What goal is the goal of psychoanalysis?

What is it that only *it* can do?

To answer this I think we must look at its method, to ask if there is anything it requires that only it can do.

Psychoanalysis has only ever had one requirement, one aim, one goal of its own. There has only ever been one request. A request that Freud enunciated, often found difficult to follow, but which was realisable for each participant. In the name of psychoanalysis he asked the patient to speak whatever crossed his mind. The goal was free association.

In the 'Two Encyclopaedia Articles' of 1923 restating the goals of psychoanalysis he discussed '*The "Fundamental Technical Rule" of...*"free association"'.

> The treatment is begun by the patient being required to put himself in the position[2] of an attentive and dispassionate self-observer, merely to read off all the time the surface of his consciousness, and on the one hand to make a duty of the most complete honesty while on the other not to hold back any idea of communication, even if (1) he feels that it is too disagreeable or if (2) he judges that it is nonsensical or (3) too unimportant or (4) irrelevant to what is being looked for. It is uniformly found that precisely those ideas which provoke these last-mentioned reactions are of particular value in discovering the forgotten material.
>
> (1923a: 238)

Asserting this fundamental rule, Freud implicitly addresses the types of resistance to free association, including those of outright disaffection, but including the embarrassment of speaking something seemingly idiotic, or distracting, or far beneath the lofty tasks of psychoanalysis. To this list of resistances Freud later added many more, especially those created by the transference, and those driven by the peculiar character of the analysand.

But Freud's and other analysts' subsequent concentration on the resistances and the technical tasks involved should not obscure the revolutionary moment created by the goal of psychoanalysis. When Freud arrived at this point in his technique he not only fashioned a method that was forever distinctively psychoanalytic; psychoanalysis as a moment in Western culture founded a new and radically liberating state of mind. Few other intellectual traditions had been as linear and goal-directed as Western consciousness, which, let us be reminded, remains highly focused, directed, and aims at a special day of deliverance when the faithful will march into the Promised Land, or in the secular world, privileges hard science which delivers on the promise of objective cross-verifiability. To ask Western man to discover truth by abandoning the effort to find it and adopting instead the leisurely task of simply stating what crosses the mind moment to moment is to undermine the entire structure of Western epistemology.

For the patient to successfully attempt free association the analyst had to adopt a particular position. If Freud specified a goal for the patient, he soon discovered a corresponding one for the analyst.

> Experience soon showed that the attitude which the analytic physician could most advantageously adopt was to surrender himself to his own unconscious mental activity, in a state of *evenly suspended attention*, to avoid so far as possible reflection and the construction

of conscious expectations, not to try to fix anything that he heard particularly in his memory, and by these means to catch the drift of the patient's unconscious with his own unconscious.

(1924f: 239)

Not only had psychoanalysis asked its patients to adopt a new and radical position, it now required the practitioner to join him in a complementary frame of mind. Once there, in this unfocused and dreamy state – what Pound called 'the obscure reveries / Of the inward gaze' (in 'Hugh Selwyn Mauberley') – the analyst would, without concentrating on it, discover that the patient's 'associations emerged like allusions, as it were, to one particular theme' (239). So unlike the mantra-like states of certain Eastern religions, the reverie created by psychoanalysis yielded themes from within the self that would otherwise have remained outside of consciousness. No mere recreational development, it was an enormous step forward in Western epistemology.

Free association was the only goal of psychoanalysis. It was also the most distinctive feature of psychoanalysis, and one that immediately radically repositioned Western man's relation to himself. It was the method by which unconscious trains of thought – in the patient and in the analyst – could come into consciousness. Many observations have been added to this discovery. We know that it sponsors regression in the transference as one becomes more childlike in returning to forms of expression more typical of the self's earliest life. It also makes the speaker more porous to slips, fragments of phrases and images and invites the self to experience the form of its own unconscious. It also devolves false self, as in the spontaneity of the analysand's free association one perceives what Winnicott meant by the true self – in this case, speech, as verbal gesture, a moving of inner possibility into lingual realisation. We add, as well, the free associative process that moves in thick silence, as well as in loose speech, and the associative that operates according to the use of the object in the transference and the countertransference. To associations that move in the symbolic and imaginary order we must add the affective order, the mood movement of speaking, one that resides in a curious accompaniment of body and voice that directly affects the other. When we think now of free association we include all these dimensions which refer to its many elements: non-verbal, verbal, imaginary, symbolic, affective, and so forth.

Some of what has been added would seem to qualify the basic rule.

Certain associating patients, for example, would seem to be evacuating the contents of their mind. Others would do so in a subtle way to accommodate to the interpretive wishes of the analyst. Others function so concretely that their discourse seems hardly free, much less associative. In 'A short account of psycho-analysis' (1924f) Freud wrote:

The choice of free association as a means of investigating the forgotten unconscious material seems so strange that a word in justification of it will not be out of place. Freud was led to it by an expectation that the so-called 'free' association would prove in fact to be unfree, since, when all conscious intellectual purposes had been suppressed, the ideas that emerged would be seen to be determined by the unconscious material.

(195)

The associations would be less than free, as he would stress in other writings, because of resistance. Indeed, much of the subsequent history of theories of technique could be understood in terms of comprehending why ideal free association is not possible. Yet the restrictions on free association, either that created by the thread of thought that ties some of them together, or those imposed by resistance, reveal their shapes freely. They are established in the psychic atmosphere of a type of freedom that openly betrays its restraints. Free association, then, was never intended to provide an ideal talk in which the observer noted from the train all the sights seen on the journey. Given Freud's phobic anxieties about train travel, perhaps he noted the presence of resistances in his choice of metaphoric vehicle. In theory one should be able to ride this train without hindrance. In practice it would generate and deploy the unconscious conflicts of the mind.

In its simplest but most important sense free association occurs when any speaker begins to lose his line of spoken thought as *other* thoughts arise and break the continuity of manifest ideas only to reveal in time hidden strands of thought. Anyone given enough talking time will free associate, as verbal coherence breaks down and new and divergent, if not conflicted, ideas come into voice.

When speaking we find that inner thoughts arise in the back of the mind, discordant with the spoken narrative. We are thinking about something other than what we are now talking about. These thoughts are in complete free association as the speaker is willing another line of thought altogether yet being interrupted by new thoughts which if anything prove distracting and unwelcome. Psychoanalysts often see this through the patient's change of voice, as he will speak with less investment in the spoken word. 'Do other thoughts occur to you' is all one need ask to help the patient abandon one line of thought for another which is more immediately charged with feeling and meaning. It takes time before a patient truly realises that it is okay to abandon one narrative for another, resulting in an occasional manifest confusion in the interest of materialising the unconscious.

When the patient realises he can break the manifest sense of a narrative, in order to speak the newly arrived – such as when he interrupts himself to report thoughts passing through the back of his mind and when he does not have to 'relate' to the analyst by trying to make sense of a shift in thought then he is, in Winnicott's sense, 'using' the object. Free association as such a use of the object is understood by both analyst and patient to be a necessary destruction of relating, as the patient needs to create himself in the presence of the other without being hindered by the supposed conventions of relationship.

Freud recognised two fundamental dimensions to free association and in effect gave them two names: '*freie Assoziation*' for the associative movement of spoken thought in the session and '*Einfall*' for the sudden dropping in of an idea from out of the blue. *Freie Assoziation* may refer more to the logic of the freely associated as the unpremeditated chain of ideas constitutes a freedom of thought functioning only through association eventually revealing latent thoughts not immediately manifest in the sequence of ideas. An *Einfall* enter consciousness suddenly, often with no apparent connection to previously spoken ideas. Perhaps the mentality created by *freie Assoziation* potentialises the arrival of the sudden idea.

Indeed in the frame of mind termed 'evenly suspended attentiveness' the analyst's thoughts will occasionally break away from the patient's speakings, travelling far from the here and now into the 'somewhere else', yet curiously, when returning to the present the analyst is now 'full' of x (i.e. the self on the verge of realisation and thus full of itself) driven by emerging thought pushing towards consciousness, queuing up on the springboard of speech. Speaking creates intermediate objects, between the patient's utterances and his own and the task is to speak x to the patient: an insight, or seeing into, is revealed, but the work of the seer is also evident. All along, of course, in his silences and sometimes while speaking the patient has also broken away from the manifest encounter to travel along lines of association, only to return full of x. These departures and returns, from manifest to latent, are associations serving the work of the unconscious in the analytical partnership evoking not only the patient's interest but their desire. Like seeing the adult walk, or swim, or ride a bike the patient wants to develop skill in the area of analytical work. It becomes a desire of the ego and in time and through practice this skill can reach its aim.

Sometimes a patient's free associations are indeed fundamentally performative acts, aiming to affect the analyst, calling for interpretation of the associations as forms of enacted relatedness or anti-relatedness. But when a patient is truly free associating, then he is rather oblivious to the presence of the analyst as a relational expectation, who is now more like the screen described in classical theories of the analyst's function. Certainly the analyst must not take offence that the patient is not 'relating' to him, as that is exactly the point. The speaking of deep free associations uses the analyst-other as an object exploiting their suspension of the relational perspective to liberating effect as the self finds in such paradoxical intimacy a deep mutual involvement in a process that deconstructs relational possibilities just as it joins two subjectivities in separate worlds of thought.

Freud repeatedly stressed that free associations destroy the manifest text of the dream and as discussed in the last chapter, this destruction serves the purpose of breaking open the figurative visual order into the symbolic universe of language: if a picture is worth a thousand words, then these words shall come forth in the free associative dissemination of the dream. All patients, however, resist this destruction. Indeed to dream is a kind of gift, to be accepted and valued as is. It is the thing itself. Seeing is, after all, believing. The dreamer has just seen the object of belief and now only needs to report it. When Freud broke it open by asking for associations to individual elements he separated the person from this object rather like removing the infant from the mother's body. In the regressed state of foetal return, hallucinating its objects, the dreaming self is partially returned to the mother's body. Speaking it now to the father analyst, the patient wants to assert the solitary privilege of communing with this maternal oracle, but the father insists upon its being broken down into parts and transformed into word presentations. The patient is somewhat compelled to leave the pre-verbal world of the image to enter the symbolic world of words and their histories. In the Freudian method, therefore, the work of analysis accomplishes separation from the maternal object.

The speaking would, however, be a compromise – a sleepy, dream-like utterance carrying forth the mother's body through the paternal order. Freud's method – inseparable from its relation to the dream – constitutes a psychic movement, from thing presentation to word presentation, from imaginary to symbolic order, from the visual to the verbal, from the maternal order to the paternal order. This same movement occurs every time the patient tells a story (of let's say, the events of the previous day) and the analyst asks for associations, pointing out a word and requesting other words. 'What do you mean associations?', 'No, I've presented you with the truth itself, I have nothing further to say', or 'What has this question to do with my anguish?', the patient protests, either silently or in speech.

For the story is to be taken at face value. It is acceptable if the analyst functions within object relations theory, pointing out how the characters and events of the story portray either parts of the patient engaged with one another or parts of the patient engaged with aspects of the analyst. The analyst points over the shoulder of the patient into the dream – 'look, that's the greedy part of you there and over there...that's the me whom you portray stealing your valued possessions' – and even if the patient is distressed by the content of the interpretation they are still reassured that the story is left intact. Object relations is picture-book work, moving the story from one place to another, from the manifest content of the dream text to the manifest content of the analytical partnership. Freud's technique was more radical than this. By asking the patient to free associate he requested the breaking up of the object relational world and both patient and analyst felt the de-figuration of the dream text, broken up each time by the thoughts arising out of them. Left to itself, object relations theory will always return self to other through the here and now transference interpretation, enclosing the self in the cosy if solipsistic world of infant and mother; the Freudian action breaks this tie, sending the self into an uncertain and anxiously open-ended future.

Free association facilitates unconscious vision. Disseminating ideas suggest a future, realised if envisioning is allowed. In this respect, the free associative moment is a prescient present tense, evoking links to the past as it senses its future. This integration of past, present and future in the movement of ideas always gives to psychic reality an inner sense of intuitive vision, as the network of thoughts arising out of all prior moments of thought articulates one's idiom into a complex form of memory that simultaneously functions as a resource for subsequent unconscious perception. The discovery and use of free association as a method of cure implicitly recognises the value of facilitating the movement of this network, so essential is it to all the senses that comprise human intuition.

Even as an analysand reports a sequence of events from the prior day, certain words used, images described, or feelings conveyed in the voice strike the analyst with their psychic weight. They are pregnant with other meanings and when the analyst repeats them very often they open up and deliver varied ideas, memories, or feelings sequestered in the manifest. The free associative always releases the unconscious from the blissful ignorance of consciousness, a setting free that is inevitably disruptive to the conventional thesis that ignorance is bliss. 'The secret of psychoanalytic method', writes Barnaby Barratt,

> is the very engagement of a discourse where fixity and certainty of any proffered epistemic configuration are dislodged in response to the movement of the immanifest, the animative temporality or libidinality of 'being itself' as something radically 'otherwise' than semiosis. What psychoanalysis offers the subject is thus its discourse as *otherwise*.
>
> (1993: 42)

'The course of free association produced a plentiful store of ideas', wrote Freud (1923a: 196), recognising one outcome of this unconscious work. Included in this store would be ideas opposing the further dissemination of latent thoughts as well as the silences, hesitations, gaps, and refusals that express the patient's resistances. But accomplishing this stance, talking with no agenda other than reporting the ideas in one's mind at the moment, would always be a matter of degree. What was not equivocal was the stance. Indeed the position occupied in the name of free association was already a psychic accomplishment, fulfilled and failed in differing ways, but always opening the self in a manner heretofore unimagined. It was and still is the most revolutionary accomplishment of psychoanalysis. And if it seems to disappear[3] from the psychoanalytical situation (the patient speaks, but seems not to use free association to express himself), then it will exist fundamentally in the mind of the analyst, which he brings into spoken reality through associative work with the patient's 'material'.

Perhaps because the goal of psychoanalysis is partly accomplished so easily and immediately it is all too easily undervalued. Furthermore, it alone does not cure the patient. The analysand's illness remains to challenge the analyst's skills and is so absorbing, it is understandable that the analyst may have little inclination to pay credence to the momentous change in the patient who decided to enter analysis. That entering may be part of the most important accomplishments of our civilisation, but the patient still proceeds to pose his illness and the analyst sets about his tasks.

Nonetheless, I believe that under the sway of the patient's demand and our own therapeutic ambition we have marginalised the accomplishment that is free association, although two works, Anton Kris' *Free Association* and Barnaby Barratt's *Psychoanalysis and the Postmodern Impulse* argue cogently for the value of the freely associated. ('the central point in psychoanalysis is the commitment to the free associative method', Kris 1982: 7). The diminution of free association begins in Freud's work as well. He revised his own therapeutic wishes, indicating over time many differing goals. As Sandler and Dreher point out in *What Do Psychoanalysts Want?*, initially the goal was to uncover latent instinctual wishes, then to de-repress forbidden ideas, then to systematically remove resistances, then to liberate the libido from pathological attachments, and then to free the ego from its disturbed investments. These changing goals reflect important shifts in Freud's model of conflict and, as with the psychoanalysts and schools that followed him, such goals are not universally subscribed to by all psychoanalysts, arguably reflecting the desire of the analyst within the love relation of theory. But such goals miss an essential point. They do not address the question I have already posed of what precisely it is that psychoanalysis has as its goal, which only it can bring into reality, and through which it can accomplish its aims.

Some would argue that free association is the method rather than the goal of psychoanalysis, at which point a goal might be stated, such as uncovering unconscious conflicts. The same might be said of the goals of science. It could be argued that scientific method is the means of achieving various aims, such as the objective discovery of physical facts. In fact, psychoanalytical method and scientific method (to which we could add literary critical method and other methods of examination) are distinctive, peculiar to themselves. The goal of any bearer of a method is to bring it into place, and whenever any practitioner nominates goals transcendent to the method he is almost inevitably in conflict with the terms of the method.

Indeed when any practitioner – psychoanalytic, scientific, literary – names goals of the method, the ends do not justify the means, they erode them. Looking back over the history of psychoanalysis, we see how the scores of goals articulated by differing practitioners have indeed marginalised the means – free association – and in doing so have unwittingly removed the distinctive character of psychoanalysis from its nominated practice.

This should not surprise us, especially when we appreciate the understandable and inevitable tension between the goal of free association and the wishes of the analyst to understand the material: as free association unbinds meaning – in what Laplanche terms and celebrates as the 'anti hermeneutics' of psychoanalysis – while interpretation creates and binds meaning. No sooner are such understandings established than the workings of the unconscious, evident through free association, break the interpretation into particles of meaning, which constitute a 'use of the object', hopefully celebrated by the analyst's unconscious working along similar lines even as such use disperses his interpretive creations.

Under the force of a patient's illness the analyst's vision is narrowed. The transference and its called-for countertransference structure the personalities around the patient's presentation of illness. Day after day the material may seem strikingly familiar, the same themes, same devices pushing the analyst toward the same interpretations. It is against this background that the free associative method becomes a third object vital to the presentation of psychoanalysis at this moment, for without it the analyst would simply be left to indoctrinate his patient. It is exceptionally difficult, at times, to request associations as this may seem fruitless in terms of the apparently redundant nature of the patient's interests. Yet often enough, even in the midst of such tenacious certainty the method springs a surprise, and the patient says something surprising. In these moments the method cures both participants of the strangleholds of pathology.

The free associative partnership based on unconscious precedents is a kind of rediscovery of something long since known, a partnership that in the first place is constituted in the maternal order, when self and other are absorbingly engaged in the nutriments of communication by association. Is this partly why free association is marginalised? Does it suffer the fate of the mother and of woman's work: taken for granted and overlooked? If so, then it bears the fate of all deeply creative assumptions: it ceases to invite thought. More than once one hears – 'oh, of course, free association, well we know that this is very important...but' – and as an assumption it is quickly passed by. It thereby endures the fate of many good ideas, which are so immediately convincing or effective that the mind then moves on to other ideas, while ironically enough, bad ideas seem to generate more thought.

Further, the hubris of each analytical school's certainty of possession of the sole truth of cure and its political valorisation seems a hallmark of the paternal order. Pushed aside and marginalised again and again, the fact of free association, and what it does, may have to be discovered and rediscovered again and again, as it has in the celebration of Bion's remark that the analyst must do without memory and desire.

Interest in the transference has to some extent reached an extreme as some analysts, in the name of what is rather clumsily termed the 'here and now transference interpretation', assume before the session that the patient's discourse will describe his experience of the analyst in that moment. The task is one of translation: from the patient's associations to the analytical relation. For many this is a development not without irony. As the patient's associations are now resolved by reference to a pre-existent manifest text, the deep work of the unconscious is ended with the brisk work of interpreted relatedness. Can free association proceed in a climate of such equational predictability?

Perhaps only when the analyst abandons memory of this technique and the desire to implement it.

There are at least three domains of 'goal-keeping' in psychoanalysis: the individual analyst and his patient, the analyst in his group with his particular ideology, and the fundamental method of psychoanalysis which thus far survives the differing (individual and group) applications. Each loses meaning when it drifts clear of either of the other two partners, in what finally constitutes a family essential to the practice of psychoanalysis, one that must endure conflict between its participant members. The analyst at work on a task with a particular patient may be uncomfortably at odds with his more typical way of practising. They may change their technique but be uncertain if their clinical judgement will prove well-founded or ill-judged. In following the dictates of an ideology such as the here and now transference interpretation, psychoanalysts may find themselves in conflict with the goal of analysis (free association). This may be troubling. If so, it is an essential distress, as analytical theories will often be in seeming (or actual) conflict with the aims of analysis. Only time will tell.

The goal of analysis will inevitably be in conflict with the changing aims of the analyst with the individual patient, and the ideologically derived psychoanalyst who practises in the name of a group. This constitutes what we might think of as the psychoanalyst's essential vulnerability. They will never find themselves in a place in which they can satisfactorily declare themselves to be following any of the above goals to their satisfaction. Whatever the individual vicissitudes found in each of the three positions above, they are in conflict with one another. A conflict that shall never be resolved, given its essential function of serving the differing masters: individual, group, and universal.

The goal of the practice that operates under the name of psychoanalysis, however, may not exhaust the theme of the goals of psychoanalysis. Psychoanalysis arrived in our culture at a particular point in time and was immediately adopted and used by the non-clinical community, from surrealist painters to novelists, philosophers to historians, sociologists and anthropologists to theologians and lawyers. We are still unclear about the unconscious significance of the arrival of psychoanalysis. Certainly we know it signifies a type of questioning, one that mobilised what we now think of as post-modernism. If he chooses, any speaking subject will discover that discourse fragments narrative coherence and makes all of us less convincing and yet far more interesting.

Irksome as it might be to the practitioners of psychoanalysis, the movement that is psychoanalysis – differing now from the IPA psychoanalytical movement – cannot be so easily identified, regulated and anticipated. What can we imagine if we ask of this object, what are its goals? What are the goals of psychoanalysis as it drives part of our contemporary culture?

We may recall that in the 1960s there were two eminent interpreters of the cultural significance of the arrival of psychoanalysis. Both Herbert Marcuse and Norman O. Brown saw it as an occasion for the liberation of needlessly repressed sexuality. Relatively few cultural historians have endeavoured to address this particular object – psychoanalysis as it operates in the cultural field. Yet it is there. If in North America and England today it appears in the media as a relic of a pre-scientific era, signifying atrophy of thought, those same newspapers may address another psychoanalysis, holding it responsible for the climate of vilification operating under the name of the recovery of repressed memories. In the borderline world of the written media, a single page may declare psychoanalysis to be an irrelevant relic and an immediate cause of widespread social disorder.

Intriguingly, however, the abuse movement has resituated psychoanalysis around sexuality. It has thus returned by the repressed to a task of one hundred years ago as once again we consider how symptomatic disability can be caused by sexual conflict. Is this surprising? Would it be possible for psychoanalysis to be separated from one of its crucial cultural tasks as the field in which sexual conflict is addressed? It would appear not. Indeed, psychoanalysis as a cultural object seems to owe much of its energy to the anger directed against it for being either totally irrelevant to the question of sexuality or completely responsible for the climate of perverse sexual practices.

As a cultural movement psychoanalysis will be invested with differing goals. As a cultural object it will be saturated with projections and yet unconsciously be rather well comprehended. If some hate it, as they do, they do so for good reason. It addresses unbearable issues. As a project that pointed toward the investigation of unconscious phenomena it clearly headed into troubled waters right from the beginning.

Freud rejected the notion of a direct psychoanalytic *Weltanschauung*, although it entered through a back door of sorts when he attached the psychoanalytic view of the world to the vistas of science. 'Psychoanalysis, in my opinion, is incapable of creating a *Weltanschauung* of its own', he wrote in the 'New introductory lectures on psycho-analysis' (1933a); 'It does not need one; it is a part of science and can adhere to the scientific *Weltanschauung*' (181). But often when he linked psychoanalysis to science he suggested a direction through which psychoanalysis could assist culture: 'Our best hope for the future is that intellect – the scientific spirit, reason – may in process of time establish a dictatorship in the mental life of man' (171). This seems very much the enlightenment Freud arguing that psychoanalysis as a branch of science can contribute to the welfare of men through relieving the psyche of unconsciously motivated ignorance that biases the personality toward more irrational enterprises.

But psychoanalysis observed an evolution in mental structure. In 'The Future of an Illusion' (1927c) Freud pointed out a 'mental advance'.

> It is in keeping with the course of human development that external coercion gradually becomes internalised; for a special mental agency, man's superego, takes it over and includes it among its commandments....Such a strengthening of the super-ego is a most precious cultural asset in the psychological field.
>
> (11)

Insofar as insight into unconscious conflict is part of the developments of the superego, then psychoanalysis could be seen as performing, in Freud's view, a function in what he termed the 'evolution of culture'. A civilisation, he argued, goes through 'psychical modifications', which consist predominately in 'a progressive displacement of instinctual aims and a restriction of instinctual impulses'. This has led, he later wrote to Einstein (1933b) to 'a strengthening of the intellect, which is beginning to govern instinctual life, and an internalisation of the aggressive impulses, with all its consequent advantages and perils'. Once one has developed a 'psychical attitude' derived from that development in civilisation that gains the intellectual skill of which he wrote and the inhibiting effect of the superego then one has a *'constitutional* intolerance of war' (215).

Freud celebrated this progressive path, but when one looks at the method that he created, matters become more complex. 'What we call our civilisation is largely responsible for our misery', he declared in 'Civilisation and its Discontents' (1930a: 86). The price of civilisation is the suppression of instinctual life with all its consequent ill-effects. One loss is man's more harmonious relation to his bodily processes, especially to his anality. Before he was erect, according to Freud, man's relation to his faeces was an object of some olfactory delight. With the progress of civilisation he is alienated from his own body.

It is of more than passing interest that Freud's method returns man to the horizontal position (albeit on the back rather than on all fours) and elicits a mode of thought and expression that evokes instinctual states (and their resistances) which crowd the mind with material from the very parts of the self that civilisation would prefer to launder. For Marcuse and Brown this was the point of departure – a radical new vision of a liberated man. And Freud certainly played down the anti-civilised valorisation of psychoanalysis. He tended to celebrate the ego's mastery of its instincts, and the role of insight in this process. He commented less and less on the evocative function of psychoanalysis. For if we follow his argument, then psychoanalysis is a kind of '*nachträglich*' or deferred action, a moment in time after the trauma of renunciation accomplished by civilisation in which the loss is not only thinkable but traumatically so. Psychoanalysis becomes a type of deep symptomatic moment, in which the self realises its illness in the presence of one who is presumed to know and who holds the self in place and progressively interprets the nature of the trauma to the patient. Gradually the recumbent self manages to stand on his or her own feet. Only as they walk into the consulting room for the last time will they do so not as a witless participant in cultural suppression, but as a wise accomplice in an act of renunciation that would make him or her ill.

If we agree with Freud that there is mental development, then psychoanalysis may have become part of a goal of civilisation. If so, it is a rebellious goal server, deepening man by unbinding the soul from its strictures, freeing it through association and placing before it mysteries it cannot possibly fathom. The method, then, is enemy to such a goal. If the gain is a non-pathological strengthening of the superego through the mediating works of the ego, it is accomplished by a compromise formation in which free association serves the instinctual needs of the self to be created anew, each day, in a freedom of mental life that is unavailable for the organisational aims of a self or a society.

7

MIND AGAINST SELF

We give so little thought to the relation between our mind and our self that the distinction may seem puzzling, yet psychoanalysis illuminates this pairing, as free association elicits puzzling ideas that bring the self to look upon the mind differently. To some extent this is a particular relation between consciousness and unconsciousness as analysands speak in order to discover what is on their mind.

In analysis one develops a certain suspicious respect for what the mind produces and comes to understand the oscillating rift between comfort with one's thoughts – feeling no split between consciousness and mental product – and the schisms created by free associations which often sponsor unpleasant surprises.

Lacan exploited this clinical fact in his theory of alienation between the imaginary and speaking selves. Whatever we imagine we think, when we speak we usually say something different from the imagined. This rift announces a gap between the imagined self and the speaking subject and it is the latter's contribution – which surprises the speaker and no doubt frustrates a longing to have speech validate thought and imagery – which Lacan understood as the true voice of the unconscious, this 'other' that is the irreducible subject.

Those not cultured in Lacan's thinking might simply note that when coming to talk about what is on the mind, it proves to have a mind of its own: largely unresponsive to will, speech follows some other dictate. This leads to a certain amused appreciation of the undermining effects of the mind that is assumed to be the source of these slippings.

There are certain forms of mental life, however, where the split between the self and its mind is so severe that the person can bear it no longer and seeks treatment.

One morning Leonie as usual got in her shower. She had put the kettle on for tea, which her flatmate would make in about fifteen minutes. As she stepped into the shower her thoughts turned to certain reports due at the office that day. These musings were interrupted by a command as she told herself to turn the hot water nozzle up. She turned it too far, however, and the water was uncomfortably hot. She wanted to turn it down but her mind issued a new order: turn it further. The water was now very hot and she was in considerable pain. 'Turn the nozzle all the way to the right and remain where you are', it said.

Leonie does not recall how long she remained in the shower tray before her flatmate, noticing the steam escaping from the gap between the door and the floor, rushed to her rescue. An ambulance was called; she was taken to hospital where she was treated for scalding and referred to the Department of Psychiatry for treatment.

Although this was the first occasion that she had been told to do something in the shower, the inner voice that commanded her was all too familiar. She felt she had to obey and could only accept intervention from the outside such as when her flatmate rescued her. Trips to the supermarket were ordeals. A week before she had been shopping when her mind told her to take all the asparagus tins from the shelf and pile them neatly in rows. An assistant asked what she was doing and in considerable embarrassment she said she was part of a school service project. Her lame excuse was senseless, as she was in her early thirties (hardly school age) and could see this made no sense, but as he had released her she fled to another aisle. It was a feature of these commands that she often found herself performing irrational acts in public and did not know how to explain herself.

Freud sometimes understood this conflict as a battle between three mental agencies: the id, its ego and the superego. Thus something in Leonie's id pulsions is too toxic for her ego and is passed to the superego for severe moral processing. She is therefore given punitive commands, but in the compromising world of this tripartite structure, the demands of the id are partially gratified (even if bizarrely so) – the auto-erotic impulse of solo activities bringing shame and punishment.

Freud's theory is that superego is an agency that internalises the function of the parents, especially the father. As it derives from an object relation it presumably inherits some aspects of what took place between parent and child. In psychotherapy it became useful to consider her symptoms as a form of 'tough love' parenting by a powerful mother or father. Indeed, she had developed an ironically unconscious admiring relation to the commanding mind. More than once I noticed her pride in narrating its capacity to demand irrational acts of her.

She was a visibly stiff woman. She never turned her neck to the left or right but would move her entire body. She walked across the room like a cadet on parade and sat in a chair like a statue. She knew that she rarely acted spontaneously, but when I drew to her attention the fact that her mind, while punishing her with some of its commands, nonetheless allowed her to do crazy things, she smiled. She could see that.

It also made sense to her to see how lonely she was and how this commanding voice was rather like a conspirator with whom she was in a powerful and secretive relationship. In time we could see that in a supermarket or mall she had her impulses to do something naughty. Gradually self and mind reconciled their differences.

It made sense to tell her that I reckoned she was lonely as a child and needed increased parental presence. When a child feels that way, I said, then sometimes a part of the mind takes over and becomes very parenting. By adult life, however, she found herself increasingly alienated and fearful of the commanding part of her mind.

Another patient, Penny, was hallucinating and delusional. She would smell the presence of the pop star Michael Jackson, or John Rut, a childhood sweetheart. She was convinced that a particular radio DJ was sending special messages to her over the air. Every so often she would suddenly glance at a part of the room, her eyes moving in a REM-type pattern and eventually she said she was seeing things.

She was extremely anxious about these hallucinations and delusional thoughts. Her mind had become a dreadful and terrifying object from which she tried to hide. She did this by watching TV for hours on end, sometimes urinating in her pants rather than going to the toilet, lest this be an occasion for such thoughts.

By detaching the mental contexts from intrapsychic personification I found it easier to think about what her ideas might mean. So when she said, 'X has raped me!' I said, 'What an upsetting idea!' When she said, 'I smell Michael Jackson!' and was now under his influence, I would say, 'So what do you imagine him doing?'

The psychotic patient lives in a universe where the mind is perceived as an endangering presence. People suffering from such illness will go to considerable lengths to avoid coming into contact with their mind. By asking for elaboration I tried to break the spell of her mental contents.

Defence against thinking increases the rift between self and mind. The person's sense of self is of a highly restricted and anxious being with hypertrophied consciousness. It is as if any of those thoughts safe to think may be cognised, but because any specific idea is intrinsically subversive (i.e. Lacan's symbolic), anodyne ideas are valued and polysemous words avoided. The self tries to launder the mind of disturbing contents. Psychotic patients, therefore, prefer to live in seclusion watching TV and having the TV do the 'minding'.

A mind boxed in like this only becomes more toxic: the tragic fate of the psychotic is that he knows he is feeding his illness, his alarm increasing as idiomatic mental contents are forced into entry through short bursts of intensely vivid hallucinations or delusions. The formulation of a delusion is a compromise between no thoughts and hallucinating ideas and can be regulated. Penny believed a particular radio talk show host was talking to her. But as he was only on at a certain time during the week she made appointments with her madness and had weekends off. As no other radio or

TV figure was part of the delusion she limited this side of her psychosis to one person.

A delusion becomes a regulated system of ideas that may distinguish the mind as an object although one can see the person trying to identify with the mind's product: putting time into it. So delusion would seem to be a comparatively safe psychosis, enabling one to feel harmonised with the mind whereas the hallucination ordinarily takes the self by surprise.

Another patient, Hector, sat in his first consultation crouched over, brow furrowed, lips pursed, eyes now and then rising abruptly to glance at the ceiling before being buried beneath a scowl. What was he thinking? That would seem to be the problem in and of itself. When Hector could bring himself to say what he was thinking, it was like unpacking the entire contents of a microchip. He would meticulously account for all the thoughts and how he understood them, describing all the associations that were embedded in a single profound thought.

For example, he spent the best part of three sessions telling me who his sister was. This was not a matter of explaining that she was four years older than him and had left the family when he was six to attend boarding school. Nor was detailing for me her prior and subsequent history sufficient. He expounded at great length on her tastes and attitude of mind, from her literary interests to her fashion sense, to the way she had decorated her room, to the types of men she liked, from the objects she bought as part of her small porcelain collection to the cinemas she preferred, from the parts of her mother and father she resembled to the ideological positions that had mattered to her in debates with all family members. Rather than gaining relief by such unravelling utterance, Hector seemed if anything more troubled by his failures to get it across to me what he was thinking about. He spent the best part of an hour asking in the very first – as he put it, 'philosophical' – sense what it meant to have a sister. What would it mean to her that she was *his* sister. What did it mean to be a brother?

He talked about the felt disappearance of the truth his mind contained, believing that the more he talked the more he was failing to communicate. As he often said, once he decided it was time to tell me something he had to try to get it spoken as close to what he felt internally. But rather than abandon the talking, he intensified his efforts to get the essence of his sister into speech. When he would commit a parapraxis he seized upon it as potential evidence of yet another strand of sister material and would milk it for what it was worth.

After weeks and months of this accounting for his mental objects it was possible to objectify the process, to begin the analysis of a relation not to a sister or to a father or to an opera he had seen, but to his mind which housed these objects. A hallowed temple holding all that was ever to be important, he likened himself to its servant – a librarian – fulfilling his duty to house the records of his mind and do his best to disseminate the truths it held.

As Winnicott emphasised in his concept of the mind psyche, in his childhood Hector had turned to his mind as a companion – one in which it was extolled and he, in himself, simply served. A feature of his transference was his belief that I should share in his reverence for the products of his mind and he was quite pleased to exploit my ordinary analytical silence to this effect as for a long time it felt to him that I was worshipping his descriptions. I gave him the time which he felt was owed to such intense talkings.

Do disturbances of the relation between mind products and a self teach us anything about the ordinary relation of a mind and self?

We have argued that the mind is ordinarily at peace with the self until a mental product gets the self to reflect on a content, thereby drawing attention to the mind. Repeated traumas of this kind eventually lead to an over-awareness of the mind as an object capable of disturbing the self. Or in Hector's case the mind's contents can seem so profound that it is always a serious question whether one should ever bother to speak, since to do so is such a pitiful act of representation.

In the first instance the self becomes aware of the mind as an object when it thinks something disturbing, while in the second instance the mind would go almost unnoticed, so encompassing is it, until one tries to speak it, in which case it seems a forlornly lost Delphic oracle.

This view acknowledges a distinction between an experiencing self that might appear mindless and mind. But what would a mindless self be?

We know, of course, that our thought processes do not cease. Once someone has learned to drive a car, for example, they no longer need to think about it; in an emergency, acquired knowledge enables them to react instinctively without first having to think what to do. The same is true of ordinary self experience. When we emerge from mindlessness, called upon to think about something, we do not think about the thinker thinking – i.e. mind as object – we just think and that's it.

Mindlessness then may refer to a state of unconsciously informed being, when we are operating at so many differing, intersecting planes of ideation that no single train of thought could carry the dense dissemination. We are mindless not because nothing is happening inside but because too much is taking place for us to represent it.

Self experiencing is a palimpsest of many elements: conscious thought, inarticulate forming ideas on the margins of consciousness, unconscious disseminations, images which pass by in incomplete form, polysemous words pregnant with meanings, somatic drives, body memories, body attitudes, and intersubjective engagements.

It seems to help us think some of this to bifurcate the mind in two: a thinking part that addresses a naive self as listener and a listening-experiencing self that emotionally or intuitively tests thoughts. So if I say to myself, 'Have a look at the theory of the superego' and the idea is conveyed with a certain feeling I may respond at first 'I already know about that'. An intrasubjective conflict may ensue for a bit, but then I will return to unity of self. Moments after such a split I might be thinking 'I think there is a relation between self as object and superego–ego relations' and in thinking this I do so without a mental division.

Mental conflict jars the self out of mindlessness (Eastern religions' dissolution of the ego) and sharpens the division that is mental structure. Severe, premature conflict in a child creates premature knowledge of mental divisions. The structure of the mind seems to compel too much notice, rather like a car driver having to think about how the engine works.

Before this threshold is reached, before the individual objectifies the unconscious agencies behind clashing feelings and ideas, mental conflict often invigorates the self. Indeed, such conflict appears to heighten conscious contact with predominately unconscious ideas and inner experience, sustaining a good polarity between periods of mindlessness and moments of conscious conflict. The mind does not feel like an alien object during these ordinary toings and froings, but what it produces – i.e. its contents – impress the self. All seems well.

The mind becomes what Corrigan and Gordon call a 'mind-object' when repeated severe conflict calls upon the self to regard its mind with alarm. This polarity between the conscious subject and his unconscious life is at the root of many mental illnesses, be they obsessive-compulsive, schizophrenic or depressive. Indeed, in the next chapter we will examine this in greater clinical depth as I describe a person deeply depressed by his mind's assaults.

The task of psychoanalysis is to release contents from their container, which has assumed an allegorical power paralysing ordinary intrapsychic life. By thinking the thoughts in the presence of an analyst, who breaks them down, they lose their manifest innervating truth and disseminate into multiple ideas. In many respects, psychoanalysis reaches its maximum clinical effectiveness with the psychotic patient as the analyst is not disturbed by the patient's mind and breaks its power by breaking down its contents.

When the contents of a mind break down they lose their customary character and when they are understood the mind loses its status as an alien object. When Penny smelled Michael Jackson I said that she felt like a boy-girl which gave rise to many associations, and the figure of Michael Jackson eventually dissolved in its mental contextualisations.

In turn, it does not matter if 'asparagus' (see p. 76) which gave way to 'ass-dis(parage)-us' revealed a meta-truth – perhaps these associations were correct, what really mattered was that Leonie learned how free association breaks down incarcerating ideas. If objectified as an object, the mind at play may be, as Lacan has it, the other (mysterious, out of reach, ultimately subversive), but it also may be an essential amusement.

As I analysed Hector's treasuring of his mind, how he formed it into his own household god, he grudgingly accepted that in order to keep it divinely powerful he had to sweep out of mind and speech verbal confusions that implied that his mental contents were not in some well held, totally static mental place, but it was speaking that broke up what he assumed to be an inviolable place. It was not that he failed to speak his mind properly – as he preferred – but speaking revealed that conscious mental contents were only ever part of one's desires and beliefs.

Some psychotherapists and psychoanalysts believe that psychotic patients are best treated by ego supportive measures, which it is argued should not encourage a discussion of the unconscious ideas floating around, since the psychotic ego cannot process work at this level. Although there are undoubtedly times when it is essential to help the patient fight off the fearful entry of molesting ideas, it does not make sense to me to do this as a matter of course. Psychotic patients may think bizarrely or concretely, but encouraging them to speak their mental productions can detoxify their cathexes (as foreign and endangering), revealing unconscious meanings which can only be grasped by psychoanalytic listening.

We may wonder if the view that psychotic patients should only be treated by ego support and medication unwittingly and unconsciously bears a projective identification. The clinician comes to regard his patient's mind as a dangerous object, not to be disturbed, so defences against its power are shored up. It is not difficult to see how this, ironically enough, sustains the core pathology, and even if it mildly mitigates it, since at least now two people share the experience, both sustain the conviction that the mind is too dangerous to approach.

When the psychotic regards the mind as endangering he inspects its structure. Words are broken down through repetition to see if they retain meaning. Repeat a signifier such as 'chair' a hundred times and what it signifies seems to evaporate. Where did meaning go? Looking carefully at the ordinary traffic of the world the schizophrenic wants to know how it all works. How does one naturally enter a stream of people walking on the pavement? How should one look? At what pace? Everything subjected to thought seems to disappear. Scrutiny is devastating. The implications of what would happen to the self were this to continue apace are clear. The psychotic hypothesises the evaporation of self and lives in ever present fear of this realisation.

The schizoid patient has long been regarded as a sound candidate for psychoanalysis, but analysts have always recognised this patient's strange use of free association to supplement a split between the reporting self and ideas from the internal world. A voyager, a film-maker, a star-gazer – whatever metaphors we choose to describe this person's stance toward his mind, psychoanalysts are well aware that it is the object relation in question that must be analysed along with those contents reported. Otherwise such patients can use the analytical process to simply elaborate their schizoid position.

It was Bion more than any other psychoanalyst who focused on what a mind might be to any self. First, it was not something which could be taken for granted. It grew only if thoughts occurred which required it. The more that the infant or the child thought, the greater the requirement to think. He borrowed from, and rather ingeniously changed, Freud's theory of mental functioning as outlined in the 'Formulation on the two principles of mental functioning'. The pure pleasure principle would conjure only objects that were to satisfy the drive, but when hallucination of the breast failed to bring about satiation, the infant was forced to turn increasingly to reality to find the mother and to communicate wishes and needs. Mental functioning became more complex and distinguished as a result, and in Bion's extension of Freud, the mind grew as a result.

What would one's relation be, however, to the mind as the agency of self: one's evolving relation to it throughout a childhood, into an adolescence, and through the life cycle? Kleinians have written important essays on the early loss of mind or hatred of mind as an object that produces unwanted thoughts. Previous analytical thought concentrated on the denial or repression of certain mental contents, but Bion, Rosenfeld and others discussed the attack on the mind itself. Clearly when the child's mind seems to continually produce toxic contents a child may attempt to nullify thinking itself in order to find some protection against intrapsychic trauma. A child seeking safety along these lines will then choose to be as mindless as possible and may to some extent be successful.

When the mind strikes such a person, it often does so with merciless terror. Take nightmares. A child waking in the night, certain that the room is populated with monsters, will need to talk to his parents and receive comfort. Their minds put him to rest. He gradually takes comfort in knowing that this terror which seemed to be so real was 'only in his mind'. *Only* in his mind? This is reassuring? It becomes consoling because he also finds that the very agency that produces such frights also has available to it other processes – such as reflection, talking, and perceptive reality testing – which are capable of detoxifying the more disturbing creations of a mind. In this respect, then, the presence of the parents, who sit with the child and talk through the troubled dream, is a vital generative opposition to the trauma of a mind, because it is rather like two or more people 'putting their heads together' to find that 'two minds are better than one'. On certain occasions when one is overwhelmed by one's own mind, the presence of other minds not caught up in such toxic contents is invaluable to one's subsequent uses of one's mind. For at the very least the child discovers that next time they can run to the parents' room to talk over what occurred to them – 'putting heads together' – and by adult life, when momentarily overcome by the products of a mind, he puts 'two heads together' by creating a friendly assistant who stands 'outside' the turmoil and chats with the mind-consumed self.

We have seen how the obsessive-compulsive individual receives irrational commands seemingly from a mental area outside the ordinary domain of mental life. Not from outer space as with the schizophrenic – who may actually look around the room to see where the voice came from – but on the rim of ordinary consciousness. Freud's image of the superego sitting on the shoulder of the ego is a fitting image, but in Leonie's situation, she was ordinarily aiming to keep this unwanted guest outside her inner field of vision. The obsessive-compulsive, we know, does not wish to come into contact with certain libidinal aims and their objects. Thus important mental contents are banished from consciousness and go into a kind of intense exile, only to return in disguise. Their rigidity is no different from the intrapsychic rigidity when one part of them is forever wary of something upsetting the applecart, something unseemly, messy or humiliating, something one does not want to smirch the self. Such patients express a distaste with the analyst's interests, which may throw the analyst into a countertransference where he feels disinclined to raise certain issues, lest he embarrass himself and his patient. Both may feel the force to move away from certain contents which may be mutually upsetting; focusing on mind as object, we can see how here the mind is a kind of spoiler and shitter, putting people in embarrassing situations. It is a kind of mind-body, or more accurately, the mind-as-bodies ally. To think certain things is to act bodily, to have an awareness of one's body that would be unwanted.

All along of course a developing child is made aware of their body in a very particular sort of way, an issue to be discussed at some length in Chapter 13. They note that they have a body: they can see their arms and legs, their feet and their belly. They can look at their face in a mirror. They clothe themselves and are increasingly familiar with how they can change their appearance in this way. Freud insisted that in addition to this body we keep in mind the child's other body: the one that asserts itself in the mind as the scene of their instinctual life. So they feel the surges of their impulses and of their desire, of their excitations and exhibitions, of their erotic arousals and their body interests. This body that plays upon the mind the obsessive displaces with a sanitised one, ritualistically cleansed of excitational evidence. The obsessive pits two bodies against one another: the mental body and the carnal body, the safe body of appearance and the disquieting body of fantasy. The obsessional child either displaces the carnal body into the field of the actual, into an object which then must be avoided, or eliminates the body through rituals meant to keep the self and its others safe.

By latency, however, a child is increasingly aware that their mind, which they know to be the author of dreams and which re-presents the physical body in specular yet passionate situations, is home to another self than the one seen by mothers, fathers and witnessed by the I in the mirror. This other self is to be forever unseen, always inherently secret even if talked about, full of contradictions yet seemingly enhanced by the capacity to bear opposites and differences. The Oedipal child who has perhaps been taken up in the world of the maternal and paternal order, who has moved through the anxieties and passions of love of the mother and the father, is soon stopped short not by paternal law or a specific bodily anxiety, but by something rather more arresting – the realisation that one's mind is increasingly too complex to be ordered in neat preoccupations, however meaningful. So the arcadian world of the mother's love and her wonderful yet fearful godliness and the tribal village of the father's quests and conquests fade into forever remembered – and revised – myths of being; the truth is, however, that one's inner life is never to know such reassuring legends, however full of frights they might be. A child discovers he is to think of many mothers and fathers, to hold many versions of the same object, all to be categorised under the name of mother or father, but not holding an integrated or unchanging being. The vicissitudes of lived experience inevitably call into mind many differing others and corresponding selves, felt through the ordinary intensities of any day.

This mind that now presents itself to a child as their object is another country where they alone shall live. They can tell someone about this country. They may hear stories about others' countries and find similar objects in both. But no one can live in their country except themselves. What each person does with this recognition is of course open to the greatest possible variation. The schizophrenic, already terrified by the contents of mind, is long since armed against experience of it and if the radical anti-psychiatrists romanticised what they took to be the revolutionary consciousness of the schizophrenic, they did so knowingly casting off knowledge of the schizophrenic's passion for the routine and the banal. Very few schizophrenic patients are as interesting as the literature would have us believe.

Eventually the child may find they are gifted or talented in certain mental areas such as maths, literature, biology or music. The mind can be tested with an IQ test, but this is not a self test and in this respect the mind is seen as independent of the self. A child may also be good at football, dance, athletics or basketball and the body and its co-ordination can be tested. For the self we have other tests such as TAT, ORT and Rorschach. In this perfectly customary sense, then, the mind is also an object in its own right with implications for our fate. If we have been fortunate enough to be endowed with certain capacities and if our environment has favoured them, then it may be our fate to live up to our...do we say mind or self? Perhaps we are inclined to say our abilities, which would include cognitive (i.e. mental) abilities and capabilities of the self.

Some time in the course of childhood, however, and certainly by and/or during adolescence, the individual, who already knows that their mind is a complex object, realises that such complexity may reveal itself most tellingly in disturbed ideas. This is a mixed blessing. The disturbed ideas become more familiar than the everyday evoked intensities of ordinary life and thus are capable of being remembered and even studied. Assuming that mental illness is something which occurs in the mind and restricts its functioning, such illnesses take up more mental time than they should, and bring the individual round to the mind as an object of worry or consideration. It is at this point that a child may experience his first insights, when he looks inside his internal world at his mental contents and catches sight of his self. For example, a patient recalls that when he was about six years old he was sexually excited by the fantasy of lying on a conveyer belt that drew him toward a woman whose open mouth was about to consume him. This fantasy would occasion an erection and as it recurred it became an object of thought in its own right. He did not understand the meaning of the fantasy – indeed in a Freudian sense we could say that its enigmatic feature was intended to fool his consciousness – but the peculiarity and intensity of the thought led him to regard his mind as something which brought about curious ideas and which would need attending to at some future date.

Gabriel Marcel became a philosopher one day when he was eight years old. 'I was in the Parc Monceau in Paris', he writes,

> and having learned in response to my questions that it was not known with certitude whether human beings survived their death or were destined to absolute extinction, I cried out to myself, 'Later on I shall try to see that clearly'. I think it would be a grave mistake [he continues] to take that as nothing but a child's mock seriousness.
>
> (1973: 20)

These universal questions – about the origin of life, the size of the universe, the dimensions of infinity, and the nature of death – cross children's minds all the time and, like Marcel, I reckon that we are determined that one day we shall have our answers to them, although they will have to suffer a postpone-ment. But I also think that each of us has a universally shared experience of being arrested by conscious derivatives of our internal world – such as my patient's fantasy – in which we find our self curious. Understanding these mental curiosities will also have to be postponed, but each child will have stored important insights into themselves.

Indeed we would regard the failure to postpone such moments as rather worrying in itself, if for example, a child decided at six or seven that they were going to solve one of their idiom mysteries by prolonged periods of self analysis. That would then overly privilege the child's mind at the expense of self and might lead to the schizoid outcome of the mind becoming an object of unusual cathexis and interest. Instead what we see is an emerging rhythm of mindfulness, mindlessness, and mind objectified as an object of thought as the child moves about, sometimes full of ideas but not thinking about the fullness, sometimes so caught up in something that they are not aware of even having a mind, and occasions when they are thinking very intently about something on their mind, or in the extreme, thinking about their mind and the way it serves up curiosities of thought.

Psychoanalysis deals with the vital intangibles of life and, as our language shows, the strain of putting the unseen into a scene – of language itself: surely some will wonder how one could make a distinction between mind and self. But patients guide analysts; they say that they can think clearly but may have no sense of self – and therefore get analysts thinking with them about a self – or they say that they are 'losing their mind' and yet sometimes such a loss does not feel to them to be a loss of self. In these respects distinguishing between a mind and a self seems true to inner experience.

But how if at all do we distinguish between thoughts going into the thinking and the supposed object of thought, both of which it may be argued are mental and from the mind?

When we think now of self and mind, a phenomenological partnership, how do we imagine each? Self is an innocence, the essential naive moment open to experience, as it encounters the complexities of life. Lived experience gives rise to endless thoughts and mental contents not only cross the mind but mind becomes an area we use to signify the effects of thought. But thinking does not erase the innocence of self. The self in the dream experience is always an innocent who barely knows where it is and does not foresee what will happen next. And although by adult life we have had tens of thousands of dreams, the self in the dream remains innocent. It does not stop in the midst of dreaming to say 'Ah, yes, this is a dream. I know this experience. End of interruption', but remains innocent each time.

Self may be an essential blindness, permitting the function of a continual state of reception and surprise.

Mind considered as a special state of being is objectified by innocence as the process and repository of the many encountered other realities (i.e. non-selves) of life. It can be internally objectified only because one part of the individual sustains perpetual innocence (or openness) permitting a vantage point, an internal point of view, from which thoughts arising may be reflected upon. There is thus a psychic double occurrence; in the 'stream of consciousness' derived from unconscious interests and disseminations, ideas often pass by as a matter of course and without reconsideration. Then there is a second occurrence of 'the thought', now thought again. And who thinks this time?

A delegate from the parliament of functions, a representative from the constituency of innocence, raises a question: 'What was that?' 'Could that be repeated?' 'What do you mean?' And the other delegates convene and speak.

Of course, all the above takes place in the mind, or, is a function of the mind. And so the self is a part of the mind, the open receptive part, that is deeply essential to our faith in the pleasure of entertaining ideas, as they shall be like surprises and fulfilments.

Human experience, taken as a gradually unfolding series of discoveries, never loses a small but important space for the naive self or the innocent in us. This is, if we will, the child in us – the *ingénu* – who is ignorant of certain things until they appear before them or happen. In some respects we are always children before our minds, perpetually challenged by those deeply mysterious and compelling mental contents that arrive every day and every night.

8

MENTAL INTERFERENCE

I think, therefore I am.

(Descartes)

Something is thinking me. Where am I?

(Helmut)

Helmut lies in bed. It is eight-thirty in the morning and although he has slept at times throughout the night, his mind has been racing. It is hard to remember what exactly he had been thinking about. He could recall pondering a conversation with his brother who had told him with earnest affection that he should start up in business as an ice cream vendor. He had replayed this conversation many times. He had imagined applying for a licence, looking for a van, reading up on the production which should be so simple, but well...he just did not know. He could see his elder brother's love and exasperation, a face that haunted him. But where would he go to find a van? Where do they make them? What would his friends think of him sitting in the van? Perhaps he should hire somebody to do that side of the business. He could try to set it all up and then hire a person. But if he did that, then how would he learn the true end of the business? No one would be successful in a new venture, he knew, if they tried to run it from the top. One needed bottom up experience. He found himself thinking of the colours of the van. White with a blue line around it? Blue with a white line? Did that fit in with the customer's association with ice cream? Maybe it should be red with white lettering. What would it say? What would he call the ice cream company? Helmut's Ices? The Flavour Van? The Ice Cream Van?

What would people think? He imagined countless types of people all responding differently to the name. Increasingly exhausted by these considerations, he thought to himself that maybe the ice cream business was not for him. What did he know about it? Nothing. Nothing at all. And he had read that it was controlled by the Mafia who used it to launder money.

What would they do to him if he tried to enter their turf? Scene after scene of his ice cream truck being attacked occurred to him. They came after him in his home. They tried to kill him. They attacked and threatened his family.

The night wore on.

He thought of other forms of work. Should he go into retail sports, concentrating on winter recreation? He had friends who lived in the mountains of France, Switzerland and Italy. Long ago he had liked to ski. He could open a shop in London and one in each of the above countries. Friends would join the venture. How much would it take to invest in the setting up of such a business? Probably about £75,000, and he thought about how much each friend would or could put into it. He recalled separate experiences with his friends, going over their recent times together. There had been problems. Some disputes. Ill considerations. He had gone out with one friend's ex-girlfriend and he had said it would be all right, but of course that did not turn out to be so. The ex-girlfriend returned to her former boyfriend – the now considered potential partner – and he wandered off thinking about their recent contacts and all the ins and outs. He tossed and turned in bed with each painful thought. The business brought him back to centre, and he went back to thinking about sports shops. But he thought, one had to be a sporting type and this he definitely was not. He did not really like people. Or he thought he didn't. How do you talk to strangers who drop into your shop? Anyway, what did he know about sports equipment? Where could he go to find out? He supposed he could spend a few weeks in the Alps and travel from one shop to another. That was a good idea. He could see what they stocked and what he thought was missing. But how would he know what was missing? And what would they come to think of him if later he set up shop in competition with them and recollected that he spent time hanging around their shops not buying anything. Thus he would have to purchase something in each shop. That means he would have to rent a large car, a four-wheel drive van, but what would he then do with all the stuff he purchased?

As the clock ticked through the wee hours he became even more exhausted by his thoughts. He moved from one job to another. From the travel business to the local recreational business. From the life of the drop-out, just painting or doing ceramics, to a middle-man bringing people together who could do business. This night was no different from all other nights. He dreaded going off to sleep and stayed up till one or two. He knew that although he would drop off for ten or twenty minutes he would wake up again and then he would be launched on this endless journey of rumination. Yes he would, he thought, usually fall asleep sometime around six in the morning and get a few hours sleep, but then he would awake again, and another struggle would ensue as he would try to find some way to get back to sleep, trying one strategy after another – thinking of a woman, thinking of a vacation spot, thinking of a recent pleasant experience, squinting his eyes to force stars and trying to disappear into sleep through them – but nothing ever worked.

He would lie in bed between nine and noon just thinking. It was always the same and went something like this.

Oh God, I'm awake for sure. I can't go off to sleep again.

Well, get up then.

Why?

You have to get to work.

I don't want to go to work.

That's not a good attitude.

But there is no point. We aren't doing any business.

That's because you don't try.

Okay. I don't try. Maybe I should get up...

Yes. Get moving. Come on. Up and at 'em!

I don't know.

Come on. You can do it!

I suppose I could.

There you go. That's the spirit.

But.

But what? There you go. Getting down in the mouth again.

But what is the point? I will just get to the office. The car business stinks. My brother will only be embarrassed.

Business isn't great, but someone out there is selling cars. Why shouldn't it be you?

I can't work. I just sit and stare out the window. I don't answer the phone. I stay away from people. I feel a sick feeling in my stomach.

You are pathetic. Absolutely fucking pathetic. You are just lying here in bed, feeling sorry for yourself, doing fuck all, when you should get out there and work.

I am pathetic. It's true. What's the point in living.

Oh! Oh! So it's suicide time is it?

Why not?

So if you can't get out of bed, and you feel like not working, it's time to just kill yourself?

I would be doing everyone a favour.

Oh sure. Your dad, your brothers, your friends. They would be all delighted.

No. But they would get over it.

That's considerate.

I should do it.

Well fuck you anyway. You haven't even got the balls to kill yourself. So how would you do it?

Well, I could jump off a bridge. But I suppose if I did that...well, I might still be alive when I hit the water and funnily enough I don't like the idea of floating in cold water, half alive. Um...

You're not going to kill yourself.

Or I could take pills. I could take a lot of them and do it...well, not in my flat, because I would not want my brother to be shocked. I could go to a hotel, although then the cleaning lady would find out...I could try it in my car.

(*This script goes on and on*)

91

Okay, so I'm not going to kill myself. Oh God, I suppose I should go to work.

Well you've pissed away half the morning. Damn right you should go to work. Get up and shower.

I should do that.

Get moving then.

I'll count to ten and then do it. 1, 2, 3, 4, 5, 6, 7, 8, 9, 10.

Well?

I just can't do it.

Can't do what?

I just can't *force myself* to get out of bed. Maybe my brother will telephone me and then I will have to get out of bed. That's it, I'll wait for him to call.

What a pathetic creature you are. And you want to start a business. You can't even get the fuck out of bed. You aren't even worth a shitload of thought. Go on, lie in your own lazy excrement.

But what am I supposed to do?

Get up!

I'm too depressed!

You are depressed because you don't do anything!

No. I don't do anything because I am too depressed.

Eventually he gets up, although it is never clear to him what sponsors the gesture. He is exceedingly exhausted and first thing when up he stares at himself in the mirror, and for a few minutes engages in another conversation about how badly he looks. Worse than yesterday? Better? Signs of deterioration? So bad he should stay home? Off-putting? And so it goes. In the course of showering, without exception, he weeps. He calls out 'Father, please save me', and in so doing he comes apart. But after this cleansing, he towels off, makes some coffee, and then has a bite to eat.

Then there is another battle which can last from fifteen minutes to two hours about what he should do. Should he call his father and brother (who own and operate the used car lot where he works) and tell them that he is ill and cannot come to work, or should he bite the bullet and go to work? A long conversation can then ensue about his worth on the job. If he shows up to work – often after midday – he will retreat to his office, and spend the entire day wondering about his worth and whether he will ever sell a car.

I haven't described him.

He is thirty-five. Tall, blonde, lazy green eyes, rather handsome. Catholic, but not practising. He has been hospitalised three times since mid-adolescence. At sixteen he began singing in a shopping mall and was arrested. It was unclear whether he was just high on drugs (which he took throughout his teens and into his twenties) or whether he was also crazy. He was released from hospital after three months. In his early twenties he had another breakdown, this time unaccompanied by euphoric dissonances, but clearly a depression of some kind. His last hospitalisation, some two years before he came to see me, was more preventive. His GP, his father, his two brothers, and his family's priest all thought that he was on the verge again and mainly out of a wish to protect him, they put him into a private hospital for a week, after which they thought he seemed a bit better.

The family had met again a few weeks before I saw him. His father had a sort of sixth sense about him. He was pretty sure he could tell when Helmut was losing it, and he met with the GP in Helmut's presence. They had a calm, even congenial, conversation about how to handle Helmut this time, and hospital seemed perhaps a good idea. But the GP, who was quite experienced and thoughtful, was less than content with this notion and after considerable bargaining with the father, it was agreed to give Helmut a shot at psychotherapy. The GP had never put the patient on medication. Not because he was averse to doing so. But for some reason, he thought that Helmut was the sort of man who once on medication would stay drugged for life, and anyway he wasn't sure this would help him. There had been only modest outcomes from the medication he received in hospital. The GP made the referral, saying that he was quite sure Helmut was unanalysable and he was not sending him along for analysis. But he hoped that Helmut might gain some minimal insight into himself so that re-hospitalisation could be avoided, and perhaps he could even begin to find his way in life, with some sort of jump-start or nudge.

When Helmut arrived for the first session I found a man who looked more of a vulnerable kid than an adult. He smiled repeatedly throughout the session in a kind of forced way, trying to put on a good expression. But he was also clearly anxious and almost stuporously depressed, and as I told him so, he seemed even more confused by my – as he admitted – accurate identification of his feelings. I asked him how he felt about attending the session and he said that as all else failed he was willing to try anything, but when I went silent he asked me if I could please ask him questions: he found it easier. He asked me how one spells psychoanalysis and what it was. I explained how I worked and lapsed into silence, whereupon Helmut said that he might just as well tell me about himself.

He described his problems sleeping and the way he thought throughout the day, which I have tried to capture in the descriptions above. He occasionally showed up at the used car lot, but usually stayed at home. He described the several part-time ventures he had tried in the last few years, selling small sailing craft, self-defence alarms for women, and a credit card security system, but each attempt had been less than half-hearted and all that he accomplished was the loss of £60,000.

I saw him in twice-weekly psychotherapy for seven months. The sessions were strikingly similar. He would report at length on his paralysis at work or in the home. As he described his inability to work he spoke of himself in critical and denigratory terms. I said that I could see why he found it so hard to work, as such a critical voice would make it hard to accomplish anything. He admonished me and told me that it had nothing to do with his inner voice, which if anything was helpful, but it did have to do with a defect in his personality: he was unable to respond to perfectly reasonable urges from within himself. He said that he was disappointed in psychotherapy because he expected me to tell him what to do and to side with the part of him that did the same. But I didn't do this and this worried him. I was silent too much of the time, and this was a waste of his time, as what he needed was tough questioning and my expertise. 'I don't know why Dr X sent me to see you, but you are meant to be an expert, so I have come along, but I don't understand any of this.'

He was puzzled by my affirmation of his feelings. I said that at least he seemed convinced of one thing, and that was that he felt uncomfortable in my presence, and did not think psychotherapy would help him. I pointed out that this seemed to be the one thing he managed to have unequivocal feelings about. He caught the humour in this and said that he could see, then, how psychotherapy was helpful, as it allowed him to have a firm belief in something. For some weeks he then proceeded to talk to me *outside* of the psychotherapy structure, in that he would try to talk to me about his life, assuming now that psychotherapy had failed, but that we should now talk about what he could do next. He continued to see me because he had promised the GP that he would stick it out for six months, so he would, as I said to him, fulfil his 'sentence'.

In the first sessions he told me that his mother had died when he was a baby – he didn't know how old he'd been, but he thought it was before he was two. He also told me he was sure it had not mattered and of course he could not recall her, nor for that matter any of the details of his childhood. Memory seemed to begin with adolescence.

As the months passed, however, and the trial period concluded, Helmut decided to stay on for a while longer. There were several reasons for this. Listening to his long and deadening accounts of his internal mental life, I had repeatedly told him that with a mind that was always ordering him about I could see why he felt defeated. One session, when he told me that were it not for his constant mental approbations he would just do nothing, I said 'Really? You mean, if you did not tell yourself that you should do something, you really would do nothing? You would just sit there?' Yes, he was sure he would, for quite a long time, for a very long time. How long, I wondered. Two hours, ten hours, a day, two days, a week, a month? He was puzzled by the question. I said that he seemed to be living with a powerful idea, that unless he constantly prodded himself, he would just be an inert heap, but personally I thought this an impossibility. I bet him that if he let himself alone he would surprise himself by doing something. What, he wanted to know. How would I know, I said. It hasn't been thought yet, has it? It would just happen. However, for this bet I required two conditions. I said that so far as I was concerned, if I were to be given a fair chance, I would need two very simple things from him. (As he was full of hundreds of demands, two simple requests struck him as almost amazingly reasonable.) I said that he had to come to psychotherapy regularly, whether he liked it or not, and that he had to show up at work, whether he wanted to or not. That was all.

What time should he show up at work, he wondered? I said it didn't matter to me. Any time. But he had to show up every day of the week. (He had been staying at home and not working, perhaps putting in one appearance a week, sometimes missing two to three weeks.) Why go to work if he didn't do anything? I said that this, of course, was the bet. I reckoned that he would do something, whether he liked it or not, but to do it he would have to be at work. The same was true of psychotherapy. He had begun to skip sessions, missing one entire week, and I told him that he had to come. What was the point, he queried, if it wasn't working. I said it couldn't work if he wasn't there. In any event, he agreed to this bargain.

Weeks passed. Quite to his surprise he discovered that indeed I was to win the bet. He found that if he simply arrived at work and sat at his desk, although an entire day would go by without his doing anything – not answering the phone, not opening letters, just looking out the window – that two such days did not occur in succession and he would just do something. He would walk out onto the car lot and suddenly go up to a customer and talk about cars. Or he would go to an auction and watch the bidding. He would not bid as it was too anxiety-provoking, but he learned a bit each time, he would see how people valued things.

As the weeks passed into months, he found a particular set of consistent interpretations on my part useful. Each time he would launch into one of his self-instructional diatribes I would say to him that with that kind of intimidation – I would often call it the 'sergeant-major' self – it was no wonder he collapsed in a heap of desultory inertness. 'Listen', I said once, 'if I had a mind like yours I wouldn't do anything either!' To his immediate, but eventually diminishing, ripostes of 'But what will I do?' I would reply 'nothing'. Nothing, that is, in response to such internal molestings which, I argued, paralysed him and paradoxically – because they were meant to inspire him to action – sent him to certain inactivity. So just see what you do, I suggested. And that pretty much is what he did for several months. And now and then he would report in a session that he had done something and on occasion it would result in something, such as the sale of a car, or the discovery of a new source of automobiles.

We can see, in this respect, how Helmut's mind, full of militant instructions, was at odds with his self. If we apply the concepts of transference and countertransference to the intrapsychic sphere, we could say that the mind acted upon him like some unempathic, thoughtless, and demanding other, which left the rest of him feeling inert, vulnerable, close to tears, and completely misunderstood. His response to the mind's split-off activities was to collapse in its presence. However, we were beginning to see that in fact he fought back by refusing to do what his mind ordered him to do; but because such passive resistance was quite unconscious, only over time did he realise that a part of him was saying a quiet 'fuck you' to the sergeant major. I said once, 'You know, I appreciate why you lie in bed; it's a kind of defiant vegetable saying to that mind of yours "Fuck you, what can these commands of yours do about this kind of absolute uselessness?" '.

Work in this area was assisted, I think, by my attending to his differences with me. After an interpretation or comment, about which I could see he had doubts, I would say that I thought he disagreed; more to the heart of the matter, I would often say 'ah, so you think, more analytical rubbish, eh!' and he would concur, eventually taking over this more generative critical response. In fact, his disagreements were often accurate and surprisingly informative, and led to a more constructive dialectic between the critical factor and its object. We managed to enjoy these moments and the pleasure of difference was gradually, very gradually, internalised into his intrapsychic life, so the battles that took place between the self and the mind became more evenly matched, even pleasurable at times.

Eventually I thought he could use analysis, even though I sustained doubts about how insightful he might become. The reason was fairly simple. Toward the end of the first year I could see another very important dimension to his depressive illness. His helpless states were sustained conditions of need and in my view he was unconsciously calling for a maternal figure to come and rescue him and look after him. That figure had

96

been the father, who indeed did often come to his rescue, by giving him money, by telling him he did not need to come to work if he did not want to, and by worrying about him. I told Helmut that in my view his collapsed self was like an infant or small child in need of mothering rescue, which he had found in part from the father; he was therefore armed against his mind, because this mind demanded independence and motivation on his part, when what he desired was care and attentiveness.

Helmut listened to my comments with respectful silence, clearly relieved however, when I said he must be wondering what to do with these 'psychoanalytical remarks'. That I was recommending more psychoanalysis, not less, was initially received by him with a kind of amused disbelief, but certain details deriving from our work supported my advocacy of psycho-analysis.

For months I had been puzzling over his mother's death, something which he clearly regarded as completely irrelevant and analytical nonsense. But no one in the family knew how she had died, nor did anyone talk about it. Out of grudging respect for what he regarded as my intelligence he had asked an aunt about his mother's death and she had replied that he should ask someone else in the family. He took this in two ways: it confirmed his view that it was unimportant, not even significant enough to discuss, but he also agreed that it was a bit odd if she did not want to tell him because there was something she did not want to say about it. Bearing in mind that Helmut was not an insightful person, and furthermore that he tended to simply recount his daytime events with little interest in what anything meant, I had assumed the function of occasionally producing an interesting idea, one that rather caught his slight interest, even if he regarded such ideas as really quite far-fetched. In the beginning, simply to be curious about something and believe one had the right to look into matters was itself somewhat new to him.

He eventually agreed to begin analysis after a particularly difficult sum-mer break. He had spent time with his family on the west coast of Ireland, and had fallen ill with some kind of flu. His father and brothers had not only not attended to him, but gone off climbing for two weeks, during which time he had a high fever and was hospitalised. In hospital he felt he had 'seen the truth' which he took to be the 'fact' that no one had ever cared for him and he had always been deeply alone. This revelation occurred during a significant mood elevation. Out of hospital, his deep insight galvanising him, he rented an astonishingly expensive car, travelled round Europe, hit the casinos in Monte Carlo, and spent £25,000. By mid-October he somatised the manic state into a non-specific illness that was to last four months. He was flattened into a kind of depression, but still haunted by his discoveries of the summer.

My comments about his need for analysis had occurred before the summer break, but he was not initially agreeable. However, the events of the summer and his depression in the autumn convinced him that perhaps he needed to be seen more intensely. It so happened that apparently coincidentally he began to ask questions about his mother and her death. The father had managed to divert him by saying that she had died of an asthma attack, but when I recommended psychoanalysis, and Helmut told his father, it was as if in the father's mind this meant that now the truth had to be told. Visiting his father, ostensibly to discuss the arrangements for the analysis, Helmut's father greeted his son by saying he supported his entering analysis, but there was something he wanted to talk to him about. He disappeared into his study and returned with an envelope. As he told Helmut to read the letter he broke down in tears and Helmut spent the next twenty minutes reading and re-reading his mother's suicide note. His father told him that she had been a very vulnerable woman, that she had had several breakdowns, and that he had not known what to do about it. He knows looking back that he left her alone too much, that he should have sought treatment for her, and that the week of her suicide she had returned from hospital, and he had just decided to look the other way, going off to work. She killed herself when Helmut was nineteen months old. Helmut's oldest brother was nine. Neither he, nor the other brother (five at the time) ever discussed the mother's death, which whenever mentioned had been understood to be the result of an acute asthma attack.

Some months before I had told Helmut that the family's reluctance to talk about the mother suggested to me that this might not have been a natural death. On one occasion I said to him that indeed (though of course I did not know) it could have been a suicide. When he discovered from his father that this was so, it added to his growing conviction that my oddball ideas had some measure of truth to them. I said that given the uselessness of his own mentational advice to himself, I could well understand that he was not particularly keen on any mind's ideas, including my own. How had I come to my idea, he wondered? I said that it was *a feeling*, derived from the fact that no one talked about it in the family, and also one I thought he conveyed by his absolute negation of her significance. I was careful to point out how feelings derived from certain facts of life, but also that a feeling without a validating context – such as the one he provided through his own investiga-tions – was potentially misguided. From this moment he had a greater respect for my mind because it had been of use on several occasions, and he could see that although I relied upon feelings, I also needed more than a hunch to validate an idea. It felt safer to rely upon a mind that worked like that.

Beginning analysis was not easy. In psychotherapy, by looking at me, he felt that he could sense my interests and my disinterests, and now, on the couch, he did not know what I thought or how I felt. Analysis felt like being cut adrift. In the first week he was close to panic and conveyed it. It was not that I considered him on the verge of a de-compensation, but that he seemed to have no personal assistance to help him through the loss of the visual object. I said that his response to the visual loss of me brought to my mind the loss of his mother, and that at this moment he was seemingly without anyone. He agreed that he felt that he was without anyone, but added that he did not see how any of this had to do with his mother. She was dead and that was that. This simply had to do with the fact that I was out of sight and he found it uncomfortable. By the second week his mind was racing. He had a hundred things to talk to me about, to fill up the hour. I said that it was interesting how he used his mind to help him fill the void created by my absence. He agreed. I responded 'Of course I know you will find this typical of me, but again, my association is to your using your mind as companion when your mother disappears. I think we are seeing that right here and right now'. This made a certain sense to him in that although he still claimed that his mother's death simply was too long ago to have affected him now, he could see the sense in what I was saying. This was different. He had found a way to find sense in these interpretations, even if he disagreed, while before he had only found them to be off-the-wall actions of the analyst.

Our senses of humour helped us through this period of work. When I would make links like the above he would complain that I was being psychoanalytical again, and I would reply 'of course', and 'I would not want to disappoint you'. Sometimes he would predict my interpretations and I would congratulate him and tell him that I agreed: he was right. Insight was now a kind of amusement, but not one which was gratuitous: it was truly something which he expected of me, and which he looked forward to, even if he was certain to keep his side of the equation present by knocking down the comments each time. He would bring in material with a clear sense of expectation – 'well...?' – and was delighted to see how I thought. He was, looking back, finding the pleasures of mind.

For some time, however, he had complained that his father, whom he loved very much, usually showed only a cursory interest in him. He did not doubt his father's love: it was feelable. But his father only seemed to ask after him in a way that was like taking his temperature. 'Are you okay?', he would ask, obviously wondering about his mental state. When Helmut replied in the affirmative the father would sign off abruptly. The father did not want to know more about him. This allowed me to make a particularly useful transference interpretation, as Helmut was characteristically abrupt when I would make a comment that was aimed at a deeper understanding of him. For example, I once asked if he had dreamt that night and in a clipped tone of voice he said, 'Nope, nothing I know of'. Moments later while describing his father's way of cutting him off he said 'You have no idea how frustrating that is' and I told him how he did to it me, with the father's voice. He was genuinely quite stunned by this interpretation. He had no difficulty in seeing the parallel and although he was less than enthusiastic about extending it to a family principle of not wanting to know about inner feelings and thoughts, he accepted that this was in fact the case.

For months he felt his plight more deeply. He did not think about his mother, nor his life history, but the discoveries had shaken him. He was increasingly aware that his brothers, like his father, had removed themselves from any insight whatsoever. Indeed, a pattern of paternal alarm occasioned by the slightest sign of depression in him, followed by immediate detachment upon reassurance, invited a speculation on my part: it seemed to me that his father unconsciously linked him with his suicidal mother. I said once, 'You know I think your father is overly worried about you because unconsciously he associates you with your mother'. This helped us to understand the unusual concern of the father, the GP, and other members of the family about Helmut's safety: everyone had linked him to the death of his mother. It also enabled us to analyse his own dissociated idea that he might kill himself, a view which he had held since adolescence, which he had conveyed on numerous occasions to his father, his GP, and attending psychiatrists, but a view that had no conviction. He did not really want to kill himself, he told me; nor indeed did he have any proper suicidal thoughts, but with engaging naiveté he said: but it could happen, couldn't it? It took time to work this through so that he could see that he was living out his father's memory of his wife's suicide, one that the father associated with her infant, and with which Helmut had identified as he grew older.

Interpretations such as the above were helpful and the first indications, for Helmut, that thinking – the work of the mind – could assist him. For years his own mind had been occupied with militant injunctions and merciless adjudications, and he had unconsciously turned against it, becoming a listless recipient of the endless stream of berations, but defying it by embracing an increasingly vegetative existence. In turn, he became more dependent upon myself and the analysis. In the first year he had frequently complained about the journey to sessions and when he began four-times-weekly analysis, he found it unbearable and unhelpful.

He had, for example, complained incessantly about the silence. What good was it to lie in silence for four hours a week, he would ask, what were we accomplishing? Sometimes I would say that I did not know what would come from the silence: perhaps nothing at all. Nothing at all, he would yelp, how could we justify silences that produced nothing at all? I told him this did not worry me as I knew that in time something would eventually occur to him spontaneously, and he would tell me. He protested with more worry than anger, genuinely feeling that this was really the beginning of some kind of end, and soon I noticed that each session he played with a rubber eraser which he pressed and distorted between two fingers of his right hand. I said nothing about this, but he mentioned that he always did it (it had only emerged however in the analysis) and had done since childhood. I said it seemed to soothe him and he agreed; he would lie in silence for quite some time playing with his eraser, now and then complaining that the silence was useless and that we were wasting time. I have to say that I found his preoccupation absorbing and I felt quite sorry for him. Now and then I would ask after his thoughts and he would report ruminative goings-on, but as time passed I remember hearing for the first time the birdsong outside my window, and I noticed that I was now sitting in my chair in a restful posture, relaxed and reflective. I also noticed that he seemed much less fretful. And he began to talk about matters that occurred to him spontaneously: a dinner he was to attend that night and the thoughts he had about it, a woman he had met at a party the previous week, reflections on his father's way of treating him at work. As he spoke up, I would occasionally ask for elaborations, or associations. Sometimes I would add associations of my own, and now and then I would make an interpretation. The point is that by the end of the second year of work Helmut was able to use silence, to speak up spontaneously when he had a thought that carried weight to it – rather than the impinging weightless obsessions of his split-off mind – and he listened to interpretation and used it.

We could say that through a subtle form of regression within the transference he was giving up some of his inner self states to the other who used mind to help sort out the feelings and to reflect usefully upon lived experience. To my way of thinking this was the analysand's symbolic[1] return to the mother who had not been there for him in the earliest months of life.

This period of the analysis gave us the working relationship that was necessary to understand the next stage of difficult work. As his dependence upon myself increased there were occasions of sudden and virulent outbreaks of mental interference, in which he would panic and then assault himself with hundreds of recommended courses of action. As he did so he was even more helpless, saying in one session that he was certain now that he would accomplish nothing and be a failure forever. I said that I thought there was an infant in him that in a way did not want to have to think or work and wanted looking after, something he was now experiencing with me, and that this alarmed his mind which as we know had to do the looking after for him as a child. (Early in our work I had emphasised the positive side of the mind's effort to pull him up out of infancy and childhood by the bootstraps.) But there was indeed a part of him that did not want to have to do anything, and this inert vegetative self, I suggested, seemed to me the infant who was demanding that the mother return and look after him. He vigorously protested this interpretation in the beginning, but by now I knew that he had to deny all links to the mother. So I would let him fully and completely express his protest and then gently say, 'There is to be no memory of mother, no link to her, is there?' and this very particular comment unfailingly allowed him to reconsider whatever interpretation I had made. In effect a certain kind of resistance had to be worked through each time, before he could make use of analytical interpretation, but arguably such comments – the work of intellection – only felt safe to him if it took into account his aggressions, his needs, his desires, and was adaptive to his self state. Then he could use mind: mine and his.

The final part of our work that I shall report was his growing realisation that his 'failures' in life – and he had been out of work for long periods of time – expressed his demand that he be mothered. As such these failures were understandable and psychologically sensible. They were no longer simply to be the object of attack. As understandable as it was, in retrospect, that his childish mind would chastise and berate him for being childish, he had used his mind as a kind of militant other that had goose-stepped him out of his infantile self. But with the coming of his adolescence he instantiated a rebellion against this 'mind object' (Corrigan and Gordon) and refused its companionship, moving relentlessly back into an infantile state, unaccompanied by a sentient other who understood where he was. That presence emerged with the analysis, and in turn, he was able to internalise through understanding a companionable part of his mind that took his infantile states into account, that did not berate him and indeed helped him. Characteristically, then, he would tell me of moments when he had felt helpless or simply rather inert and he would say 'Well I just told myself that this was not going to last forever, and that eventually I would come out of it', or 'I was on the verge of having a go at myself, but I just told that part of my mind to fuck off, and sure enough, after a while I did know what to do'. Finally these reports of his inner contests faded away completely as the process was being accomplished within the unconscious and needed far less active use of the analysis than before.

As he realised that his helplessness was in fact a destructive protest I brought to his attention that years of day and night reversal – when he would stay up until the early hours – had been his way of protesting the absence of maternal structures in his life by in effect refusing any structure to his existence. It was only with this insight that he agreed to a more reasonable schedule of his life. Prior to this he had partied many times during the week, sometimes staying up all night, and had taken vacations on impulse. The result had been to weaken his ego even more and although I had always pointed to his lack of a structured routine as self-defeating he had refused to take this on board. At this point in our work, however, he saw the sense in my comments and gradually developed a routine that ultimately he was to find very comforting and useful.

Helmut helps us to see how patients suffering from depressive illness experience the mind as a split-off other that is remorselessly attacking them. When the depressed person collapses into an infantile state, he projectively identifies into his mind all the adult parts of the personality, but because of the severity of the collapse, these otherwise potentially helpful parts of the self become so split-off that they are virtually yelling at the infantile self to hurry up and join with the mind lest there be a catastrophic structural split. In ordinary depressions such a catastrophe does not occur. The individual may sink into helplessness and inertness for a while – a few hours or maybe one day or two at the most – and although the more mature parts of the personality may have been projectively identified into the mind, which berates the self, or into an other who is now the object of envy, eventually the person comes out of the slump, rejoins mind as a helpful processor of lived experience, and all is reasonably well. But the severely depressed person experiences a catastrophic loss of mind which increases in its hostility to the self as it incrementally receives projectively identified healthy parts of the personality. If, as was the case with Helmut, the child part of the personality hates the mind because it is identified with a growing up that is a growing away from an essential truth about one's being, then the person can sustain trench warfare between the self and the mind.

Psychoanalytical language is inexact and highly metaphorical. Were we not to have a clinical context for the distinction between self and mind, then readers of the literature would quite rightly wonder what exactly is meant by a split between them, as such terms in the very first place are by no means clear. But as always, psychoanalysts are obliged to justify their language by indicating how patients can only be properly imagined and considered through such terms. And in the case of the depressive, it is striking how this person makes the theoretical statement that the self is at war with the mind. This is not the analyst's invention, but one of the most common statements made by the depressed patient, and as such deserves even more attention. It is a startlingly precise statement of affairs. In the patient's subjective sense of self, in their own core being, they feel assaulted by their mind which pushes them further and further into a corner. They see the mind as something harmful and awful. They prefer to be asleep rather than awake, to avoid the hammer blows of the mind. They may consider suicide in order to stop the mind from attacking the self. They will engage in long, exhausting, and futile conversations between their self and their mind, experiencing in this polarisation the distinction between their private subjective state of being and the mind that opposes that being.

Of course, they know that their mind is part of them. They can even, now and then, try to identify with it, and from the lofty superego heights of mental reproach, they can even joyfully cast aspersions on the inert self, declared finally to be a thing of the past. But such moments are short-lived, although naturally they become the basis of the manic development which can last for months. Eventually, however, the person is back to square one with the mind attacking the self with renewed vigour and distaste. But because this mind is part of the self, indeed known to possess some of the most important and essential parts of the self, it can become an object of envy[2] and the person can bizarrely enough come to hate what is in fact theirs. This may give rise to that masochistic glee of the depressive who takes pleasure in turning the mind's attacks into a form of pleasure, engaging in an intrapsychic war between helplessness and intelligence, between cynicism and megalomania. Less obviously but no less importantly, the depressive person is always mourning the loss of contact with the generative companionship of the mind. The mind in health is a useful and essential companion to the self. Those particular forms of destructive views that emerge from the idiom of the self, occasioned often by the precise lived situation, or the moods of a moment, are processed by the mind: one which may on the one hand projectively identify such contents, but one which eventually is part of the reconsidering process. As a self, the individual will feel helped by the thoughtful capacity of his mind: its storage of memories of better moments with the object, its capacity to objectify guilt and consider means of reparation, its time sense which allows it to soothe the self with the notion of a curative factor in life that will assuage the self's more immediate interests.

It is interesting in light of these considerations to rethink the confusional states of the depressive individual. As we know such a person can seem quite lost. Forgetful. Inattentive. Easily distracted. Loose in thinking. Perpetually muddled. If the mind is hated then such self states become means of attacking the presence of the mind, even if, as we have seen, they invite its attack. But more than that, confusion is often an attempt to defy the mind's intellectual acumen. Confusion becomes a screen that aims to deflect the mind's attack and depressive individuals may embrace confusion in order to minimise the precision of mental reproach. Of course the self will be the victim of a mental standing order (e.g. 'you are always in such a total muddle'), but the self habituates to such crude reproaches and hides its mental contents from more precise and devastating attacks by maintaining the confusional state. Psychoanalysts have no doubt observed the difficulty in getting the confused depressed patient to free associate. This is often due to the patient's deep fear that he is now on the verge of giving the mind the material it is seeking as the object of its fierce attack. It is better, reckons the depressive, to be a silent wreck than to be an articulate conveyer of mental contents that will only render the self more vulnerable to attack. The analyst's impartial consideration of the free associations, including his analysis of the patient's moral interferences, allows free thinking to occur and in time helps the patient to see that their mind's reproaches are often very wide of the mark, as the free associations refer to feelings and ideas that are beyond the penetrating glares of consciousness. Unconsciousness then becomes a kind of new-found freedom in being, adding to the patient's sense that they may, after all, be in ordinary defiance of the moral reproach, as unconscious life is too complex for single judgements and moral injunctions. Here is creative muddle: out of the con-fusions of unconscious processes, new visions and creative reflections emerge (see Milner 1969).

In the manic state the individual identifies with the mind as an omnipotent and grandiose synthesiser of all selves everywhere, and a separate essay could be written on this side of the equation: mind as object. For in the manic state the mind becomes the treasured and adored vehicle of a triumphant trajectory over the woes of mankind. But my emphasis has been on the depressive state and on depressive illness, in which the mind is experienced as an alien object that attacks the self, driving the person into a profoundly vicious state of victimage. Psychoanalysis affords a unique and special treatment for the depressive individual as the analyst will have to encounter the patient's defiant hatred of mental processes in themselves, and the analyst's mind will be attacked and nullified. Eventually, however, the analyst can present mind as an interesting and sentient companion, one able to bear and indeed invite the subject's fury and demand. When this happens the patient begins to present increased mental contents to the analyst's mind for their processing, gaining relief, and eventually coming to believe that the mind – the analyst's and his own – can become an essential companion to the self.

9

DEAD MOTHER, DEAD CHILD

Antonio worked as an engineer for a construction company for about two years, but left some six months before beginning analysis. He complained that he did not comprehend why he acted in the ways that he did. He told me that he had found the construction company very challenging and thought he had done quite well there, but there were problems. He paused for some minutes, seemingly in contemplation, before resuming his account. He said that it had been 'interesting' how he had gone through a sort of crisis with his boss: he initially quite liked him, but then he believed his boss had been less than thrilled with him.

His boss had thought him unusually promising and they got off to a very good start. He was handed important projects, but then found himself disagreeing with one of the other projects' managers. Eventually it became clear that he withdrew into a kind of sulk in the presence of his boss and colleagues, but his employer, a hearty, well-intentioned family man, wasn't going to be deterred by his new employee's odd behaviour, and confronted him continuously over several months. Antonio thought he was always on the verge of the sack, but, as his boss informed him, although it seemed as if that was exactly what he wanted, he, the boss, was not going to accommodate him. This led to a quite profound breakthrough in which Antonio rediscovered his sense of initiative, came out of his sulk, idealised his employer, and was very content – in fact happier at work than he had ever been.

As he told me the details of this story and the tale unfolded and deepened, he gradually became less communicative. It felt like a resistance of a peculiar kind, as if he had suddenly been overcome by something. When I drew attention to anything he said, or to his silences, it lit him up and drove him to further speech; smiling, as if awakened from some distracting sleep, he would suddenly tell me in much greater detail what he had intended to discuss.

I commented on the moments when he began an hour with promise, only to withdraw into what seemed to me puzzling silences, eliciting forms of pursuit from myself. When I said this he often broke down into uncontrollable sobbing. Within a few weeks of beginning analysis Antonio, who initially seemed talkative, composed and alert, was transformed into an often mute, distraught, and lifeless looking self. It was as if 'something had come over him'. Now he entered sessions like a figure out of the 'Walking Dead' films, his face drawn and expressionless, only moving into a vestige of life when I asked him what he was thinking, this ordinary question throwing him momentarily back into something of the lively self that had entered analysis.

Still, he continued to tell me about his life outside the analysis.

It was with considerable disappointment that his employer had to accept Antonio's well-reasoned resignation notice. He believed it was in his best interest to undertake an advanced training course in engineering and he wished his boss and colleagues a fond farewell. He left after a very moving Christmas party, when the entire 'corps de construction' toasted his future, unaware that he had no course to enter. He felt a kind of inner distillation of a powerful secret, but his sadness, forlorness and sense of fatedness seemed absolutely real in response to his departure.

In these early months of psychoanalysis he told me in halting but considerable detail about his childhood and adolescence. He was the third of five children, three girls and two boys. His parents had lived in Sicily until he was four, and then moved to England, where they hoped to find a better life for themselves. This did not turn out to be the case, however, as his father struggled to find work, his mother – pregnant with the next son – was depressed and distant, and he can only recall a profound shift of atmosphere within the family.

As he described Sicily, tears welled up in his eyes. Sessions drew to a halt. He would clench his face in a fisted hand, squeezing himself back into composure. Then quite abruptly he would calmly describe his good memories and end many of these recollections with the statement that of course things changed in England. Antonio's manner of relating his story was as odd as the contents of the tale.

Following earlier observations and comments, I said that it felt like he was leading me up a very meaningful path saturated with feelings, but that he stopped his narrative at crucial moments to gain my increased interest in order to thwart it. He agreed. I said that we seemed to develop a sense of rapport when all of a sudden he changed or it seemed that something changed.

Once I said that his recollections seemed addictive, as if he were recharging the batteries of loss. He howled with laughter. He shook with laughter for a good three or four minutes. When he calmed down I asked what was so funny and he said that he was very amused with the way I had said that he recharged his batteries. Whatever merit there was to my interpretation – and unquestionably he felt strangely relieved at being seen – he was as responsive to my concentrated effort of speech, deriving intense pleasure from my 'delivery', even when deeply saddened.

One day, however, he sat down very calmly and looked at me unblinking. I waited for five minutes or so and then said 'Well...?' and he responded: 'Well...?' Thinking I had been misheard, I replied 'What occurs to you?' and he said 'What occurs to you'. It was a flat empty echo. Surprised, I said 'Sorry?' to which he replied 'Sorry'. I was more than a bit confused. It was rather hard to believe what was happening. I asked another question, which he then repeated, and then I told him that for some reason he was echoing me. He repeated the comment. This had never happened to me with a patient before, nor has it since, and I was unsure how to proceed. I remained silent for most of the hour, only occasionally commenting on his behaviour, and towards the end of the session I said that I did not know what his intention was, but it occurred to me that he was trying to dislodge me from my analytical position, to mock it and myself, and that something cynical and disturbing about himself seemed to be occurring. My interpretation was something like a stab in the dark. I actually did not know what to say. The experience, however, was of the death of communication; he was alive and in my presence, but it was as if the spirit of interrelating had been extinguished. I knew that I did not comprehend its meaning.

At the next session he smiled warmly, sat down, and began to talk about a new job he thought of pursuing. He made no reference to the previous session. I decided to see where he led so I said comparatively little. Nor did he mention the echoing session in the next week of treatment. By this time I felt I had colluded with something, although what that was I did not know; however, having given him what I considered sufficient time to tell me, I recollected the session and said that he had not commented on the session when he echoed my remarks. 'Oh! Oh that', he laughed. He laughed a good solid minute or so. 'That's nothing...nothing at all.' I did not find his laughter irritating, just rather odd. I did not know what to make of him, although the words 'that' and 'nothing' remained in mind, perhaps waiting their time for meaning.

He had no explanation, he said. He apologised, stated that it was not a nice thing to do to me, told me it would not happen again, and expressed his embarrassment. He went on to other things and I just listened, knowing of course that it meant something quite important, but as yet not knowing what.

Something of the same curious phenomenon repeated itself, however, in that moods seemed to sweep over him, altering his mentality.

Later in this chapter we shall be considering Andre Green's theory of the dead mother complex, but Antonio's mirroring of me calls up an important explanation of Green's. When the mother abruptly loses her alive mothering, the child will decathect her, he argues, and substitute 'mimicry' of her for reparation. The aim of such mimicry is to 'possess the object (who one can no longer have) by becoming, not like it, but the object itself' (1983: 151). As we shall see, Antonio took possession of me through a form of mimicry that was abrupt and bizarre; it occurred far too early in the analysis for me to understand, thereby meeting its transferential intent – to shock me into experiencing something which had no meaning, corresponding, as we shall see, to Green's theory of action that scars the self with its meaninglessness.

Over the next year Antonio undertook several jobs and the same thing happened each time. He was exceedingly promising on interview and was definitely the 'new boy on the block' for several weeks. But when the lustre of the honeymoon period waned he would withdraw and cease to work as expected. Each time his employer would initially express some concern. Perhaps he had been expected to do too much to begin with? No, he replied, if anything the work was rather simple. Maybe he was tired; he looked pale. Yes, perhaps, he would say. A few weeks of the same would pass and his employer would call him into the office to chat. These events were strikingly similar; there was little difference between the situations. His puzzled employer would wonder what was wrong and Antonio would assure him that things would be put right. The employer would reply that time had already gone toward just that. Could he not explain in more detail what was going wrong? Tears would well in Antonio's eyes, the employer would find himself personally moved by this event. Reluctantly and with solemn exasperation the boss would tell him he had no choice but to sack him.

Quite a few sessions were spent discussing what was taking place with the employer, which I interpreted in the transference and linked to early events in his childhood. By then it had long since become quite clear that he had found his brother's birth and his mother's attentions to the rival unbearable. He retreated into a sulk that lasted his entire childhood, made worse, no doubt, by the parents' apparent failure to perceive what he was doing. So far as he could make out they understood him to be quiet, shy and serious. I said that he seemed born into new situations and enjoyed a good honeymoon with mother, but after this wore off, he expressed his anger by turning it against himself. I told him that I thought he found relief in my having seen this side of him and that it was one of the reasons he laughed so frequently when I confronted him in sessions: it was a relief to be found out. We rarely referred to the echoing session, although I told him that I thought he had shown me someone else, a hated person who was meant to be shoved aside, and that it seemed to me this was his notion of what was in store for him with me.

Every few months or so he would come to a session in a very dark mood. He would tell me he was having very strange thoughts. He was certain that people on the bus were talking about him. They found his way of sitting odd and were commenting to one another about it. Or while walking down the street he was quite certain that people reckoned that he smelled. I listened and asked him to tell me all that was on his mind during such moments, and his fantasies were elaborate, dense, and profoundly paranoid. They had one element in common. Each fantasy occurred in the context of a mood of profound aloneness and I told him that however disturbing these ideas were, they were nonetheless failed efforts at soothing: he needed to feel that he was the object of some interest, even if it seemed odious. In time the person they saw was, as I pointed out, the crippled part of himself, which he felt had never been cared for, and that needed attending to. I said that he had been presenting me these aspects of himself for years, and showing it to employers, but no one seemed to know what to do about it.

Antonio found relief through my continual interpretations of the depressed and what seemed at the time the vengeful boy who did not know how to express his love and only knew how to turn things sour. Over the years, he found these comments useful, and he could take himself on in differing walks of life. He began dating for the first time, and although he had quite a few girlfriends, he eventually settled for one person. He retrained as a graphic designer and slowly re-entered the job market.

As we shall see, these interpretations were slightly aside from the core of his despair, so it is interesting to consider nonetheless why they were of use. Even if they overlooked the true cause of his anguish, they offered him an explanatory structure into which he could unconsciously project the deeper sources of his despair, and through which he could re-imagine himself and gain some true relief. In fact, however, the strange transformation of self – from ordinary thinking to bizarre mentations – came over him, as it were, from the outside like someone catching a virus. He clearly conveyed this in the way he described these states of mind and their contexts: for example, he was walking along Oxford Street when suddenly he was overcome by a strange idea, or he was riding a bus when suddenly he felt people were talking about him. I focused on the mental contents at this time, on the state that seemed to change in mind.

The mental contents in themselves were obviously of considerable interest and concern within the analysis, and revealed particular states of anxiety or depression on the day.

At first, however, their contents were reported exclusively within a paranoid context, but the paranoid milieu as exclusive narrative dissolved itself and he ceased thinking these thoughts only in this way. He would report his fantasies genuinely seeking understanding of their immediate origin.

But now and then he would tell me in darkened mood that he was having violent fantasies. He thought of punching people on the bus, or knifing people on the Underground, or blowing up buildings. When he reported such contents he would look down at the ground, hands between his legs, in a solemn rather self-executional manner. I would wait, silence would fall, and after a while I would take up the contents and ask for associations, including the day's context: what he had been doing just before such thoughts. Clearly he was not pleased about working in this manner but complied, particularly after I indicated to him my realisation that he seemed to want such thoughts to define him as monstrous. That they might mean something beyond themselves, as it were, interfered, I suggested, with his wish to see himself in a castigating universe.

Once again, my approach, though useful in some respects, continued to miss what as yet I had not been able to comprehend. I did not see that his peculiar thoughts, which overcame him when in the company of fellow travellers, were like visitations of the bizarre, sweeping over him, and carrying him off from himself, just as they swept through the occasional fellow traveller, who would see a man shifted by passing thoughts into an uncomfortable frame of mind. He described occasions when he would be talking to a passenger on the bus, only to have a bad idea pass through his head, which would then end his social engagement, rendering him a kind of headstone for the departed.

Time passed, however, and the interesting contents of his thoughts diminished as they were deconstructed by the ordinary course of his free associations. In the overdetermined world of the symptomatic, if his character structure was only partially met by this process, the works of the dynamic unconscious still revealed their meanings through the free associative method. It was not difficult to see that they dramatised barely suppressed emotional reactions to precise experiences that just preceded them. So by returning to the scene of the injury and reconsidering it, he was able to put his distress into language; this intrinsically detoxified the violent nature of the fantasies and he became less disturbed.

Eventually, however, it was important for him to understand why he had had so many violent thoughts, and furthermore, why he seemed to amplify them when they occurred.

His bitterness towards his parents was not unknown to him, and he knew that by adolescence he was unusually preoccupied with feeling a deep grudge against them, although in another part of his personality, he felt love and affection toward them. He knew that he was not being fair to them and that he was indulging his bitterness, but he could not stop it. Furthermore there was simply too much odd pleasure in acting out the same scenario with his employers, and with women friends. These enactments abated with the analysis, but I still did not understand his curious celebrations of the violent thought.

I said he enjoyed startling people and we recollected his efforts to do this with me, conjuring a violent idea to see if he could nurse it along until it became horrifying: sufficient even to scare himself. He was well aware of this. I openly wondered if during his early childhood, perhaps due to the arrival of his brother that intensified his envy, he had experienced an increase in hate and his mental contents had become too violent too early. I am thinking here of a kind of premature ego development in which the child becomes aware of his destructive feelings and ideas too soon. In his case from the age of four.

This made emotional sense to him. He remembered feeling that he was deeply alien and bizarre as a child, and believed he thought of himself like this when he was six. I said that his reports of violent mental contents had had a curious feel to them, as if he were dramatising some other self, to see what it would do or say and how it would be received. I emphasised this as a dramatic act rather than a personal commission, and he agreed that these statements lacked conviction and that he was well aware of their monstrous quality as a matter of intrigue in their own right.

From this point I said that in my view he was showing me that he really did not know what to do with his violent thoughts. They fell upon him just as they fell upon me in the sessions. They were comprehensible and upon understanding vanished. But he experienced them as containing a deep essential truth about himself that surely, due to their power and authority, displaced any notions he might otherwise entertain about himself. I said that this left him feeling that he had no option but to side with the monstrous thoughts and try to make them into his own, even if he was personally and privately horrified and confused by them.

It was not difficult to hypothesise a split in his early childhood that drove a wedge between a loving and reparative self and the hating and violent self. The increment in his hate had led to too many destructive ideas, suggesting to him as a child that he was evil, an idea to which he capitulated. As his parents were good people and as he suffered no gross abuse at their hands, his hate was compounded by a destructive envy of what was good about them, his siblings and himself that led him to despatch loving feelings (towards others and himself) with ruthless abandon. He believed he did not deserve to thrive and whenever he embarked on a new job or started up a new relationship he ruined it by turning himself into a Richard III, darkening the stages of his life with brooding malevolence. In fact, however, he was desperate for someone to 'see through him' as had been the case with one of the employers and was true of course of my work with him. All this gave him hope, but in the therapy this hope was very risky indeed and on innumerable occasions he was unconsciously compelled to prove me wrong: that he was a monster and that his good feelings were only false ephemera.

As is often the case, the analyst's countertransference can be of assistance in making a clinical decision about some of the underlying truths that patients present. Antonio's violent thoughts did not alarm me. They puzzled me. I found them curiously eruptive and oddly out of place. I took that feeling to possibly mirror his own: that they just seemed to happen, as with obsessional patients who have compulsive thoughts that just seem to fall upon them come what may. But Antonio was a likeable person and I also took this to be an indication of the effect of his unconscious love of the other. He was also genuinely cooperative and truly relieved upon analytical interpretive work, and so I knew – I thought – from this that he was not as ill as he needed to be.

Looking back now, I could put it differently: the illness he carried was from somewhere else, an 'interject' not an introject. An interject is an internal object that arrives in the internal world either due to a parental projective identification, interjected into the self, or to a trauma from the real that violates the self, or both. An introject always expresses an aspect of the self's need or desire – a complex inner organisation reflecting the vicissitudes of the self's status over time – while an interject is an interruption of the self's idiom by the forceful entry of the 'outside'. Differing types of hesitation, uncertainty, blankness and stupor reflect the presence of an interject which as the work of the other (or real) bears no internal sign of unconscious meaning: it simply 'sits' inside the self, its ideational content bounded by seizures of thought or behaviour.

At the time, however, all I knew was that my understanding of him was incomplete. There was no point in pushing it, I thought. I would just have to wait.

Antonio was spooked by his mental contents, however, so work could meanwhile take place in this area to some beneficial effect. His bad thoughts scared the hell out of him. The price he paid for years of childhood revenges against his parents, all of which were purely internal, was to cultivate a genre of horror fantasies that could scare him witless, although increasingly he realised that they also amused him. Or more pertinently, when he had a bad thought he would set up a cinema within himself, popcorn stand included, and sell tickets to the other portions of the self which in states of carefully deployed innocence could walk into an unfolding scene of horror to their extreme fright. But as with the horror film addict, such scenes were also exciting, and of course it was a great relief to have survived.

Those for whom life is a trauma register this fact in a very particular way. When Antonio's parents moved from Sicily the entire family endured a trauma together. His father removed himself from the children, not because he wished to, but because circumstances in his new country required that he work long and hard hours. He missed his children. Antonio's mother was saddened by the move and she lost her intimate relation to Antonio; indeed her mood seemed a curious witness to the truth imposed by the event.

Antonio recollected the small village in Sicily where he spent his first four years. His father managed a small citrus collection centre and was a man of considerable repute in the village. He can remember the way his father would walk down the street, received by people who clearly respected him: he was a proud and accomplished man. His mother did not work, but she and her sisters and relations would sew, cook, talk and enjoy the children together. Antonio's memories of the nooks and the crannies of the house, the garden, and the perimeter of the house were finely detailed.

The move to England annihilated all of this. The father could only find menial labour and his spirit was destroyed. The mother had lost her family and the village she loved. She went to work for the first time, continued to have other children, but could not find a way to re-root herself. Antonio's family moved house several times, eventually settling in a rather dismal bungalow in south-east England where they lived a joyless life, watching television, occasionally talking about Sicily, and avoiding at all costs upsetting anyone in the family. Each member seemed to be nursing a private devastation and no demands or reproaches could be made without one person or another immediately becoming grief-stricken.

An event had, in other words, profoundly altered the family. Antonio's parents collapsed along with him, in response to the event, which then assumed its priority over them, and indeed over the effect of the personal.

Event-traumatised individuals live in a rather suspended state, defined in part by the intrusion of the real into the personal, and the fascination in popular culture with the 'walking dead' – disturbed in their natural migration from the death of the body to its burial by a *natural event* (usually a sunburst, a peculiar storm, or radiation) – testifies to the distinction between the event-inspired trauma and the person-inspired trauma. Indeed, Mary Shelley's *Frankenstein* and the subsequent figures of scientifically resurrected corpses cannily represent the position of the family aiming to recover from a deadening experience which left the family in limbo. The family tries to doctor its murdered participants back into a form of life and to some extent succeeds. Antonio's mother took a certain grim pride in the fact that they all survived, although each of the children was in his own way a kind of walking dead, a revived corpse which could exist, but whose gait was evidence of a death and depressive transformation. The transforming figures – the mother, the father, the family culture – resurrect the children in the wake of a trauma that has left them all shattered, but inevitably the act of transformation is saturated with grief. In putting the pieces of the family back together again the members cannot overcome the effect of the event and this informs their subsequent selves.

Antonio felt himself to be a reconstructed child. Devastated by the move which had wasted the family, he intended that it not be forgotten. His remembering took the form of mutating himself in the presence of the other, transforming what appeared to be an ordinary amiable relation, into a bizarre eruption that drove the other into a corner. As we shall see, however, this devastation-by-a-move proved so malignant because it, in turn, remembered an earlier devastation by movement. But we shall come to that.

Although Antonio was shattered by the family's move, the mother's pregnancy, the birth of his brother, and his mother's withdrawal from himself and his other sisters, he always knew that she loved him, as did his father, and yet he felt deeply harmed by both parents. I have pointed out that the full course of the trauma was really only achieved through his response to these events, when he personalised them through hatred of his parents, which in turn maximised the hating parts of his personality. This had a knock-on effect. He developed a monster self which subsequently began to bother and shock him. He felt possessed by evil, yet he could almost turn it on or off as he chose. If a bad thought crossed his mind, he could cast it aside one way or he could convert it into a trailer for a feature film that was soon to follow, and he could darken the self like a cinema dimming the lights to better see projecting images.

He became something of a dramatist. It would be incorrect to state that his dramatisation of his early life was an hysterical action, in the sense that it was a form of reminiscence, but it is true to our understanding of what that word means, to use it obliquely to refer to his cinematics as theatre. Each dramatisation seemed to take him by surprise, but of course we know better: there was always an entrepreneurial part of the self present, ready with projector and screen, to stage a film if he so wished. The other half of him – the innocent – did not know of this self, and so he was routinely shocked by the arrival of the other side of himself, which left him shaken and forlorn. Here we can see the two stages: the arrival of a shocking event (the thoughts themselves), and the effect of such arrival upon the self (to create a sense of evil).

The child who has been disturbed by an event that too early in life sets him to hating his parents for it, casts himself into a very anguishing form of hell. The pain caused by the original trauma is exploited by the child to become his primary sense of self, and the pain displaces the open-mindedness and emotional receptivity of the child, who closes himself around anguish and manufactures internal objects to play out the rage of the distressed self. The unconscious guilt that is generated by the abuse of the actual parents, through grotesque caricature in the internal world, only makes matters worse, as the child must then seek negative *qualia* in his relation to the parent in order masochistically to impale himself upon parental presence whenever possible. The unfortunate consequence of this all too effective strategy is its success. The child hides his violence, cultivates bad parental objects, substantiates his hate by focusing only on bad moments with the parents and by negating anything good, all done so often within the schizoid realm of a false self that can appear quite superficially benign. Antonio acknowledged that so far as he could tell his parents thought he was just a bit too serious and solitary. He was quite sure that they had no idea what was going on in his mind.

Obviously, looking back on the echo session, we can see that Antonio launched his other half into the session, aiming to cause me not only an experience of the bizarre, but also to show me something that, as it were, would totally disappear in the next session. It was a transference of the purely internal world and as I did not actually live there, except as a specular other, I was in the first instance only an echo of myself. So when he echoed me, he simply kept me locked up in the internal world that is not meant to have a true engagement with the other. But of course this was the challenge. Did I see what happened? Or didn't I?

Did I experience a radical change in the atmosphere of our life together? Was I forced into being an outsider, thrown into a dissociated state, observing the world from a place of anxiety?

Antonio once used the term 'mutant' to describe himself. When he said this he rather bellowed emptiness but there was nothing humorous at all. To his pleasure the joke was only to be on himself. The word stuck in my mind, however, and it was only after some time, when we were reflecting on his early life, that I said it seemed an apt description of a self that was changed by a sudden event. As the years passed I reconsidered some patients with whom I had worked and realised that they too considered themselves mutants, people suddenly altered by a radical change that created a new and grotesque breed, but one that also often heralded a permanent change. One that could be passed down from one generation to the next, creating a separate race, like a group of vampires that live a separate life hidden under their tombstones during the day.

These persons are often schizoid personalities, although I think schizophrenic individuals also testify to a sense within them that they have been dramatically changed by an event. The schizoid character, however, seems to recall easily the period of self mutation. The schizophrenic can only mythologise the moment of mutation, calling up extraterrestrial forces, or actual genetic mutations, or germs in the environment, which permanently altered the self. Both nonetheless recall a moment of mutation when they became different, leaving them with a mutational self, which bears in its inscape, the self that existed before the trauma, the event that was traumatising, the altered self, and what Winnicott termed 'the caretaker self'. Knowing they have endured a change to their personality, such individuals must call upon a certain kind of personal parenting to hold themselves together, lest their new character break out into its own form of madness. Schizoid stiffness or schizophrenic cold alarm are efforts on the part of the ego, to hold the mutational self in place.

People who feel they are mutationally changed rather than psycho-developmentally evolved convey this sense of fatedness by creating a curious atmosphere around themselves, achieved through odd gestures, idiosyncratic movements, and curious verbalisations of their states of mind, which give off the feel of an impending climactic change. Something is in the air. Something may be on the verge of happening. The world is not to be taken for granted. What we think of as human must not be assumed. They have experienced a change in the self due to a change in the atmosphere of childhood – like radiation or chemical toxin that mutates the folks of the horror genre – and they not only remember this atmospheric change, but also believe it has altered them forever.

It is not surprising that individuals like Antonio who have suffered from the events of a life are deeply wary of any subsequent change, even if it is theoretically for the better. The fear of psychoanalysis is understandable; the analytical process is the theatre for psychic change, so brings to the mind of an individual a deep fear of the harm which processes beyond the control of the self can inflict. This person has much in common with those who bear in them a knowledge of the structure of evil.[1] This knowledge has specific characteristics. The self in distress is offered assistance by one who appears good and thus elicits trust and dependence from the distressed, but who then uses the appearance of the good as a lure for a catastrophic reversal, when the distressed now finds himself at the destructive mercy of one who will turn need into a life-threatening situation. At the root of such knowledge is the experience of good and the trust one puts into the world for well-being, a belief that is radically destroyed by the other and results in different forms of self destruction.

Although Antonio has knowledge of a structure of evil, in which the good can be seemingly presented in order to change itself into malevolence at the expense of a trusting other, he is not a walking killer – someone who identifies with the act of murder; but he feels himself to be a walking mutant, a limbo man, between life and death. What he has to his benefit is the memory of parental effort to revive him, even if parental acts of reparation were overly saturated with a grief that made the ego a depressed caretaker.

The knowledge, however, of having once been in good psychic shape as opposed to that self derived from an intervening trauma, creates in this individual a deep memory of two selves: one that can thrive, the other which destroys life. Antonio's other half is the alternative self he became under the force of circumstances and with which he is identified. In his personal relations, as in the analysis, he ruptures the world created by the good self, with a suddenly arrived mutation, that heralds the transformation of lived experience from benign to traumatic. The people in Antonio's life are forced to endure a sequence of actings out by him which has a memorable beginning, a middle and an end. It is like a happening that has turned things sour.

Towards the middle of his analysis, Antonio's comprehension of his identification with the rupturing event led to the crystallisation of new material. It became clear that he did not want to leave the structure of his transference, one that involved his repeated presentation of what Andre Green terms 'blank mourning'. For some time this had taken the form of his retreating into a sulk to be rescued by forms of interpretation on my part, which in turn became the object of interpretation in its own right. Now it seemed that this forlorn testimony was meant to be a presentation to me, a gift to my creativity: he would be bereft, I would transform him. The cumulative effect of this enactment, however, revealed love 'in the maternal necropolis' (Green 1983: 167) as this grief-stricken self was a kind of Sleeping Beauty to be awakened by the kiss of alive speech. It was never intended, however, to change in its structure, as the dead object was always meant to be a lure for any presumed live object in a romance of life with death.

As this became more comprehensible, Antonio also made several crucial visits home, returning to sessions after weekends with his parents. No sooner was he in the house than he felt gripped by the family atmosphere, one which he always thought was defined by the catastrophe, but one now reassessed. He told me how he witnessed his father frequently trying to help his mother sort something out – in cooking or tidying up – but that she seemed incapable of being moved to receive assistance, wedded instead to the agony arising out of the smallest of problems. In a rather sudden flash of insight Antonio wondered if perhaps the move to England had been necessitated by maternal despair with Italy, one which the father may have tried to remedy by leading the family into a promised land. He reconsidered his long-held view that the family was somehow a passive victim of the move.

At the same time I took a different view of the transference. What did it mean, I asked myself and eventually my patient, that Antonio's ruptures were of so little deep distress to the other? For however frustrating it was to his girlfriends to find him withdrawing, or to his employers, or to myself in working with him, he dosed the disappointment with an astonishing flourish of masochistic skill, transforming the other's disappointment into bewilderment and finally into a kind of remove. This dissociation aimed, however, to preserve the imagery of withdrawal, to prevent its eradication through the other's expression of anger. He was to make himself into a still life, a picture never to be forgotten, forever engraved on the other's mind. 'Behind the dead mother complex', writes Green, 'behind the blank mourning for the mother, one catches a glimpse of the mad passion of which she is, and remains, the object, that renders mourning for her an impossible experience' (1983: 162). Behind this drama, or one should say, projected by this drama onto a transcendent screen, is a picture of passion: of a self forever forlorn, unforgettable, inconsolable. 'The subject's entire structure aims at a fundamental fantasy', Green continues: 'to nourish the dead mother, to maintain her perpetually embalmed' (162).

Antonio broke off relationships in order to pass on to the other a part of the mother's dead soul, a picture-fetish of the dead mother that becomes the love object. 'Thin husks I had known as men / Dry casques of departed locusts', wrote Pound in the *Cantos*, 'speaking a shell of speech... / Propped between chairs and table... / Words like the locust-shells, moved by no inner being; / A dryness calling for death'. When Antonio died before the eyes of the other he returned in their minds as an after-effect, a dryness calling for death.

The answer to the question, why was this not so disturbing, began to form itself. Had Antonio been too off-putting he would have been dismissed and hate aroused in the other would have mitigated the other's guilt or remorse; but by dissociating self and other from his mutational moment, he froze self and other before a painting, at an exhibit formed by the absent object, and one far too puzzling to evoke customary rage.

It is important to bear in mind a difference between mutational and developmental change. The individual who is altered by trauma transforms this deficit into the structure of a wish and henceforth seeks dramatic events as the medium of self transformation. The person who has simply evolved, disseminating the idiom through its choices of object, gets on with the quiet aspects of this rather remarkable unravelling. Such an individual finds the peace, solitude, contemplativeness, quiet urgency, conflictual density and subtle shifting of an analysis almost like a true home for the psyche-soma, while the mutational soul finds its atmosphere arcadian and therefore frustrating.

Those who have suffered the trauma of an event cannot successfully identify the personal with the structure of an event, because although it involves people, it is beyond the purely psychical. It does not have an originating subjectivity, a locale within the self or the other. It is beyond the person and yet person-created. The child who has been mutated by the event develops an attachment, therefore, to the nature of mutational eventfulness rather than to the presence of the other. They seek malignant events like some seek relations with people.

But is the dead mother's death not a personal death? How could it be regarded as an event from the real?

Depression often descends upon selves. Although it has a psychic origin and an unconscious meaning, it may overcome the self the way a virus grips the soma. The kind of death suffered by the mother in the dead mother complex is also dead as a psychic event at the time of its occurrence; although it has meaning, the meaning is lost to the mother experiencing it. While despair, sadness, or frustration sweeps into the psyche of all mothers (Eliot: 'the certain hour of maternal sorrow'), troubling them to think themselves through the moods, the dead mother refuses her own moods, killing off contact with the processes of inner life. As she dissociates herself from her affects, she stands as a continually stricken witness to the unforeseen misfortunes imposed upon her by lived experience and its after-effects. After-effects are not for her; she is dead to them.

Returning from one of his home visits Antonio described his mother's response to a failed family outing. They had intended to walk in a park but it had rained and the father and another sibling had suggested going to a museum instead. The mother disowned this solution, instead dying with the turn of events, transformed into a stricken being. Antonio was stunned by the realisation that he felt, ever so briefly, an erotic response to his mother's collapse, as if she were offering herself to the gods: a sacrificial gift...the newly dead to the long since dead.

Of course it may be argued that each and every one of us knows the experience of mutation. Certainly we can reflect upon significant events that had an effect upon us and we know something of the mutational moment, when we are different due to a precise experience. But the traumatised person has experienced a process of continuous radical shifting from his idiom to something else and his self is derived from an event and its structure. There is a special sense of the self as a born again monster, one killed and then resurrected in a new form, mutated by the trauma, which indeed becomes part of the newly created visage.

If the event is a *Nachträglichkeit*, in the case of Antonio, an evocation of the death of the mother, then becoming the something else is an act of secret devotion to the mother's dead body.

A split in the self is established very early in childhood. The individual has a sense of the old or true self which once existed. Then there is the false or mutant self, derived from force of circumstance. That ordinary intrapsychic object relation between the internal *I* and the *you* that derives out of the natural internalisation of the fundamental relational structure between self and other, is transformed by its grotesque double, one in which the *I* is the vestige of a former true-self structure – that is, it is the place of the observant consciousness – but now relating to a *you* that is a new creature. This new creature gazed upon from a dissociated I bears *its* own grudge, as it was created out of the unnatural, 'Frankensteined' by the science of events which no human other could successfully manage or repair.

If the malignant event is the descent of death into the mother, who offers it as her passion, then the child of such circumstance may auto-eroticise his own dissociation: out of his death and the sprung double – from old self to bizarre new self – arrives a love relation.

The individual traumatised by the event, then, believes that he or she is parented by something other than the human, by the molecularity of accidents committed in the presence of others but not intended by them. Such people are surprises. They do not have an inner harmony, or live within the generative illusion of understanding (of self and other) but instead regard with positive fright their inner life as an event that displaces their observant interest. Antonio, for example, could not entertain a passing thought – such as an aggressive fantasy or a sexual wish – without believing that this inner content was on the verge of overpowering him and becoming an event in the real. Sitting on the Underground looking at an attractive woman the thought would cross his mind that he was going to go over to her and touch her breast. This thought seemed a dare. It was as if his unconscious were speaking to him thus: 'Ah you complacent idiot. You think you are master of your own house, do you? Well you are about to be overpowered'. Antonio would break into a sweat, tense his body, grip himself, and look for the first place of exit. That is, unless he could laugh. If he could laugh his haunting laugh he could unconsciously identify with the power of the unconscious to unseat him and find solace, as if he were replying: 'Yes of course you can get me to go over there and touch her breast, indeed to french-kiss her, and then fuck her in front of everyone. What a scene that would be, huh!', whereupon he would imagine the shocked look in the eyes of the other passengers, and this would then be like a kind of practical joke. He could triumph over his anxiety by laughing.

When this occurred he would have to laugh, but knowing how odd this could look, he would put his hand over his mouth so as to control the obvious signs of a guffaw. But he knew that his laughter was visible. So he would close his eyes and rock slightly, trying to indicate that whatever was amusing him was a spontaneous internal event and had nothing whatever to do with the people around him. This was the best he could do in an otherwise acutely embarrassing moment. Although the laugh ended his conviction that he would act out the event, nonetheless his oddity gave rise to a recognition that he looked bizarre to the others, and this confirmed his view that he was a mutant. Indeed we may see how his conviction that he would become prey to an acting out – transformed from the psychic content to the actual event – mirrored his early life history and bizarrely recreated him according to the unnatural. Thus each and every day of his life he was reborn by the event.

On other occasions, however, he would suddenly stop being charming and step into a morbid state of self, dead of face. Fellow travellers, he could see, were quite stunned by this sudden reversal of social fortune. It looked, he reckoned, as if something unforeseen had happened to him.

Either way, he believed that he left people with a haunting picture of him, which in time we understood to be a kind of love bracelet.

The individual lives now outside himself, considering himself an outsider. Thrown into the outside by the structure of events, he now is *there* in the place where *it* happened, and in that place he observes the self that is mutilated by the course of events. He carries the structure of this phenomenon within himself. Sometimes Antonio would startle another person and bring about a dissociated moment. Sitting opposite a passenger on the train, his nose in a book, he would speak clearly but seemingly from nowhere, saying something that seemed to have nothing to do with the appropriateness of the occasion. 'Your socks are rather nice', he would say to a fellow passenger as the train whisked by the familiar places. The passenger rarely answered, so disembodied was the comment. I can only surmise that the passenger may have wondered if, in fact, he truly heard what he heard. But I reckon he knew that Antonio had in fact spoken these words and that furthermore he was presaging the possibility of an odd moment. Antonio would note the discomfort aroused in the passenger. He would cross his legs suddenly or bustle about in his briefcase. After a few minutes, the passenger might go and sit elsewhere. The point is that he had introduced a dissociative factor in an otherwise ordinary situation, interrupting the other's harmonic relation to himself as an object, throwing him outside the internal place, into looking at the actual other, looking at himself through the imagined (and presumably mad) eyes of the other, now quite uneasy about what would happen. He traumatised the other in the way he himself had experienced the traumatic. A human being was present. But the human being had become either the author or the associate of the eventful-as-disturbance, which now seemed beyond human comprehension and human resolution. The shudder that runs through the body of the unsuspecting bears momentarily the effect of a micro-trauma, a small token of the mutational self's being.

What event had destroyed the mother? Where did it come from? What was its character?

Antonio was an Iago–Othello all to himself, presenting the 'beast with two backs' to the other, witnessing the auto-erotic primal scene: the happening between forces of intercourse taking place solely within the self. How would an Oedipus enter this space? Where is the point of entrance? Was the event that deadened the mother from the outside, or, did it arise from the inside, from some unknown and unperceived place?

A schizoid person like Antonio who is alone most of his life shunning close or colleagial relations with others naturally increases the power of the internal voice, that subvocal medium through which we utter our thoughts and talk to the self. The inner voice lies between the dream – a more deeply and purely internal phenomenon – and speech – when the subject enters the interpersonal world through utterance. The inner voice receives the imagery and textures that derive from dream objects but also imagines social encounters in which one must make the self sensible to the other. It is a kind of messenger from the world of dreams to the domain of speech and from the society of actual others to the culture of pure wish.

Demons were originally understood to be intermediaries between the divine and the mortal, spirits that passed freely from one domain to the other, performing a valued function. By transporting the texture of his inner dialogues into social space Antonio transferred his inner world into the outer world unconsciously aiming to put before the other the nature of what he found so disconcerting. We cannot blame the fellow passengers on the train for their discomfort with his disembodied utterances; he was putting them in that internal space in which he lives as the constant recipient of such shocking commands.

Was the mother deadened by a nightmare or her mother's bad dreams, 'night-mers'? A dream from which she recoiled, disappearing from life and its after-effects?

This inversion of a self, in which the inner world of self and object representations is oddly externalised, reverses and yet expresses the effect of the traumatic upon a self. The move which dislodged Antonio from his unselfconscious personal development forced him to be prematurely aware of his inner objects and in turn to associate these mangled selves and objects with the outcome of the move. They were internal mutants which he felt had to be transferred back into the external world from where they came: shoved back into the real.

We think of psycho-development as evolving stages of mental tasks, each incorporating the accomplishments of the prior challenges that constitute a maturing of the self as it encounters increasing complexity in the world. Each stage is marked by a feature of its rite of passage and the oral, anal, phallic and genital stages all indicate complex challenges in the negotiation of body change and intersubjective engagements. Each stage re-invents the self's interests and desires as well as its anxieties and depressions. But ordinary people also think of life as marked by important events that challenge or inspire one to differ from former selves and to inaugurate new perspectives. Thus most of us learn from experience and are continually informed by our life.

For someone like Antonio, however, life is not marked by such stages. There is no history of seminal moments. Instead all of life seems to have been arrested and stamped by one event that stops any further psychic development. Psychoanalytic treatment, by its very nature, challenges the stasis of such a person as the associative process, and the analyst's off-beat interpretations vary the patient's frozen accounts and destabilise what has become a frozen narrative. The transference returns the self to its arrest in time and from there needs and desires arise that enliven a moribund soul. Antonio did change, very, very, slowly, over eight years and he did come to a path of psychic development which now and then he travelled, occasionally jumping off for a moment's self arrest – but then returning to take part in the spice of life.

'The transformation in the psychical life, at the moment of the mother's sudden bereavement when she has become abruptly detached from her infant', writes André Green, 'is experienced by the child as a catastrophe; because, without any warning signal, love has been lost at one blow' (1983: 140).

It was this loss, in one blow, that Antonio presented to me in the transference in the early years of our work; a loss that took the form of a sudden change of his mood, without warning, indeed without any apparent meaningful affective context to himself. His own transformed moods seemed not to be of his own making. And although he acted these blows upon the other, more often and more pertinently, he enacted maternal detachment, by suddenly acting out an apparent passing idea, and abandoning any sentient effort to comprehend himself in the moment of the enactment.

When Antonio fell in love with Melinda he celebrated the moment of un-enactment, a spell, when he felt the sudden arrival of the catastrophe from within, but he 'stuffed it'. Days passed and it remained un-enacted. He recalled a time some ten years earlier, with Gretchen, whom he loved very much and who was totally besotted with him. They had spent the day walking along the Thames and were having a coffee, before heading home for dinner, when suddenly his entire self state changed. What is the matter, she wondered. Nothing, he replied. To each query, he replied nothing. In one hour the relationship, which had been building promisingly for over one year, was destroyed. He said he wasn't feeling well, told her he needed to go home, and he left her in the cafe. He refused to answer her phone calls, did not open her letters, and months passed. This pattern was enacted repeatedly. And although of course she felt abandoned, the abruptness released by Antonio was for him a form of self abandonment, a 'meaningless' indifference to his own fate. Actions committed by the self seemed not to be of the self. They were the work of some other. And in this respect, such an odd attitude – customarily seen in psychoanalysis as the split-off portion of the personality (correct in some ways) – was in fact a recollection of an early fact of his life.

The catastrophe of abrupt detachment, argues Green, 'constitutes a premature disillusionment and...carries in its wake, besides the loss of love, the loss of *meaning*, for the baby disposes of no explication to account for what has happened' (1983: 150). By removing himself without explanation, Antonio presented a catastrophe that bore no meaning either to Gretchen or to himself. Instead he succumbed to the very event he unleashed, following its logic, turning the stunning effect into the stunned self. As Green argues, the child de-cathects 'the maternal object' and forms 'unconscious identification with the dead mother' (150); in Antonio's case, he follows the event which he enacts and derives his character from it.

And in the period of separation from Gretchen? The character of this isolation? Let us read Green.

Arrested in their capacity to love, subjects who are under the empire of the dead mother can only aspire to autonomy. Sharing remains forbidden to them. Thus, solitude, which was a situation creating anxiety and to be avoided, changes sign. From negative it becomes positive. Having previously been shunned, it is now sought after. The subject nestles into it. He becomes his own mother, but remains prisoner to her economy of survival. He thinks he has got rid of his dead mother. In fact, she only leaves him in peace in the measure that she herself is left in peace. As long as there is no candidate to the succession, she can well let her child survive, certain to be the only one to possess this inaccessible love.

(156)

We may see how the strange contentment that came over Antonio during his enactments, especially in the transference, dulled what one would otherwise have imagined to be an exceedingly irritating effect. Instead the auto-erotic theatre of this love relation pulled its punches, he curled into himself, mother

124

to his mother, other to himself, in the beginning his end, in the end his beginning.

Solitude *changes sign* – from negative to positive. This changing of the sign is part of Antonio's transference. The transference serves a sign function, rather than a symbolic meaning, one of the reasons why it is so curiously empty of meaning, yet powerful as an emptiness.

'That's nothing...nothing at all.'

Nothing?

Nothing will come of nothing.

A no-thing.

A nothing brought into the midst of filiation. Think of *King Lear*, a nothing carried by a daughter to her father in his departure from rule. Abruptness giving birth to catastrophe. And the mother: where is she to be found in the play? Perhaps recollected in the change of sign from the positive to the negative which was meant to be positive; a breach created between father and daughter, to commemorate what? The daughter's love of the father? Or memory between them of maternal absence, celebrated in the abrupt catastrophe: sudden decathexis of love (Lear: 'We / Have no such daughter...nor shall ever see / That face of hers again'). And whose face has not appeared in the play? Whose presence is virtually unmentioned? Whose name signifies the eradicated? Perhaps, however, maternal abandonment can only announce itself in pure absence of representation, a sign that moves as an effect through the other who shall never know it, only act it.

Antonio's 'nothings' were the verbal sign of maternal absence, born upon the mood of catastrophic departure.

We may now look back on the view that it was the move at age four which was the sole cause of Antonio's mutation. In his repetition of love followed by radical decathexis Antonio demonstrates the disappearance of love from the self, leaving either a mordant presence, or, after sudden withdrawal, a totalising absence: compelling the abandoned to retrospectively assume that signs of love and affection were only appearances. The move from Sicily is engraved in Antonio's mind partly because it is memorable and partly because the family recollected the traumatic effects of the mother's de-cathexes by leaving the country. The family (mother included) could now give location to this trauma and safely grieve the loss. No one was held to blame. No one was responsible. The move, like Lear's apparently wise retirement, released the 'no-thing' born in human character, now external-ised into the collective of man.

The wave of depression. The sudden loss of cathexis, of love invested in the child. What dies in Lear, as died in Antonio's mother, is love unaffected by passing moods, shifting circumstances, quirks of character. A self is overcome by '*x*', forced out of its love. Antonio's sudden departures recollected maternal decathexis, but the dissociation precipitated by this catastrophe allowed the infant a backward glance, catching a glimpse of the falling hands, enough to find in this maternal departure an erotic distillation: the tug of love crystallised by the vanishing. As Antonio withdrew into 'born again' narcissism, deriving out of the dead mother complex, self love is fixation on reaching for the dying love object. Her laugh is not the giggle of the mother at play in peek-a-boo, but the haunting bellow of a ghost who leaves the abandoned with a lifelong riddle to haunt the self. Antonio's sobbing would often follow prolonged, unreal, laughter. The belchings of death.

In the later years of the analysis, I found a certain line of comment increasingly meaningful. You were tempted to withdraw from Gretchen (his girlfriend) to see if the catastrophe of withdrawal is real, I told him. It is all too real, I added, so real as to be beyond belief and therefore – you hope – in the world only of bad dreams. I said that I thought he wanted to test it again and again, to try to make it only a nasty turn of events, and not something that came out of the real to affect him.

The passing of time, and the fact that he was now in his late thirties, assisted the line of thought: to continue would sustain proof that we are really alive, not figments of our imagination, that we can really suffer the consequences of our decisions and that our lives really are affected. Really.

When I spoke to him like this from where did I speak? In the textures of dreams and associations? In the opaque house of memory's mirrors? In the opera house of object relations?

No.

I spoke from a place into which maternal love vanished, from the rim of dreamland, psychic life, and its object relations, a border from which a type of perspective is achieved. I was outside the scene, outside the transference, outside the analysis and it was from there that I could speak to him and see his recognition of a need to speak to the other on that border. In the oddest of possible ways, by speaking from the outside, I gradually put Antonio back into life itself, a necessity forced upon me from communiqués transmitted from the strange country we call transference and countertransference.

> And as imagination bodies forth
> The form of things unknown, the poet's pen
> Turns them to shapes, and gives to aery nothing
> A local habitation and name.
>
> (*A Midsummer Night's Dream*)

10

BORDERLINE DESIRE

Some years ago, well into the analysis of a borderline patient, it seemed that her frequent emotional storms – occasions of profound fragmentation – were a curious object of desire. When emotionally upset by something recollected from her life or something I said or did not say, did or did not do, her feelings rocketed into that enraged homing intensity typical of the borderline person except that she was insightful enough to let me know that once the experience arrived it was feverishly embraced. What does this mean and what can it tell us about some, if not all, borderline people?

Customarily we give objects of the internal world a figurative character. A good object, a bad object, a bizarre object, call to mind a specular other, in one form or another. But what if the primary object is not so figured? (Not any object, because of course all persons form internal objects.) What if this paradigmatic object of objects formed within the first years of life is experienced not only as disruptive but as disruption, represented as emotional turmoil?

For the borderline person, an affect resides where otherwise the matrix of an ordinary object, the 'material' of representation, would begin to live. As feelings are the object, borderline collapse is sadly ironic: it conjures the dreaded object of desire.

One day my patient flew into a deeply disorganising fury when she felt I made an insensitive comment. No longer idealising me, she now believed I was useless and untrustworthy. Her intense pain joined fear that she had mangled me and led her to believe I would seek revenge. But despite these and many other threads woven into her emotional state, her turbulence also seemed blissful. This forceful movement into an object was gained by a devolution of herself into invading furies, but it was as if she had found an other, someone missing for a while, but someone she knew very well, who could receive her evacuative shitting and vomiting.

'You have seized my comment with intense pleasure, as if I have given you an opportunity to be stirred up yet again', I said. Even though she pursued her object – now in the form of fragmented elemental turbulence – she felt closest to me when I became the occasion of such anguish. Later in the

127

session I commented: 'I think this stirred-up-you is in a most familiar place, as if you are hugging something you cannot bear, but cannot bear to lose'. Another day I said: 'I think this is a kind of mamma whom you do not want to leave, a mamma-feeling that allows you to empty yourself into her, and for her to empty herself into you'. Many times subsequently I would remark: 'You are enraged with me now I have become the disturbing spirit, who now it has at last arrived, you do not want to leave you'. Other times I would say: 'By upsetting you as I have, I think you feel I have offered you this shit-fitting mamma, and you are confused because you both want this and abhor it at the same time'.

Work with borderline people suggests the following hypothesis. Whether inherently disturbed as infants, or disrupted by the environment, the primary object is experienced only as a recurring effect within the self, rather than a specular phenomenon to be introjected as part of normal development. Like the wind through the trees, it is a movement through the self. When any emotion hints at the presence of this object, the borderline person is always tempted to find this object by escalating an ordinary feeling into a disturbing experience.

This maternal effect does not inform the self in a nourishing manner, unconsciously communicating one's idiom through its discrete effect on the other's unconscious. Devoid of the essential cumulative designs of maternal desire shaping the infant's needs into a sensibility with a future to it, it is pure chaos.

The borderline person experiences any ordinary affect such as irritation upon missing a bus or anxiety about a friend's lateness, as the awakening moves of the mother, calling the self to its customary 'affectionalism'; all life must be judged in terms of how it makes the self feel, and feelings exalted to an oracular place destined to determine all meaning.

This turbulence of mind, however, is not well served by the word 'affect', as this mentality is occluded by violent ideational intensity – a thinking and thinking and thinking again and again about x – often followed by fruitless talking that floods the mind with excessive and overwhelming mental content. Linked to the feelings and mentations are unforgettable scenes composed of fragments of visual and auditory images, mnemic beacons drawing mental life to the dominating impact of the dreadful. (For Lacan this is a primordial layer of representation, composed in part of the gaze and the voice.)

For the borderline person, thinking or speaking this object does not bring the expected relief. Instead there is a painful 'widening gyre' of thought, defying the centre to hold it.

A patient. 'After a while, I lose myself in this craziness. It has no coherence to it, no boundary, yet it feels like a comforter.'

Put in a familiar vernacular, these people are 'into mind fucking': either molesting their own psychic life with overwhelmingly disturbing thoughts or fucking with the other's mind by endless anguished talking, forcing this primary state upon the other, to establish true intimacy. Feeling invaded, the other may take evasive action. The borderline person, on the other hand, feels that however disturbing the relation, it is nonetheless the source of deepest truth and beauty. If this is a phallus, it is a maternal phallus, delivering its power (as the affective) into the other, an intercourse that consigns the other to dyadic oblivion, as out of this passion, nothing emerges.

But finally even the borderline person suffering from too much – or being too much – retreats into self isolation for recovery before inevitably returning to the object of desire.[1]

Arising out of an intense emotional moment, this turbulence grows in complexity as it becomes a type of communication solely aiming to embody this object through figurations of affect, thought and speech.

Even though this turbulence exists as the place of the primary object, the borderline person forms tertiary objects outside the dominating realm of the primary state. Such objects bear the character of false self work, constructions brought together in a fragile and deliberate way – an avoidance of an essential truth. They screen the self from otherwise oppressed mental states regarded as too dangerous to be liberated. One may think of Dante, who, transfixed and tormented by Beatrice, stares at her across a room, momentarily fearing that others have seen his love object. 'At once', he writes, 'I thought of making this good lady a screen for the truth' (1962: 7) calling to mind the way borderline people create screen objects, stand-ins for the sequestered objects of desire, but enough to get many of them through childhood.

When this primary other becomes disturbance itself, as Dante hints, the emotion is the thing.

> It...could be puzzled at my speaking of Love as if it were a thing in itself, as if it were not only an intellectual substance but also a bodily substance. This in reality is false, for Love does not exist in itself as a substance, but rather it is an accident in substance.
>
> (1962: 53)

Borderline persons fall into fragmentations. They seem psychically accident-prone, thrown into torment by the apparent insensitivities of the other. But what if the primary object for this person is the accidental? What if the infant or child experienced the mother as disruptive movement, eventually knowable as a negative transformation of the self? An accident in substance? If so, then the object of attachment is the deeply disturbing emotional wake of the other which includes the fright, rage and destructive hate aroused within the borderline self, a persecutory anguish that further binds the self and its affective object in a psychically indistinguishable combat of negative forces.

Like Ahab following in the wake of his tormentor, Moby Dick, this person follows the object that stirs the self. 'Ahab never thinks; he only feels, feels, feels; *that's* tingling enough for mortal man!' he says to his crew a few hours before his death. In the same passage he thinks next of the wind: how it can be a 'vile wind' that blew 'through prison corridors and cells, and wards of hospitals and ventilated them, and now comes blowing hither as innocent as fleeces' (Melville 1967: 460). There is, says Ahab, 'something so unchangeable' and strong about the wind that blows one across the seas. 'Would now the wind but had a body; but all the things that most exasperate and outrage mortal man, all these things are bodiless, but only bodiless as objects, not as agents' (1967: 461). The object as agent has a particular kind of body (that different sort of thing in itself of which Dante wrote), a primary object that we know as its effect.

That 'tingling' of which Ahab spoke, or the love-wracked state of Dante and other poets who wrote of their loves as afflictions, may be the psycho-sensational trace of a particular object of desire. Roused by the other, perceiving it primarily sensorially, the self brings it into the transference by instilling in the analyst's countertransference a sensationally rousing storm of feelings that bind the self and other in a con-fusion. Not a confusion of thought as such, but a merging through affliction, both participants linked by racing hearts, adrenal highs. This desire is not from the instinctual core of the self, working its way to the wish proper; it is emotion evoked by disturbing impact. Once roused, the fury of the self's persecutory force assumes a life of its own, becoming a body shaped and sustained by fury.

Borderline persons often sustain this object by marrying a person who continuously rouses them. They may also cultivate a borderline object by taking up a cause such as victims' rights or environmental protection, where a single infraction – a case of harassment or toxic spillage – allows self-afflicted turbulence to escalate into the furiously widening gyre of psychic apocalypse. The borderline object functions as an emotionally impacting stimulus, that upon evocation arouses the sensorium. The fact that the (borderline) object is most often on the border of the external and the internal – linked to an external happening, yet immediately evocative internally – testifies to the unconscious place of the borderline's primary object: an outside that is simultaneously an inside. The self is on the border of a simultaneity of valorisations: the object that impacts the ego and causes it alarm; the object that is formed by the precise character of the subject's internal life at the moment.

Borderline personalities will often try to share a borderline object with others – an attempt to break bread in the communion of turbulence. They have an uncanny knack of bringing up topics designed to evoke maximum emotional impact on the other, often unconsciously playing on the other's situational vulnerability. Self and other are briefly merged through shared anguish, although the non-borderline personality will usually rebuff efforts to turn personal distress into a festival of anguish.

Recognition of his desire enables this patient to consider his resistance to psychic change, and working this through occasions a very particular type of anguish. Outbursts can often be seen as defiant resurrections of an attachment to the primary object: the affect as thing.[2] The kind of truth that is disaster, one which devolves ordinary life into madness, is tempting indeed to the borderline and less than the catastrophic feels lifeless: a strange irony indeed, compounded by the grizzly emotional fact that the absence of catastrophe feels self destructive. As he searches the empty seas for the white whale – his tormentor – Ahab's profound loneliness illustrates powerfully that empty space following the other's vanishing.

Turmoil is the presence of the object.

As quiescence is abandonment by the object, it becomes a pain inflicting void.

Psychic emptiness then is part of the primary object's residence within the self, an inevitable outcome of its moving effect. Stirred up then abandoned, the self is full of enraged anguish and then empty. Fullness and emptiness not only remember this object, they constitute it.

Renewed emotional turbulence is strangely nourishing and usually preferred to the void. Feeding off the emotional tempests provided by the other, searching for catastrophe from which one takes succour, is by no means unknown; literature and art have many examples of the self feeding off rage, or jealousy, or loss, as the borderline turns the object-as-agent into a feeding occasion in order to transform a traumatic relation into something of a nurturing one. Unsurprisingly, the analyst's good enough technique is often experienced as strangely depriving, seemingly preventing such feeds, so misunderstanding may be sought in order to gorge the self on disturbed states of mind.

A vertiginous self, always on the brink of catastrophe, the borderline patient awaits catastrophic moments in order to 'milk' them. Turmoil is hard to resist: 'I know I like to live on the *edge*', one patient told me, referring to a kind of low-level thrill, never knowing whether he would fall into the maelstrom of intense conflict or pull himself back to safety. The edge or the border. A line which this personality knows only too well, a feelable border which he traverses, balancing himself, coming continuously close to falling, yet often able to bring himself back.

As mentioned, borderline personalities often seek work in disaster relief schemes or victim support services. They have an uncanny knack of knowing that such victims are disturbed by the object as agent, by something impersonal yet familial, something that touches the core of a self and lives in malignant residence. They know what it feels like to believe that one's life is now irreversibly defined by a shocking event, but their unconscious addiction to that shock, their search to revive it in order to gain excitement from it (to be close to what is believed to be the ultimate knowing truth) makes it difficult for them to really wean true victims from a life catastrophe. We know only too well the unconsciously devoted victim: the man who never recovers from an automobile accident, the woman who never recovers from a rape, the man who cannot talk about anything other than an earthquake he was in. The cathexis of the object is barely hidden, whose memory stimulates the sensorium and gathers the person into his truth.

Borderline sensationalism binds the self as the ego fragments. It is as if the self, failed by an apparent object, attacks it violently in mind and comes to pieces in the process; yet paradoxically, coheres the self by shit fits: mental torment is both the other disrupting the self and the self's grasp on its reality. In their most extreme states of rage (usually during hospitalisation), borderline patients will literally spit, shit and urinate, partly as an attempt at recovery through libido – a libido turned to the body and contributing to a psycho-sensorial sensationalism supporting the body ego. One is reminded in these moments of the excretory territorialism of the psychotic who uses faeces to mark his living space and preserve his valued objects. More typically, however, the borderline person is suffused with mental pain and rage, using affect, in an autistic-somatic way, for its sensational effect, rather than its communicative function.

An example may help to bring this into focus.

Clyde was a nine-to-five man who dreaded the workplace and preferred home life where he lived in anguished enmeshment with his borderline wife. His work as a security guard meant that he had few conversations with people, but he had lost so many desk jobs due to argumentativeness that policing now seemed to be his fate.

When he awoke in the morning he rushed to the front door to get the paper and broke it open to the sports page where he regularly followed the reports of five favourite teams in basketball, American football, baseball, ice hockey and soccer. Many of his neighbours no doubt did the same because when one team wasn't doing so well one could take heart in the better fortunes of another, but Clyde always focused immediately on a team's poor performance. 'Jesus Christ to hell', he yelled to his wife, 'listen to how these assholes did yesterday!' and he would read scathing reports by sports writers to anyone within listening distance. The sports report concluded, he would then read the stock market report, where he had a few diverse stocks – perhaps wisely selected as poor investments – enabling him to explode over their failures. Then he would read the weather report, followed by the political news (he hated both political parties) so that in the ninety minutes or so before leaving for his job he had worked himself up into a near blind rage, producing more than enough negative food for thought to last him through the day. When an occasional passer-by would ask him how it was going he would say 'Jesus...those Mets. Do they stink!', seeking out fellow sufferers in what would often amount to short but intense snacks on the negative.

One of his sons, now in analysis, recalls a typical moment:

> He would be talking to a coach, or the President, or a Congressman, yelling at the top of his lungs. He would begin by saying, 'do you know what I would like to say to that asshole?' and he would be looking at you directly in the face, as if you were the asshole. You didn't dare say no and when he told 'him/you' what he thought, it was like you were caught up in some terrifying nightmare. He had no idea of the effect he had. And on the few occasions when we would be out at the local restaurant, we all dreaded the inevitable moment when he would explode over the memory of some offending team or person, because then he would go into this rage, head beet red, arms flying about, staring you right in the face, and of course, you imagined that everyone in the restaurant would think he was furious with you. So we all devised this technique of mirroring him. We would shrug our shoulders, say repeatedly 'yeah, God that's awful', doing anything to indicate we were talking about someone who was not there. But the thing is for him that someone was sitting right across from him, no matter who unfortunately happened to be there.

If nothing else, Clyde always had his primary object with him, through thick and thin. His son unknowingly witnessed his father's evisceration of the other by the pure force of the primary, and even though the son was not a borderline personality, he felt the object preoccupying the father. 'My father was a storm', he said,

> a storm, always a storm. When we heard the front door open always at 5.45 I felt his effect on me before I even saw him. It was awful. I only felt better when he was away and later, when I left home, it was the greatest sustained relief of my life.

It is unfortunate that many well-intentioned therapeutic endeavours designed to get the borderline patient to understand and use boundaries, find socially appropriate expressions, and adapt to their surroundings, often support this person's false self. Here the false self is a move to be without affect and to avoid engagements that will stir the self. The patient himself may be unusually 'contractual', trying to settle conflicts by redefining agreements and gaining assurances. When I arrived two minutes late for one person's session, he spent that hour and the next two enumerating agreements between us for what was proper under such a circumstance, trying to get me to sign a contract, so that if I did it again I would be bound to receive a just retribution from him. This false self, however, is constructed against any feeling. As feelings are unconsciously exciting, rousing a hunger, the borderline feels himself sliding into a relation defined by turmoil. So when the analyst makes a mistake the patient does not know what to do. Has the analyst momentarily offered him succour from the primary object – i.e. 'Hungry for something? Do you wish to feed off this?' – and is the borderline person tempted?

A borderline session will often begin with the customary niceties before invariably the patient brings up a negative object. If encouraged to say more or feel more then the patient will work himself into a lather, feeding on the negative through the unwitting help of the therapist. Or if not invited to do so, he will touch on turbulent areas like touching base with totemic objects that reassure the self of its location. Or commonly, the patient will seek a narrative escalator in order to ascend from lower-level irritations to the heights of rage, beginning with minor irritants on the way to the session, to distressed recollections of ill-treatments by the other, to negative ideas about analysis and the analyst. This negative transference, however, is usually avoided, as once it is released the patient is haplessly attached to the therapist for life. Even though this is desired, as we have discussed, it is also an otherwise doomed and futile relation. Only through interpretation of its basic structure can the patient be eventually separated from an object that destroys the self's sanity.

Psychoanalytical writers from numerous schools of thought have quite rightly emphasised the nature of the borderline person's developmental deficiencies. In focusing on borderline desire, I wish to concentrate on a particular clinical problem. If we see desire for turbulence not simply as a decompensation occasioned by internal objects falling from a structural place or triggered by blows in reality, but as a conjuring of the primary – the self feeding on its own anxiety and hate – we may see why this person pursues the very disturbance with abandon. When the patient understands that they take a form of pleasure in communing with this object, much of the seemingly senseless chaos of borderline attributes makes dynamic sense. 'I know what you mean', said one patient, 'I have always gotten off on it [turmoil], like some kinda sexual thing'.

However painful it is for the borderline patient to discover through analytical interpretation that their coercive emotionality and clinging grievousness is the realisation of a wish for a state of mind that is the object of desire, it eventually enables them *to see* the unconscious gratifications sustained through their character, ones which when lessened allow redistribution of pleasure along different lines.

Until then, borderline desire seeks what the patient experiences as their deepest truth. Behind the ostensibly offending other (whether the analyst or someone else) is the intangible ghost of a profoundly familiar other who inhabits the self and becomes indistinguishable from it. This desire does not have to seek the object, it knows that this intangible force will visit the self regularly enough, in life events or in memory, and when it feels itself being called to this communion, believes it is moving toward some awful truth that is at the very essence of the formation of the self. The borderline's desire is to meet this truth and to be moved by it.

11

PASSING ON PARANOIA

A woman in her mid-twenties whom I will call Marge told her therapist that she needed psychotherapy because she was isolating herself from people. On the verge of marriage, she and her boyfriend often quarrelled and she was especially haunted by his remark that she didn't know what she was saying. She was also particularly distressed by her mother's apparent alliance with the boyfriend and by a recurrent maternal comment, 'Don't worry about her, she is just being dramatic'. Being in the midst of arguments had been a feature of her childhood as she and her brother had sided with one or another of the parents in their countless disputes.

At first the therapist found Marge exceptionally talkative and personally urgent. She observed the therapist's face closely and listened attentively to what was said. From the beginning she was preoccupied with a disturbing image. She imagined that at that very moment her mother and her boyfriend were having a conversation and her mother was telling the boyfriend what a rotter her daughter was. As she conjured up this scene she became extremely distressed and the therapist was impressed with the intensity of Marge's paranoid frame of mind.

She missed the first scheduled session, leaving a message on the therapist's answering machine to say she was out of the city on business.

In her first three sessions she spoke in the same pressed voice, describing innumerable disturbing scenes from life. She recalled dreams and disturbing comments made by people such as her father which she found profoundly shocking. Apparently her father assaulted her with singularly caustic remarks that stung her deeply. She recalls one phrase – 'You are a thorn, a thorn in my side' – as particularly devastating; it prompted recurring images and when becoming intimate with someone, she imagined herself covered in thorns, which pushed through her skin.

The therapist found her narrative compelling, but she was distracted by the patient's cancellation of the first session and increasingly perturbed by her lateness. She was fifteen minutes late for the first two sessions and a half-hour late for the third. At the close of the third session she said she thought

136

she would have to reduce the number of sessions from two to one as she was afraid she could not afford to continue the treatment as is.

It is interesting to reconsider her idea that her mother bad-mouths her to her boyfriend, one that disrupted her conversation with the therapist. When she cancelled the first session the therapist wondered about the consultation, going over it in her own mind. Had she missed anything? She picked out salient details which might cohere around the question of Marge's ambivalence. The fact that Marge provoked the therapist's internal questioning by coming late was the object of the therapist's first reflection. One of our observations can be that the patient told the therapist about feeling attacked by a twosome (mother and boyfriend) who harboured bad thoughts about her at the same time that she elicited negative views of herself in the therapist. By cancelling and coming late the patient compelled the therapist to review the consultation and to focus on the analysand's negative transference.

The patient interrupted that potential free play of association between herself and the therapist by forcing the therapist into an unusual amount of internal conversation with herself. It was the equivalent of the scene where the mother talked badly to the boyfriend about the patient in that the therapist was now talking to herself about the patient, behind the patient's back in a way, just as the patient imagined her mother to be doing.

As is usually the case in the beginning of psychotherapy, the therapist wanted to listen to her patient with an open mind. With little knowledge of the patient's history, present state and personal experience of therapy, the therapist was invited to form an intrasubjective relation based on insufficient data. She was lured into a paranoid process of mind mirroring the patient's own self state as the self is forced to construct an idea of the other from painfully insufficient data.

The patient has also created a situation in which internal relations aggressively usurp self–other relating. By the beginning of the third session the clinician was full up with private inner reckonings and anxious inner conversations, that displaced consideration of the patient's narrative. As she listened to the patient she could not reflect on the material in an analytical manner, was unable to associate to the patient's comments and found herself preoccupied by the distressing tardiness of the patient. She felt somewhat slighted, was suspicious of the patient's true inner feelings which she believed were not being represented through the patient's bubbly conversational mode.

Perhaps the patient knew this. Perhaps she knew that she had acted upon the clinician to bring about this state of affairs, sensing now that the therapist was engaged in another relation (i.e. to herself) that usurped self–other relating. She knew that as the therapist was developing a suspicious construction of events, that in time she would find it hard to keep this secret set of views and feelings to herself, and thus attack the patient.

If the patient is conscious of the above, as I think she is, she is unconscious of the way in which she seeks to convey her state of affairs.

In a sense, this is an attempt at intimacy, even if it is achieved through cruelty and suffering. The patient conveys her conviction that the deepest heartfelt feelings are born out of suffering and cruelty. Such states are not conjured up in order to give pleasure, but because the paranoid patient feels split between a false self replete with phoney representations and a real self composed of pain that derives from the gap, the difference, between a potentially good inner world and a desperately false representational order. Such people often feel that their parents have been deeply false, describing often very cruel things they have said or done which have caused them considerable pain. Over time, the good moments with the parents are regarded as superficial and meaningless as the child waits for upsetting actions or comments which seem more true to the relationship.

Is this a description of cruelty in the parent? Possibly, but not always. It seems to be the cumulative outcome of a subtle but upsetting discrepancy between the parent's ordinary false self and recurrent breaches by some other self, such as an outburst of bad temper, or a passing cloud of depression. This may be simply a parent who, when depressed, collapses into occasional bitter views of self and others (including the children) which is rather shocking or it could just be the recurrently sarcastic parent who now and then stings others with a sharp tongue.

Such parental traits do not alone create a characterological reaction formation of similar type in the child. There must be other contributing factors and these will vary. Marge was excited by parental conflict into an Oedipally driven primal scene urge – she wanted to get to the true scene of true action. The closer she got to such truth the more powerful she felt. Her selective over-emphasis of her father's hurtful caustic comments underscored her sense of there being another side to her father, one she did not ordinarily see. Unconsciously she aimed to ally her inner state to this secret father whom she insisted she knew better than anyone else did, and she unconsciously solicited and married this feature of his personality.

A curious form of envy develops in this kind of paranoia. Marge felt furious that her father kept his secret self from her. She was irate that he could do this, particularly as she felt incapable of such self protectiveness. She was always breaking down into paranoid scenes, rupturing her false self with discordant statements from certain internal states. Where did the father get such an ability to calmly keep his nasty suspicious feelings to himself? Damn him! At times she seemed to draw an Oedipal conclusion: he and the mother derived their smug abilities from mutually empowering intercourses which satisfied the need for confirmatory sexuality, a bargain all the more effective as it partly rested on the elitist act of banishing the children from sexual co-partnership.

Thus when the parents argued she seized the moment. Intriguingly enough she took the mother's side against the father even though he was the parent to whom she felt most closely allied. The conscious view was that because he was the more competent and attractive of the parental couple it was her mother who needed her support, but her unconscious aim was to join the mother in order to break down the father's infuriating composure, even if, as frequently happened, the father ended up making sarcastic remarks to other family members.

Hurtful though such remarks were, they were also wonderful as she had gotten to her father, forcing him to reveal this other secret self where she was convinced he truly lived and which resonated with her own sense of a self divided between her false appearances and her secret real feelings. In fact, we may conclude that she was partly convinced of the father's state of mind precisely because this was true of herself: she was unusually full of hateful feelings and she demanded that the other be this way too. Her rivalry with her brother had increased the economy of her hate and had excited a scopophilic impulse as she watched to see if more scenes of birth and siblinghood were on the way. By insisting that all people harboured a nasty real self with surreptitious aims, the patient just about managed to ward off a persecutory guilt over her own destructiveness.

In the transference she aimed to split the therapist's internal life (between the ordinary internal I and you) into a premature and intensely divided state. With little knowledge about the patient's state of mind, the therapist was left cohering around crude feelings that displaced perceptual reciprocity with projective speculations. By displacing discourse with private affect, the patient tellingly invited her therapist into a paranoid world, which ultimately took the therapist to the heart of the matter.

This fine art of pathology we now take up in the next chapter as we discuss the skill of the paranoid schizophrenic to drive the analyst into somewhat mad states of mind.

12

OCCASIONAL MADNESS OF
THE PSYCHOANALYST

Hospitalised some eight months prior to his acceptance at the hospital where I was working, Nick was regarded as a more than potentially violent patient, who had, in fact, drawn a knife against his mother and chased her about the comforts of their home in the fashionable suburbs of a mid-western town. He was eighteen, claimed to have dropped acid four or five times a week for five years, and had experimented with as many drugs as he could find (or manufacture), except heroin. He had discharged himself from hospital against medical advice after pressuring his parents to taking him back home. In the course of this prior hospitalisation he had been restrained on a few occasions, and because he was too disruptive he was isolated to protect the other patients. The Director of Admissions found him cooperative but extremely suspicious and monosyllabic. He appeared polite and formal in an eerily false manner, and the consensus of the hospital staff was that he was likely to 'blow'.

Before introducing Nick, it is worth sharing some of the thoughts I had before meeting him, for, whether a colleague refers us a patient for private practice, a patient telephones us on his own initiative, or a hospital assigns us a patient, we read or hear about them before we meet them. Some analysands, and Nick is one of them, develop a reputation of some notoriety and they enter the conceptual space rather disturbingly. Indeed, a Nick fosters a troubling reputation partly to enter the other's conceptual space on his own very particular terms.

Like most psychoanalysts, I value my peace of mind, or the reverie of evenly suspended attentiveness, and part of the pleasure of analytic training and experience is to develop an inner area for the reception of disturbing patient communications, which nonetheless is sufficiently containable so as not to disable the container itself. Just listening, being part of a structure (the analytic process) which has its laws (absence of socialisation, economy of intervention) that enables me to freely associate and concentrate on certain interesting figurations of meaning that develop from time to time is a pleasure. Every analyst who works with the neurotic patient, particularly the good hysteric, knows what a pleasure it is simply to be the analyst who analyses.

Then there are the Nicks. As this stocky, red-haired young man with thick forearms sank into the chair opposite me on our very first meeting, I was instantly not my psychoanalyst self. At the time I did not know why; in fact, I did not even know this was so. In hindsight I must have been uneasy, carrying him inside me in that pregnant period from referral to 'delivery' at the consulting room door. For here was a most bizarre infant. He sat staring at me with a fixed gaze, a slight smirk playing across his face. After a long silence, I asked him how he found things here. He allowed this question to hang about long enough for us both to feel the echo of its emptiness before he replied 'fine'. After a pause, I said 'What is fine?' and he said, 'I am comfortable'. No doubt struck by the sanguine paradox of his apparent ease juxtaposed to my unease, I replied 'What do you find comfortable?' to which he said 'everything'. After a seemingly endless session I managed to extract from him the news that he liked the hospital because it was an open unit and he had found the other patients 'nice'.

What I did not know then was what was so disturbing about him. For example, I was not yet aware that although he stared at me, he did so at a precise, unvarying angle – not exactly out of the corner of his eyes, but at a slant. I was also aware only weeks later that every five minutes or so he would rotate his head to the left, to look to the window side of my office. It was not the action of a person looking out of the window to capture the view, it was more like the mechanical movement of a TV monitor, scanning the space with intentless emptiness. I saw him do this, wondered if he were hallucinating, and I asked him if he had just had some thought, to which he replied 'no' after, as usual, leaving my comment to hang itself in silence. What I did not notice at that point was the effect this bizarre rotation was having on me. And although I noted that Nick sat perfectly still for his sessions, I did not realise that for the first weeks, he never moved in the chair. He never crossed his legs, or changed position. He placed both hands on the armrests and they never moved, except about twenty minutes into each session when he would reach into his left shirt pocket with his right hand, to extract his cigarettes and lighter. With his left hand still holding the chair arm, he would remove a cigarette, bring it some twenty inches or so in front of his face, then horizontally bring it to his mouth where it would sit for a few seconds before he lit. Then lighter and cigarettes would go back into the same pocket. Both the rotation of his head and the lighting of the cigarette occurred without any sympathetic movement in his own body. On reflection I can say that his monosyllabic responses were simple, isolated vocalisations, as detached from meaning as his movements were detached from his body.

During the first weeks I worked too hard to engage him and as I did so, I was annoyed with myself for straying from the ordinary analytic position that I enjoy so much; I was cross with myself for the many empty questions I put to him and for my sense of being false. I was simply trying to get along with him, in order to establish some rapport. All the work of the hour came from me as Nick would sit in utter silence if I did not initiate, sustain and develop knowledge of him.

My voice was shallow and strained, empty of 'affect-ions', despite the fact that it is through our wording and our telling that we convey our frame of mind from moment to moment (see Chapter 14).

With my false self, I was able to extract details of his life history and learn more of his hospital experiences. He said that his problems began when he moved schools at age seven. He had felt an oddball at his old school, but his classmates had liked him, while at the new school, he had been an object of intense persecution, which he dealt with by increasing his oddness. He would stand in the playground engaged in an isolated idiosyncratic display of sign language, gazed upon by classmates who were meant to believe this represented some superior knowledge. As discussed in Chapter 13, the child's body signifies much of his state of mind and Nick's odd body gestures alarmed his schoolfriends, an anxiety that carried Nick's own panic over embodied being.

I said the move to our hospital must have been like the move at seven, and how clearly determined he was to try to be liked. I tried to discuss his fears with him, but he insisted he felt fine, that I was a good therapist, that there was nothing to know about him other than the disturbing move at the age of seven.

Each patient suggests an environment within which both are meant to live a psychoanalytic lifetime together, and the analyst must suffer the illness of such place. As I look back on these first weeks with Nick, it is clear that of the two of us, I was the one undergoing a psychic change – for the worse. He remained his oddly inert and suspicious self, while I became progressively more irritated by my questions, or interpretations which felt compliant on my part. I was ill at ease, struggling fruitlessly to get to that place that I like to be when working as an analyst, but Nick had me out of that place: removed from my analytic identity, alarmed by a seeming inability to arrest my progressive false adaptation to the analysand. As I coaxed him to speak about his life, employing as many subtle interactive proddings as I could, I began to loathe him, and to really hate the content of my remarks, the sound of my voice and the shallowness of my personality. In my view, I had regressed by splitting my personality; out of touch with my real self, I had been taken over by a false self increasingly unable to be effective. The only real state of self I was aware of was my intense irritation with the situation and my role within it, although my hate – due to this regression – was of no use to me, or my patient.

Faced with a lifeless, dismissive, yet bizarre other, I split off my private inner reality, which I could not bring into the hour. Was I living through an early relation that characterised Nick's life? Had he been there before me?

Had he been forced to give up his sense of identity and put it outside the space of interrelating? Was he showing me something of the personality of the other, who displaced his true self from its idiomatic use of the object world?

As the weeks passed into months I worked to diminish my false self adaptiveness. I would greet Nick at the door as he came into the room; he would sit down and then a silence would descend upon us. It is not something I can describe.

A deep fear of ? enveloped us, perhaps that fear that occurs in an ordinary dream in the split second before it becomes a nightmare.

As the days passed, this feeling intensified. As he rotated his head, I would say 'You are looking at something?', to which he would reply 'No', followed by a long silence. One day he said 'You hear it?' 'What?' I replied. 'The fly.' 'What fly?' 'The fly', he said. 'Where?' 'Over there, by the window.' I could neither see nor hear anything, and hadn't seen a fly since the early autumn. It was winter and there was snow on the ground. Ten minutes of silence ensued. 'It's still there.' 'This fly on the wall?', I queried. No reply. Another long silence. I made an interpretation: 'As we know, you often look to that side of the room, where I think you feel there is a fly on the wall observing us, listening to us, and troubling us. But I think I also trouble you, and you may feel spied upon by my listenings into what you say'. A long silence followed. 'No, I don't. You are a good therapist.' Then the dense silence descended again.

The chairs in the consulting room were large, soft leather objects that exhaled when you sat on them. If you moved about, the chair echoed the shift of the body. Yet Nick sat in the chair and made no noise. This noiselessness contributed to the ever-increasing eerie strangeness of this place, as if there must be no sound to announce our existence. Looking back, I think I almost stopped breathing. I rarely moved.

Then an extraordinary event. Amidst this fear-ridden silence Nick moved slightly in his chair, and the leather uttered a material shriek. We both jumped. My heart was pounding with anxiety. But why? Over what? The sound of leather squeaking? I can recall thinking, 'All right, that's enough, God damn it! This is ridiculous'. I was furious that it should come to this. Although I did not know what to say, I was determined to speak.

> I want to try now to think out loud with you about what has just happened. When you moved – ever so slightly – your chair made a noise and we both jumped. Why? Why should this be so? Is it the case that you have no right to move, lest you scare yourself, or me? What is it that does not permit movement? No. What is it that does not permit your existence? It's as if you are hiding from a monster! And what is this monster? Where is it? Is it me? Am I a monster: a Bollas monster?

A disembodied laugh ricocheted off the wall. Nick had not laughed before, if that's what this fit could be called. The next day walking down the hallway, he called out 'Hello there, Monster!' That dreadful silence had ended.

What had analyst and patient lived through? I think of it as a fight for survival, when one's very existence, one's right to be alive, is challenged by the insidious yet indistinct presence of the other. I had regressed from an over-talkative false self to an endangered and frightened being. I had no psychosomatic aliveness to me. I was all bunched up inside, barely breathing, without body movement: a lifeless non-entity. Although this environment was promoted by the analysand, I was more aware of my inner madness than the patient's frame of mind. His behaviour, as I have said, was a constant. Dominated by a nameless fear, I had lost the integrity of the psychoanalytic process.

Nick and I did, however, share a common response to the world in which we lived. We were both startled. And when I became furious, I sensed that my anger, my protest, and my effort to speak was somehow spoken for both of us. It felt as if I were standing up to something, to establish a right to speak my mind.

By fostering a deadly silence and killing off interrelating the patient sponsored false self adaptiveness in me. Not unlike a defence the patient had adopted earlier in his life when presented with a similar killing of human intimacy, although Nick concealed his false self adaptation by conjuring what Erikson termed a negative identity (1968: 172). But the intensity of my fear cannot simply be occasioned by the bizarre behaviour and hostility of the other towards me. As we know, it's the marriage of the actual happening and projected inner states that produces an emotional crisis, and my fear was so compelling because, having become a false self, my hate was split-off and projected into x. Not into the patient *per se*, but into the environment inhabited by the patient and myself. My fury over our startled response can be seen, therefore, as my partial recovery from this pathological process. Perhaps my hate had become useful.

Nick emerged from this silence to become a comparatively talkative patient, though not to the point where I could ever relax into the analyst's position. However, my troubles were by no means over. 'By the way', Nick said watching me intently, 'I had some great pot last night'. As he knew, this was against hospital rules, as was his consumption of booze, which he also told me about. Indeed, each session was now spiced by an announcement calculated to provoke me. 'Sue and I were at Safeway the other day, stole a whole carton of M & Ms'; 'I went to the bar across the street, and guess what? They served me!'; 'I found a whole stash of mushrooms. I'm going to fix them up'. I was aware that his actings out were intended to offend me, but initially I was uncertain what precise object relational meaning lay behind the acting out.

I was aware of a new kind of anxiety, an intrusive worry about what he was up to. Whenever Nick attended a session, I would have difficulty listening to him because I was wondering if he had perpetrated some of the misdemeanours reported at morning conference a few hours earlier. My knee-jerk response was to want to lecture him about hospital rules, but I kept such responses to myself, saying instead that I thought he was trying to worry me, which I think gave him pleasure. Soon he complained that he thought it was a drag that the hospital had so many rules. He wanted to be free, and taking drugs, or boozing was his way of exercising his freedom. I disagreed and said it seemed quite the opposite: he was provoking the hospital into noticing, monitoring and eventually restricting his movements. He eventually compared some of the staff's scrutiny of him to his mother's fretful and intrusive eyeballing of him. As far back as he could remember, she was always peering into his room. There was no latch on the door so eventually he tried to rig up a warning system to alert him when she was opening the sliding door. In early adolescence he had also put towels on the floor against the door to prevent his mother from detecting whether his lights were on. While he complained about his mother's intrusiveness, it was clear he had also developed a technique for provoking her, by leaving evidence of his drug habits lying about the house for her to see. Although I realised that he was bringing out the worrying and intrusive mother in me by informing me of his intended actions, Nick himself was not aware of this. However, when I told him what I thought was happening, there was a glimmer of recognition that psychoanalytic interpretation might be useful.

My own regression in the countertransference, however, was characterised by a particular frame of mind, a fragmented position, littered with unintegrated islands of affection, interest, coldness, withdrawal, overconcern, indifference and so forth. Around the same time it so happened that Nick's mother wrote to the hospital with her personal history and details of Nick's early life. It was a deeply moving account of her early failure of her child. Some time after his birth, she became preoccupied by the terminal illness of a member of her family and Nick responded by clinging to her so that she barely had a moment to herself when at home. Her preoccupation with her relative's illness continued, and, when Nick was three and a half, she found herself feeling intensely cold toward him. She wrote of how she rejected him, and how Nick subsequently detached himself from her, apparently killing off his feelings for her. As the years passed, she was haunted by what had happened, and when Nick began to take up drugs and act bizarrely, she could only be intrusive. In effect, she did not know how to live with him.

Nick's descriptions of his mother's personality seemed accurate enough for me to match them with my countertransference, and now with the mother's account of herself, I was quite sure that we had moved to a new level of object relating. But understanding an unconscious process and interpreting it, does not necessarily add up to psychic change, and Nick's actings out had now caught the attention of the nurses in the activities centre and therapists in group sessions. I knew that the best way for me to work with his enactments was to interpret what he aimed to bring out in me, and the sadistic but organising pleasure of this object relation. In so doing, I felt that we were slowly emerging from the paranoid atmosphere of a particular child–mother relationship, and by managing to contain and process the distressed mother he brought out in me, I was succeeding in working our way out of pathologically regressed object relations. But the hospital's understandable response both complicated and intensified the endeavour.

At almost every morning conference, when the nurses read their reports of the day and night before, Nick figured prominently in the news. In his first weeks at the hospital, he was rarely mentioned, and I had looked forward to the morning conference, as an occasion to sip coffee, listen to the 'Under Milk Wood'-like narrative of the different patients' night-time life: their nightmares, sexual adventures, political intrigues, etc. I could greet colleagues, gaze at one of the attractive nurses and catch up on local hospital news. It was a nice start to the day. When Nick's name was mentioned in connection with the disturbing pot, I was shocked out of my dormantly pleased state into an altogether different frame of mind. I was more a creature of my respiratory system, anxious and barely able to think what to say. I knew that eventually my colleagues would ask me to help them understand what was happening. I knew they didn't want to do this as this was an intrusion in the therapy, but it would happen. As the news continued, with nurses now reporting rumours circulated by patients about Nick's misdemeanours, I found myself engaged in the much more difficult struggle to prevent the patient from succeeding in his unconscious effort to become a behavioural object.

I think this struggle occurs in most treatments of a psychotic patient, as the analysand unconsciously tries to force the analyst into regarding him as a creature defined by manifest behaviour. By acting out against established hospital rules and routines, the patient coerces the environment into reacting to him as a phenomenon defined by his actions. Indeed he becomes associated with acts: 'Well pot is around, so what was Nick doing last night?' 'We have had a report from the police of a shoplift at a local store. Anyone know where Nick was yesterday afternoon at 4:00?' The response is understandable and in a way as it should be, but the effect may be to render the patient into a thing.

To become a thing, an unreflected-upon source of reaction defined by manifest acts, is one of the unconscious aims of schizophrenic object relating. The schizophrenic intends to deaden the other's psychological empathy, just as he has muted his own inner life. During this long spell in Nick's treatment, I emphasised how he was aiming to be viewed as a thing-creature-of-habit, and to bring about in the hospital a cold hatred of him. Fortunately, as he knew this to be so I could work this through with him. At morning conferences my colleagues and I were frequently in necessary conflict with one another. They would announce his transgressions and consider courses of action, while I would remind the group of the psychological meaning behind these actions. It felt at times as if the nursing report of his actions and the administrative response was pure Beta (Bion's term for mentally undigested facts) and I was pure Alpha: thoughtfulness working on the Beta. But because this was a good working group, creative polarisations were possible and I always felt an underlying support for my conflict with the behavioural view of the patient. Regrettably, because many psychotic patients get hospitals to see them as a behavioural thing, they are treated with a mixture of chemotherapy and 'supportive' psychotherapy.

Before discussing the underlying issues in this case presentation, it is worth summarising the stages of regression and recovery within the analyst's countertransference.

1   The stage of a splitting of the analyst's personality into false self adaptiveness, leading to a loss of a sense of personal reality in work with the analysand. This is partly due to the patient's presentations of deep maternal refusal (of interrelating) with the analyst experiencing the child–patient's loss of personal reality.

2   The stage of terror over survival, as the analyst is overcome by a dreadful silence which immobilises his psyche-soma. This is understood as the patient's presentation of maternal hate, of death wishes against the aliveness of the child. The fear, however, is intensified by the child's responsive destruction, expressed by the analyst's countertransference. The analyst, having split his personality, has projected his hate into the environment, leaving him only a part analyst. The analyst, shocked out of this by a moment within the session mobilises his fury into speech. Aggression becomes a useful means of survival.

3   The stage of the worrying mother, in which the analyst takes on the mother's personality as the patient now switches the analyst's subjective position from the child's place to the location of the mother. The analyst uses understanding and interpretation to recover from regression into the mother's madness.

4   The stage of the desubjectification of the patient in which the patient aims to coerce the analyst and community into regarding him as a behavioural object. To think or not to think about the meaning behind the patient's actions is the question, with the analyst working to transform the mother's deadening of meaning into meaningfulness.

To treat a severely disturbed patient means that each analyst will have to live within that disturbed and disturbing environment created by the analysand.

Many analysts, but notably Searles (1979, 1986), and Giovacchini (1979), have written about their own mad internal states while being with a borderline or psychotic patient.

In such situations, the analyst may experience in-formative regression, unconsciously determined by the patient's projection of parts of the self and parental object world into the analyst's psyche, thereby communicating his experience of being and relating. When this is true, the analyst must hold himself within these regressions, giving time to the other parts of his personality, so that the information being processed, part of the unthought known, can be worked upon by the parts of the analyst's personality that are still available to reflect on experience. All clinical situations are an interme-diated psychic reality, and during work with a psychotic patient, the intermediate nature of an hour assumes a greater significance in the analyst's mind than it does with the neurotic analysand. Healthier patients create meaning that can be reflected upon within the hour, an outcome of their intrasubjective work. But the more disturbed patients cannot do this, and the work of the hour takes place in the intermediate area of experiencing, as the analyst, now bearing split-off portions of the patient's true self and its object experiences, is not sure at any moment who is carrying what and why at that time, the lack of boundaries a familiar condition for work in the intermediate area. As time passes (and it is interesting how time assumes a different and curative function in this situation), the analyst is able to transform an informative object relation into thought. When he can objectify his countertransference position, he then 'puts' it into an interpretation. In these moments analytic insight and interpretation are in the first place curative for the analyst, and only gradually, through holding interpretation and the passing of time, does the patient get better.

When I use my known countertransference to interpret something of the patient's madness it is only because I have comprehended what I think and feel. Such insight is ironically licensed by pathological structures, for, as mental illness forecloses the freedom of unconscious life it makes it possible for us to see unconscious organisations. The patient's pathology – which limits the self – creates restricted forms of being, thinking and relating, and through its transference becomes a structure that suggests the countertransference.

Strictly speaking, psychoanalysts do not know their countertransference. It is too unconscious. Far too complex to be imagined let alone interpreted, ordinary countertransference is the matrix of any self's processing of the other's idiomatic uses of one's own self, a strange symphony of interanimating souls fundamentally conveyed through the changing idioms of wording and telling one's mental life.

13

EMBODIMENT

A child suffers humiliations. Could it be any other way?

Less conscious of the meaning and effect of his actions than the adult, he is often hard pressed to explain himself.

A twenty-month-old girl joyfully paints the wall of her room with her faeces. Her mother's considered negative response comes as a shock. What she has done is wrong and she should not do it again. And yet decorating walls with her poo feels natural and rejection of her paintings seems a repudiation of her bodywork.

Even if she is expressing an anal attack on the mother's body, she is unaware of this. The mother's intervention takes place in the realms of consciousness, so, to some extent the child is made aware of the inappropriateness of her action by the mother.

Consciousness arrests the unconscious.

A three-year-old is at play with a neighbour's child of similar age and in the course of playing 'bang the trucks against each other', knocks his friend's finger, causing tears and the arrival of an adult. 'What have you done?' Stupor. 'You mustn't hurt other people.' Distress verging on tears. 'Now tell Terry you are sorry.' Tears. 'It's no good you crying, it's Terry who's been hurt! Now stop that crying this instant.' Unfortunately the adult's understanding of what has happened is not the same as the child's, if we allow for the fact that in playing 'head-on' banging, the idea of consequentiality did not come to mind.

A five-year-old goes up to his new-born brother who trustingly chortles at such wonderful company. The older brother feels a surge of hate displacing his pleasure and drops a toy on his brother's head, bringing howls of pain. 'What's happened?' yells the distraught mother. Stupor. 'I don't know', replies the child. 'You don't know?' 'He just cried.' 'Well what did you do? You must have done something!'

Let us think about this. This child is certainly aware that dropping a toy on his brother's head is responsible for the tears. He also felt hate and knows he wanted to hurt his brother. But is he speaking an entire untruth when he disclaims responsibility? If we bear in mind that children live within the terrain of childish psychic reality, where the fantastical and actual meet up in untaught ways, it is partly true that he actually does not know how this happened. He doesn't know how he dropped the toy, any more than he knows why he felt hate, or why he felt pleasure before that. These states of mind and their actions just feel rather arbitrary. They just are. The notions of causality and consequentiality are not yet fully grasped, even if they are cognitively understood.

But how can this be?

The clash between these two sets of truths resides in that discrepancy between cognitive and psychic reality. Cognitively a child knows that dropping the toy on his brother's head will cause pain. In psychic reality he knows that it is an expression of murder, but also that it never happened. In the milliseconds following its execution he is sure it happened some other way; he didn't intend the toy to do this, it just occurred.

Is he lying? In some ways. But at the same time he behaves in a manner quite consistent with the child's sense of reality, in which actions are entirely open to imaginative revision. So he can say that what happened in fact did not happen and he can come to believe this.

Children live much of their life in fantasy – in one imagined event after the other – often simply daydreamed, but occasionally played out in action. As these playings and actings are to some extent the stuff of internal imaginings, a child feels licensed to reverse consequentiality by simply changing the course of internal events. So this boy can believe he did not drop the toy: his brother knocked it out of his hand and unfortunately hurt himself.

But let us consider his initial response to the mother's 'What happened?' which I have described as 'stupor', a moment's speechlessness. To fully comprehend the course of this child's emotional truth I think we need to honour this abruption in his social grace. The stupor is real. Why? Because he is asked to account for actions and events in the real which he cannot do. When he dropped the toy it seemed more a deeply private internal happening than an action in reality, an event inside the psychic envelope of the body ego, rather than a gesture in the real. But the child discovers that it has happened in the real and his psychic envelope has been breached by social consequentiality.

Curiously enough, guilt may be a relief. The boy did feel like killing his brother; he did drop a 'bomb' on him, and as he gradually accepted the reality of his action he felt his brother's suffering. A child who commits a destructive act is sometimes emptied by it, almost as if he projects his violence into the other. The self is empty too because with the intervention of a parent (and later the mind) the subject psychically leaves the scene. Experiencing guilt, then, is filling – indeed we speak of someone being full of guilt. It displaces the empty state by the return of affective responsibility, which restores parts of the self lost in the act of aggression and the act of denial.

But such guilt can only develop if the child does not for one reason or another eradicate his deeds with a new version of past reality. If, for example, the father enters this scene and is too harsh, the child may militantly will himself into a fantastical denial. With the sort of child I shall soon be discussing, however, the stuporous state is most powerful. The child remains paralysed, speechless, perhaps simply staring at the enraged parent. Following the laws of denial, this child cannot easily move into speech, either to accept the deed as done or affirm another version of the event along the lines of psychic reality.

The stuporous child is caught in limbo, with no place to go, characterised by a sort of terror within, a horrifying retribution against the self by enactments of psychic reality. Blankness becomes an important self state, occurring at the border of the psychic and actual. Some of these children will eventually start to blank themselves in advance, preserving an apparent not knowing to avoid psychic pain, resulting in a kind of violent innocence as the child gradually destroys the links between his psychic dreams and actual behaviours.

We can probably assume that, initially, the child will deny the intentions behind an unfortunate or destructive act; but because his inner sense of guilt, linking an intrinsic psychic state with social disapproval, reinforces his guilt, the child will eventually begin to think about the effect of his action on the victim as well as about how he is viewed by others.

We are all no doubt familiar with the sort of child who commits an act of aggression and then immediately presents a blank self to the enquiring adult. This is often a tell-tale sign of the child's guilt. But equally there are some children who automatically look stuporous and who accept blame for their actions even when they are truly blameless. Are they affirming the original confusion between the intrapsychic and the interpersonal? Does it matter whether they actually committed the misdeed because they can certainly imagine having done it? In this case the stupor seems defensive, arriving automatically in anticipation of social disapproval and merging the intrapsychic with the interpersonal so as to cancel the integrity of both. If one can be regularly blamed for deeds not done, then one can equally be blamed for deeds done, a kind of unconscious cynicism that absolves the child of anything like reflective consideration of his actions.

Each child differs in his or her development of an introspective capability. Certainly it is heightened during the Oedipus complex when the child assumes multiple points of identification and achieves a richer and more varied perspective on the self and others. But it also marks a time when each person comes into continuity of self consciousness.

Children lost in fantasy or unconscious actions, however, remain comparatively deficient in their ability to think about what they are doing. Any adult witnessing a child at play or engaged in actions can easily interrupt and identify what the child is up to. The surprise in each child at such a discovery suggests that children feel unseen in their playings and enactings, perhaps because they lack self observation.

Putting the self into the real through play, children are engaged in a kind of embodied dreaming that brings elements of inner life into the world. The quiet, continuous embodiments of dream mark the passing of time with signs of the child's idiom.

Perhaps self observation needs to be delayed until the child feels embodied, until they feel they have put their sexual, emotional and memorial life into the world. For this to happen they will need to enact the inner self repeating and inventing, bypassing the censors, in order to achieve relative integrity of representation. Thousands of such doings constitute the work of embodiment.

But what is meant by embodiment? We have a clue in the theory of the libido, a specifically psychoanalytical idea that identifies the child's evolution in consciousness through the organising passions of the erotogenic zones. From the oral, through the anal, to the phallic, these passions are like stages in the development of the child's sexual being, experiences that link the child's bodily excitements with consciousness, so that through the development of the libido, the child comes into the experience of their body. However, children who are schizoid or who suffer inhibitions do not develop in quite this way: erotogenic passions are not enacted in and through the movements of the body or the manipulation of the actual world, but only gain representations in the mind. Mental representation of erotogenic interest is important, but if the child cannot move this into the body's being, as it were, then something is missing.

But how is it possible to talk about moving a mental representation into the body's being? How is this accomplished? What does it look like? And what is meant by the body's being?

In an oversimplified sense this may refer to the body's participation as a spontaneous signifier of mental and emotional states. It creates its own meanings in the spirit of Winnicott's true self as a designator of aliveness. As it conveys the subject's desire it is open so far as the body's signifying capacity is concerned. Naturally, flushing of the face, rapid breathing, erect nipples, an erect penis, will convey sexual desire and to this extent the body is clear as a signifier, but its gestural punctuations of our silences or speeches, our initiations or our responses, is mysterious, if common. In this respect the body is a rather ambiguous expression of the unconscious, as its signifieds are often unknown to the other and the self. If we surrounded ourselves with mirrors to witness our body we would arrest it as signifier. Even when we see ourselves through the pallid shades of the video camera, we only ever see a glimmer of what we have expressed.

To express our being through the body we cannot bear it close witness, a rogue presence of unconscious communication. If the developing child feels increasingly free to release the body to its being, to embody their subjectivity, they will develop a very particular expression which we know as 'sensuality'. This capacity to use the senses is an acknowledgement of the body's freedom of movement and the sensual self has matriculated desire into gestural being.

But sensuality is not achieved by self alone. Freud's emphasis on the instincts is partly correct and enables us to elucidate the course of an instinct, but on its own it is more a theory of the auto-erotic – only half of what comprises the sexual. Although he wrote of the mother's sexuality elsewhere, it does not feature in his instinct theory. Not only is the mother the first sex object, he tells us, but she finds her infant erotic. Maternal libido cathects the infant's body and expresses itself through a laying-on of hands in the innumerable caresses that stimulate and gratify the body. A mother's kiss eroticises the infant's body that responds through the pulsions of the instinct.

The first and most essential fusion of the instincts of love and hate, life and death, sexuality and aggression is not achieved in a vacuum – the outcome of the infant's psychic economy – but is demonstrated in the sensuality of the mother, who combines love and hate in her way of being with the infant. When she laughs with deep love and says 'I am going to eat you all up', all the while pushing and shoving the infant's body against hers, she fuses sexuality and aggression into a dynamic pair that constitutes a vital contribution to the child's embodiment of their internal world.

Embodiment refers then to the subject's abandoned expression of internal states through the body as signifier, the yielding of the psychic to those natural embodying pathways, in which psychic states translate spontaneously into physical expression. The mother conveys erotic meaning through visible and invisible caresses, and joins the child's erogeneity – their instinctual discovery of the body as a colony of pleasure zones – with spontaneous expression of the other's desire.

As we shall see in a moment, embodiment allows us to speak of disembodiment – a movement away from incarnated being, back into the world of exclusive mentation, including all the manifestations of disembodiment known to psychiatry: derealisation, dissociation and out-of-body experiences. On these occasions something happens to divest the body sense of its abandoned incarnation, the mind leaves the body to see it as an object, or the subject feels strangely odd within the confines of his own body. The cumulative movement of embodiment and the radical moments of disembodiment nonetheless constitute a unique expression of non-verbal meaning: something like the self's rendering of its idiom through free expression, or its radical withdrawal.

Imagine two children with different lives.

Child A is spontaneously expressing his sadism with a new toy which he bangs about and the father intervenes to say 'My God, look, you are destroying that new toy: this is shameful'. Stupor. Denial. Arrival of mother who chides the father 'Don't be so harsh. He is enjoying his delight with his new toy. Toys are made to be used'.

Child B is at play and only one parent is present. 'You are ruining a perfectly good toy. Stop! Look at what you are doing!!' Stupor. Denial.

As B looks at his actions through the parent's eyes, he cannot successfully deny his embodied actions. A child can deny speech, affects and moods, but if caught red-handed, denial is impossible. The child suffers a humiliation, which I will define here as a 'committed action', resulting in a slight separation of the subject from his own body, as he sees his body self through the accusing gaze of the other: a gaze which needs no evidence other than what lies before it. At the same time the body self is rooted in space and time by the accusing gaze of the other. If a child also feels a psychic alliance with the accusing adult – the superego – then they will feel an even greater shift of identification, as they identify with the parent.

It is as if one's soul departs from one's body, entering into the other, leaving the body an inert, heavy, spiritless container. This split between a part looking at the self through the eye of the other and a part being so scrutinised, constitutes the experience of humiliation. I wish to emphasise the subjective feeling that one's body is guilty dross, valueless as it is the signifier of the damned. To fully identify with it is to be pulled by its heavy slipping mass into the maws of perpetual damnation.

In the moment of humiliation time stands still.

Child A's spirit also leaves his body but he sees himself through two sets of eyes, one damning, the other saving. If one is to leave the body, best go to heaven, where, through the eyes of the defending angel, one can look lovingly on the frozen body.

It is easy to see how B, continually arrested by parental disapproval, can develop a fear of the evil eye, that catches the true self in its actions, sending the body self to hell. If a child is unfortunate enough to live with a parent who is unusually censorious then he may develop an identification with the parent's evil eye, thus aligning with a particular kind of mind in a split with his own body. Such a mind is precocious and paranoid and regards the true body self with mistrust, leading to a false body signifier, since the true body self is denied. The aim is to protect the true self from being killed and sent to hell, or more accurately to prevent the timeless sense of damned imprisonment in a deadened body that is filled up with hellish affects.

One patient who had suffered repeated humiliations as a child handled his adult body like a crane operator manipulating parts of a building, lifting his arms and legs with great detachment. He looked at his body with ill-disguised contempt, at times almost with alarm, and he felt that it smelled badly. Another patient took an altogether different position. Humiliated by his mother and three older sisters, who would sit on him and mock his genitals, he developed a muscular physique and became disturbingly expert in the martial arts. He was sent for treatment by his university tutors in the Physical Education Department because they found his behaviour menacing. He would point to someone and politely, eerily, challenge his fellow students to tell him how they would kill him. In therapy he told me with pleasure how his body was a killing machine, with account after bloody account of how he would have killed person X or person Y, whether a casual passer-by or a friend. He had dealt with a mind–body split by putting his mind into his body, to the extent that it became the machinery of his mental aberrations.

This patient identified with the evil eye. He believed that his survival depended on his capacity to use a menacing gaze, which he would cast upon his potential opponent. In this respect the evil eye is an interesting condensation of two splits. The superior eye, split-off, endowed with menacingly intrusive intelligence, seems to verify the notion of that superior sight the adult has into the child's behaviour, displacing the child's own eyes into himself. (Prize fighters, on the verge of bodily catastrophe and humiliation, trade glares at the beginning of the contest, seeking possession of that humiliating stare about to strike one of them.)

With Child A and Child B, however, the child leaves his body because of parental judgement, examining the body as an offending object. This psychic disembodiment deprives the subject of the benefits of sensualisation. This is a vast subject about which Kenneth Wright (1991) has written a fascinating study.

Sensualisation is a form of embodied perception and reverie-like physical expression, the subject moving in the physical world of body-to-body communicating. Sensualisation is the realisation of the body's capacity to receive and convey such communicatings, expressive of one's inner reality through incarnated being and also as a receiver of the other's equally sensualised intelligence. Disembodiment, which leads to de-sensualisation, disables a person in what we might think of as a rather sophisticated, but in some respects quite basic, form of intersubjective capability.

These accounts of humiliation, based on actual interventions by parents, are not the only occasions where this type of mind–body split occurs. Psychoanalysis teaches us that an individual can intrapsychically cultivate an internal evil eye that could, in itself, sponsor disembodiments. One does not need an actual other to intercede and break in on unselfconsciousness to create the trauma discussed in this chapter; as we know, a sudden interdiction by the superego can affect someone in the same way.

The structure of this particular trauma, however, resides in the first critical interventions by the other, when parental consciousness interprets unselfconscious child action correctly. Consciousness of unconsciousness is brought about by the other, perhaps traumatically so, rather than through the slowly derivative routings of preconscious work that imbricates the progressive layers of self consciousness. A development that was to have been intrapsychic is enacted in the interpersonal field and the child's consciousness has been extractively introjected by the parent who now uses it to censor unselfconscious (or unconscious) behaviours.

A patient.

Jill came to analysis partly because she felt herself to be stupid. Although she knew this was not objectively true, she had a deep feeling that it was nonetheless so. She lived in daily fear that in any important conversation it would be very clear that she was intellectually inadequate. Her understanding that she did not lack intelligence did not derive from her own inner sense of herself but from her objective assessment of her performance.

One would not know of her fear by looking at her as she is graceful, exceptionally well dressed, poised and socially sophisticated. But over time it was clear that her embodiment of self was processed by a false mediation. It is easy to err at a moment such as this, by suggesting, for example, that she was stiff. In fact, however, all that I could say with accuracy was that she lacked sensuality although she was polished. In a way she knew this. Her body was clearly an object of careful scrutiny and ministration and she moved it about quite well. Yet one could see an anxiety in her body movements.

Although she rarely slept with her boyfriend, she was secretly passionate and generated a vivid internal sexual life. She felt that her internal representation of herself constituted her sentiently true and alive being precluded from existing.

Her psychic body was sensualised yet she lived a non-sensualised mannered body, the object of constant assessment, an investment in an elegant vessel that would not only compensate for her sense of stupidity but also stand in for a brilliant mind. Her grace was to be the embodiment of wit and culture.

In a compromise between mind and body she presented not only a split between the two but also what is perhaps more rightly termed a division or an antagonism. Her mind, rejected by the other's gaze, froze her imagined actual body in mortification, so she constructed a perfect body elegantly designed to conceal any such shame, her erotic embodiment of self only able to live in a secret inner world of passion.

In adolescence she overcame a sense of psychic impoverishment by dressing up her body, assisting its natural biological fruitions with her own finishing touches, enabling her to become part of the in crowd.

This kind of leap-frogging graduation, from awkwardness to apparent sophistication, can occur, as we know through the presentation of the body. Jill looked lively, alert and socially skilled, but when asked a direct question in the classroom or in conversation with friends, she would often feel incredibly stupid. At first she claimed that she was speechless on those occasions but she confabulated this in order to convince the analyst of the absolute inner dread of these moments. It took some time for her to see that having turned away from reality to a world of fantasy she had an antagonism to the actualities of interrelating and attacked the parts of herself unconsciously designated to learn about and cultivate the mind's relation to reality, a hostility that left her feeling blank when someone approached her mind. Her body was meant to be the mind's embodied icon, an ornamental presence sufficient to answer all passing enquiries.

In another essay I suggest that under special circumstances the term 'spirit' should be introduced into psychoanalysis, even though there would be many objections to a term laden with pre-psychoanalytic meanings. If, however, we understand spirit as the expressive movement of an individual's idiom through the course of his or her life, we may say that each of us is a spirit, and that we have spiritual effects upon others – who will indeed carry us as such within themselves, and we in turn will be inhabited by the spirits of others. Spirit is not the same as an internal representation although it does, I think, come very close to what we mean by an internal object: something deeper, more complex, beyond representation, yet there.

Embodiment, then, partly refers to a certain success in becoming a spirit, moving freely as incarnated intelligence. A feature of such intelligence is sensuality, a way of naming that presence that derives from the movement of the self's inner life into incarnated residence. Under such circumstances the body functions as something beyond derivative instinctual gesticulator or mimetic representer of internal object relations; sensuality suggests the expressive work of immanent erogeneity, which registers the history of met desire. The deepest of internal urges has been greeted by the sexuality and aggression of the mother, a combination that constitutes the sensual, and that informs the infant of a new border – the embodied – created from the reciprocal enhancement of two forces: the subject's instincts and the other's desire.

14

WORDING AND TELLING SEXUALITY

Psychoanalysis focuses on the fate of narrated or enacted mental events, especially in the dream, the memory, the daydream, the symptom, or the erotic scene.

Each is epiphenomenally vivid and yet immediately dismantled by the arrival of emerging ideas, dispersing the hegemony of any event by the work of the unconscious that keeps moving the self. 'The laws that govern the passage of events in the unconscious', writes Freud in 'An outline of psycho-analysis', 'are remarkable enough. Above all there is a striking tendency to *condensation*, an inclination to form fresh unities out of elements which in our waking thought we should certainly have kept separate' (1940: 167). And though we may dwell on newly formed unities, Freud's theory of the dream work attends to the movement of thought itself, working to break up former unities as it recombines them in new complexes.

There is an overlapping oscillation between vivid arriving mental presences and vanishing fragments working their way into a future; between the arriving dream, memory, symptom, or erotic scene that fills the self, soon to be broken up through passage of time and new interests.

Writings on sexuality tend to focus on the perversions, perhaps because they are guaranteed to come round again relatively unchanged. Otherwise, the character of the sexual – operating as it does through subtle shades of displacement – is too elusive to pin down and observe. Indeed it seems easier to focus on its stages, on each gender's experience of it, on fixations in it, than to discuss it as a phenomenon in its own right.

But what would that be?

Would it not be a mental event, the constituents of which at any one moment though present could not be accounted for? In asking ourselves to address sexuality-in-itself are we not requesting the appearance of the unconscious-in-itself? As Freud said, the ego is 'principally determined by the individual's own experience, that is by accidental and contemporary events' (1940: 147). We know that a person's sexual life is the dynamic history of the ego's inner organisation of particular lived experience driven by the instincts of eros and death, so in any attempt to investigate a person's sexual life, we can only ever glimpse it as a fragment.

Are we aware of the irony of such a partial glance? That any selection from the field of the erotic is immediate cousin to the perverse, whether the choice is made by the patient or by the analyst.

Indeed, the density of the self's sexuality – a vanishing point of never-ending convergence between psychic reality and newly lived experience – would elude any consciousness aiming to detect it; it could only be gathered into a place when distorted through the symptom, the dream, the daydream, the erotic scene, or any particular aspect of it. Freud conveys this density of sexual life when he writes that it 'streams to the ego from various organs and parts of the body', (151) creating the image of the ego as a dynamic repository of all that flows into it.

The analysand's sexuality operates less through the report of erotic fragments than through mental movement, the flow of thought itself expresses the subject's desire just as it 'tells' his history. (Freud: 'A character-istic of libido which is important in life is its *mobility*, the faculty with which it passes from one object to another', 151.) We cannot insert ourselves inside this process as lucid organisers of meaning, making it difficult to talk meaningfully about, for example, the wording and telling of sexuality.

One of the features of the perverse act is the effort to create the illusion of the self's mastery over the instincts. The Sadean hero – as with all perverse characters – presumes to reside over the scene of sexuality. A false mastery is created, rather deadening over time, no matter how fecund the erotic fantasies. Such morbidity arrives out of the pulverising effect of falsely assuming that sexual life can be mastered by consciousness, to which it must submit in the form of fully cognisant conscious ideas. Instead, the movement of instincts, operating through the primary processes of condensation and displacement, dissolves us always.

Might the moment of orgasm in the sexual act, then, be the rare occasion when two human subjects are excited by the nature of the sexual? The self finds the object of desire at the moment it is lost, and ironically finds in this loss the displacing movement that is sexual existence. Foreplay, frequently associated with a devolution of consciousness and an increase in erotic knowledge, gives way to the sense of total abandon, in which neither imagines a cessation, or undoing, of the final drive to ecstasy. But that conjugation is a moment when two lovers share between or through them the character of sexual life itself, a knowing that functions only on its own terms.

Sexuality, then, is invisible passion; or, the absent as passion. Perversion is an effort to manifest the immateriality of psychic life by giving sexuality a permanent and locatable character. In doing so, however, it transforms the absent in ways similar to the dream, the symptom, the memory: all of which partly manifest the immanent. But unlike these other mental phenomena,

159

perversion refuses the unconsciousness to ourselves, rendering us false masters of the instinct and denuding self experience of its passion.

The self in the dream knows that this is not an event to be mastered by consciousness, and our ongoing realisation that the dream is organised by unseen desires helps us to live in the larger theatre of daily life in which we know that psychic life is constructed beyond consciousness, out of sight, absent.

Thus we can no more easily discuss sexuality than we can what the dream work had in mind. What do we do?

Instead we are left to talk around it, as I shall do presently when discussing our wording and telling of the sexual, as I contemplate how voice shares something of its character, insofar as the way we word and the way we speak to our patients constitutes a psychic realm operating according to intimacies that shadow the invisible nature of sexual life.

I shall begin with a patient.

He remembers a childhood moment many times. Here are a few versions.

> I was playing with a friend and ... [pause] ... he, ah, ... or ... I ... ah ... we ... I suggested ... we look ... we tried to see ... ah ... [pause] ... who could urinate furthest. I ... ah ... think I said ... ah ... 'why don't we look at your mother's bloomers'.

> 'X' and I were ... just ... fooling around. Urinating. We – one of us, but I think it was me – said 'let's go have a look at your mother's bloomers'.

> I was with a chum with whom I had been having a contest to see who could urinate the furthest and later when we were sitting next to a low blue table with my nanny, I said to him 'let's go get your mother's bloomers'.

Although the basic structure of this memory remained unchanged, each telling slightly altered the narrative meaning.

The patient had a degree of interest in female underwear and during childhood would procure clothing from a friend's sister or mother.

Let me word that differently.

The patient was fascinated by women's panties and as a child would sneak into homes and snatch what he felt was a kind of prize.

Or another way.

The patient stole into the houses of friends where he ripped off women's underwear which he used to excite himself.

Each wording creates a slightly different event as the work of revision (*Nachträglichkeit*) resignifies the remembered.

160

The instinct, according to Freud, selects its object expediently, only to discharge the excitation. But instincts arrive in the continually changing contexts of a subject's life; an aesthetic decision performed by the unconscious ego in the service of idiom, the mood of a self experiencing its instinct will be reflected in the choice of objects.

The instinct also speaks through the performative action of the transference, when it arrives through the use of the object and its effect upon the psychoanalyst.

For example, the above patient began an hour alluding to his excitement over the idea of urination. This aroused my interest. Immediately, however, he filled the hour with laboured accounts of problems at work. With two minutes remaining he blurted out 'so to come to the point, I like the idea of women urinating on me', followed immediately by 'Why did it take me so long to tell you this?' 'Perhaps', I replied, 'because you were filling your bladder first'.

In the months prior to this comment we had examined in some detail his 'cruisings' in which he wasted a great deal of time and felt considerable despair. In childhood and young adulthood this had consisted of tedious searches for female underwear. In his twenties he cruised the streets of Athens for prostitutes, frequently spending an entire night searching and not finding the one for whom he had been searching.

He would roam the countryside collecting butterflies, his long loping body a somewhat forlorn indicator of his search as country people would comment on the unusual length of time it took him to satisfy his hobby. He would roam about art galleries for similarly long periods, any initial interest giving way to a desultory state amongst otherwise formerly exciting objects of interest.

He manifested this same drive in the transference. He would often begin an hour with a topic of some interest and then immerse himself in rather uninteresting details, usually removed from the initial object of thought, often ending the hour feeling 'wasted'. I said I thought he was cruising in the session, hoping to sustain some initial interest, but then losing himself in despair. This comment had many derivatives too numerous to itemise here, but, returning to the fragment above, certain questions come to mind.

As with any analytical intervention there are many issues I could have addressed at the conclusion of the hour. Given the content I selected, why did I word it the way I did? I could have put it differently. I might have said 'what comes to mind?' and opened up his free associations. I could have said 'perhaps you wanted me to feel the frustration over the hour that leads to a pressure inside the self, one that only seems served by a blissful evacuation'. I certainly felt such a frustration and a concomitant relief when he confessed his interest in urination.

Even if we take my remark in its strictest sense, might I not have commented on that in a more neutral manner? I could have said, 'I think you have delayed telling me your interests because you find it embarrassing'. My comment was, instead, somewhat pithy and aggressive. Nonetheless, it felt correct to me at the time, in that place, in the climate of the emotional atmosphere with the patient.

Wording determines the transformational potential of a signifier in relation to the latent contents of the analysand's ideas. Choose a word and you select a direction. Choose a word and you create force. A 'colourless' word is without force, perhaps weak, but in certain moments appropriate for considered thought engaged with emotionally powerful issues. Select a colourful word and its evocative effect contributes a meaning emerging from sprung affect and idea.

'Words have their own auditory character', writes William Gass.

> Some open and close with vowels whose prolongation can give them expressive possibilities ('Ohio,' for instance); others simply vowel heavy (like 'aeolian'); still others open wide but then close sharply ('ought'), or are as tight lipped as 'tip', as unending as 'too,' or as fully middled as 'balloon.'

'Some words', he continues, 'look long but are said short (such as "rough" and "sleight"); some seem small enough but are actually huge ("otiose" and "nay")' (1996: 322).

Telling re-delivers a word through voice. The second coming of the signifier, it conveys differing degrees of vitality in the speaker and through pitch, tone, stress, cadence and duration gathers complex meanings that contextualise and alter the strict meaning of the signifiers. 'If the analysand makes himself known by his words', writes Andre Green, 'it is completely impossible to give the words equal weight because of the different states of mind in which they are spoken' (1977: 204).

Telling reflects the differing states of mind, both of the speaker – in the above example the analyst – and of the recipient, whose state of mind is implicitly addressed in the character of the telling. Having already interpreted to the patient numerous times the anxieties and aims of his ruminations and intellectualisations, I wanted to carry in my words something of the force of my encounter with the force of his transference.

In 'Dora', Freud wrote that the 'best way of speaking' about sexual matters to a patient 'is to be dry and direct' (1905: 48) but subsequently when asking Dora to 'pay close attention to the exact words' she used he notes: 'I laid stress on these words because they took me aback' (63). Only a few years before, as Kahane points out, he might have laid his hands on the patient's head to stress his meaning, but now voice acts in the place of physical touch (1995:18).

As the analyst's choice of wording and telling contains and transforms the patient's sexual representations, a psychoanalytic interpretation of the force of sexuality reflects its mutability. No wording is without character. The words we choose and the way we enunciate them indicate the degree to which we bear within our own speech the economy of sexuality. 'In the psychoanalytic dialogue', writes Kahane, 'the intersubjective relation between analyst and analysand is constituted by the voice, which, circulating between two interiorities, functions as a kind of transitional object, binding speaker and listener in an imaginary dual-unity' (1995: 16). Not only does the function of speaking and listening in the psychoanalytical situation transform the mouth, voice and ear into a particular type of erogeneity, but the character of voice too assumes a newly found psychic property, immediate and intimate, yet ephemeral.

I kept my comment close to my patient's body, which I felt was important, but also close to his anal retentive resistances, as it was his character to frustrate himself and his objects by withdrawing vital interests in order to cruise amongst the irrelevant, or, to move morosely through interesting matter in a devitalising manner. He felt the force of my comment and took it in good humour. Its cryptic form reached him without his quite knowing why and the thoughts that arose out of it were more spontaneous than might otherwise have been the case.

Another patient says to me, 'I am taken by the thrust of your comments'. I reply 'my thrust?' Working to de-repress her sexual interests after years of rationalised denials her selection of a phallic metaphor was a crucial act. My reply was soft and unemphatic, echoing her word.

We vary the force of words in psychoanalysis through our telling. ' "Libido" means in psycho-analysis in the first instance', writes Freud, 'the force (thought of as quantitatively variable and measurable) of the sexual instincts directed towards an object – "sexual" in the extended sense required by analytic theory' (1940: 203). Wording, which determines the 'affectivity' of the signifier, and telling, which exercises through vocalisation the force of words, shadow the character of libido.

Freud often linked affects to instincts, as when he wrote of the factors that go into his theory: 'they are: emphasis on instinctual life (affectivity)' (1940: 197). Analysts are 'affect-ionate', then, as they employ signs of affect in their enunciations. In this respect, we are always 'affect-ionate', although what we convey in our differing affections is continuously changing. It is no small matter that certain analysts interpreted 'neutrality' to mean not neutral speech, but dead speech; or that some analysts interpreting the here-and-now transference in a continuous process of translation (from all these people you are talking about to you and me) do so in the growing monotony of a litaneous voice – a 'da da da da da da da da' – that kills the psychic reality of voice and acts as a kind of unfortunate verbal shaft pounding into the analysand. At the other extreme is the friendly therapist who swaps 'Hi!'s and 'Bye!'s and all the in-between effusions, achieving through excess of emotion a paradoxical cancellation of the subtle range of personal affectivity.

By neutrality of voice, I mean speech that assumes a matter-of-fact tone, a very particular affect which is often used by the analyst to sustain thought in the midst of the patient's turbulent frame of mind.

To a very disturbed schizophrenic talking about his sexual experiences, for example, I say 'you are frightened by the imagery that comes to your mind when you think of intercourse'. The wording is neutral, lacking in colour and the telling is in an even voice without suggestive emphasis. But with an obsessional patient in his fifth year of analysis, once again laundering his narratives of the forces of instinct and affect, I say 'you describe your wish to "jump" "X" as if you were thinking of shaking hands with a colleague at work'. My use of slang and somewhat rough but affectionate wording stemmed from a long history of interpretations in this area which we both knew well. The comment is forceful and does not collude with the analysand's schizoid detachment. My intent is to evoke, bear and sustain something of the sexual in work with a patient who is gifted in removing it from his character. Moments later I discussed his sexual anxieties in colourless language and with no distinctive affect in the telling. Even if the analytical literature is sparse in the discussion of the changing voice of the analyst, we convey our differing receptions, evocations, and intentions through wording and telling. By using the word 'jump' I intended to transform representation of his sexuality and aggression from desiccated prose to embodied wording.

There are many subtle ways to express affect, but none more than in and through the voice. The psychic reality given to a signifier is suggested by the character of its vocalisation and in wording and telling sexuality the analyst's interpretation partly exists in his or her voice. Affects function as inflections. Inflection refers to a 'turning, bending, or curving', to 'a change in tone or pitch of the voice', to 'the change of form by which some words indicate certain grammatical relationships'. The affective register operating as voice is inflective, as it changes meaning through the alterations of enunciation.

'The sentence is a literal line of thought', writes Gass, but 'also an apprehension, sometimes of a thought, often of a sensation. It is also aimed. It has energy, drive, direction, purpose'. He argues that we are now 'dealing with the element of desire' as 'some sentences seem to seep, others to be propelled by their own metrical feet'. Other sentences are 'ponderous, tentative, timid; others are quick, burly, full of beans' (1996: 40). 'Repetition, diction, the way language is caressed, spat out or whispered by the writer', he concludes, 'every element, as always…combines to create for the sentence its feeling. I think of it as a kind of conceptual climate' (41).

The analyst's selection of content, introduction of new words, and telling engages the patient at differing levels of consideration. He or she bears speech from the maternal and paternal orders (discussed in Chapter 4) and through his or her changing use of words and qualities of voice indicates talent to bear and transform the sexual and the aggressive.

Amongst other things, this skill develops the aesthetic capability and helps analysands to embody sexuality. Part of the talking cure is in the innumerable precise and discrete emphases of the telling that put or bring the latent contents into discourse, giving new body to the analysand's speech, helping the patient to bring the force of instincts into words adequate to bear and transform them, to weave the force of the instinct into that poetics of telling that is in itself a derivative of sexual life.

What Theseus says of the poet in *A Midsummer Night's Dream*, we may say of the psychoanalyst who words the movement of emotional reality: 'And as imagination bodies forth / The form of things unknown, the poet's pen / Turns them to shapes, and gives to aery nothing / A local habitation and a name'.

As we shall see in the next chapter, free association – the method within which such wording and telling takes place – is a new form of thinking and speaking, rather like the creation of a new art form, capturing 'aery nothings' in a net made for the unconscious.

Ordinary poetry conveys its meaning not only through the selection of apt words; through the construction of the poetic line and the rhythm of the cadence, it directs the forces it evokes through complex pulsions and deferrals, arrivals and vanishings. The analyst's wording and telling does not derive from poetry, but it does inherit that particular intelligence of form that calls the poet. A discourse not only of the body, but from the same sources as sexual life, telling works idea and affect into the structure of desire.

To some extent we develop the passion of the aesthetic with the mother. For Freud the sexuality of mother and child was the prototype of all sexuality as it was she who 'regards him with feelings that are derived from her own sexual life: she strokes him, kisses him, rocks him, and quite clearly treats him as a substitute for a complete sexual object' (1905: 223). To this one must add the logic of pulsions deriving from the child's own body which vitalises the self with its own rhythms. Anyone who is in any doubt about the ways in which the poet takes this form of knowledge and uses it to carry the reader will, in my view, have such doubts dispelled upon hearing a poet read his or her own work. In the telling the poet breathes life into his work. And in a different way, in a context and a manner appropriate to it, the psycho-analyst brings sexuality into the analytical partnership.

Through the particulars of the psychoanalytical situation, from its physicality centred on the patient's recumbent position, to a methodology which privileges the loosening of thoughts in free association, to the differing types of analytical intervention from allusive facilitation to direct interpretation, it offers itself as a type of body to the patient's psyche-soma.

The patient's unconscious comprehends its specific allure which inspires sexual and aggressive life in differing ways. A good container for sustained mutability – the character of the instinctual – the body's seductions will not be toward the erratic discharge of excitation for its own sake, but the pleasure of transforming sexual energy into acts of meaning.

Perhaps the 'ahhah' passed back and forth between analyst and patient is a *jouissance* specific to the sex life of psychoanalysis.

15

CREATIVITY AND
PSYCHOANALYSIS

In 'What is Surrealism?', André Breton recalled how he 'practised occasionally on the sick' during the war using Freud's 'methods of investigation', as he experimented in written monologue by throwing out ideas on paper, followed by critical examination. He invited Philippe Soupault to do this with him and soon they were writing automatically and comparing results. Although of course their contents varied, Breton noted that

> there were similar faults of construction, the same hesitant manner, and also, in both cases, an illusion of extraordinary verve, much emotion, a considerable assortment of images of a quality such as we should never have been able to obtain in the normal way of writing, a very special sense of the picturesque, and, here and there, a few pieces of out-and-out buffoonery.
>
> (1934: 412)

The writings proved 'strange', invested with a 'very high degree of *immediate absurdity*'. It was out of this experiment with Freud's method that Breton founded surrealism and when he asked himself to define it he wrote that it was 'pure psychic automatism', which through the spoken or written word, or some other means of expression, would reveal 'the real process of thought'. The associations created by the surrealist act created a 'superior reality' – more purely because they came from the unconscious – otherwise known in the forms of the dream and 'the disinterested play of thought'.

Breton's manifesto was a passionate attack on a trend in civilisation. Bullied by 'absolute rationalism' mankind 'under collar of civilisation, under the pretext of progress, all that rightly or wrongly may be regarded as fantasy or superstition has been banished from the mind, all uncustomary searching after truth has been proscribed' (413). 'All credit for these discoveries must go to Freud', he wrote, concluding: 'the imagination is perhaps on the point of reclaiming its rights' (414).

Freud's method of free association launched one of the more intense, if programmatic, periods in Western fine art, and Breton was not alone amongst those influenced by this way of imagining. In the novel, poetry and music, Freud's stance was liberating, suggestive and morphogenically concordant with a certain type of emergent representational freedom.

I doubt it was puzzling to artists that Freud shied away from their own particular transformations of his method. Even a casual reader would have noted his repeated effort to affiliate his discoveries with the scientific world and his odd habit of claiming that one day all his theories would be explained biologically. Readers of 'Civilisation and its Discontents' would also have noted that in his analysis of Western culture, he stressed the exchange of pleasure for civility, part of the psychical change brought about by development of the superego.

Whatever one thinks of the surrealist celebration of Freud, it is of interest that Breton and his colleagues brought to the foreground what Freud marginalised in his writings. If civilisation was a triumph of the conscience in a war with instincts and the pleasure principle, Freud subverted this reality – perhaps what Breton meant by 'absolute reality' – by inventing the free associative process.

To some extent, Freud took his method for granted, and as with many assumptions, it escaped further consideration and development. Like an astronomer who, having marvelled at the discovery of a telescope, subsequently gets lost in what he sees, he was naturally more interested in what he found through his method than in the method itself. We may see something of the same tension in much modern music, literature and painting – a conflict between examination of the method that is one's craft and concentration on what can be manifested through the process. We can paint a figure without having to scrutinise the type of thought that is painting. We can compose a melody without having to think about what a musical idea is. Or we can write a poem and not have to examine the poetic process.

Indeed this tension gives rise to certain intellectual wars, with some artists decrying the representation of the process of creativity and celebrating the figurative outcome of the creation, and others expressing clear irritation with the mimetic simplicity of a figure. Perhaps we all recognise the essentials of this debate: each side in this conflict loses meaning if its opposite is eradicated. Indeed, we know that writers, musicians or painters who profess impatience with the deconstructivists – those artists whose figures are breaking down or cracked to begin with – are also intensely interested in the process that generates their creativity.

It is not too difficult to understand at least one of the sources of this impatience. If one is too self conscious, or too self examining it may interfere with one's creativity. Perhaps the surrealist movement failed to realise its wish to employ the unconscious because an anxious self awareness in their undertaking resulted in an overly stylised art. Indeed this extreme in self observation – or representation of the character of the mind – led Dali to his celebrated 'paranoiac-critical method', which elaborated the irrational character of mental contents in order to further illuminate the structure of the irrational. Paranoia, he wrote, was the 'delirium of interpretation bearing a systematic structure' and he defined 'paranoiac-critical activity' as 'spontaneous method of "irrational knowledge", based on the critical and systematic objectification of delirious associations and interpretations' (1934: 416). The surrealists experimented with the primary process in earnest: Max Ernst used hypnagogic illusions to provide material for his collages, Miró went hungry to inspire hallucinations, coming from what he thought of as the form of the object. But they did so in a curious combat of absolute unconsciousness and absolute consciousness, rather like a meeting of absolutes negating one another.

Perhaps abstract expressionism became the vital compromise. For in the works of de Kooning, to take just one example, one can see how a technique, once sufficiently divorced from the figurative, allows for a certain type of unconscious influence that can be observed but not readily comprehended. Even as the process of painting becomes to some the aim of the painting, heralding what could become a disturbingly intrusive self observation, the result is mysterious. Even as the patterns typify and identify the works as the product of one artist, they nonetheless open the project as a question. What is this? What is one looking at? From which perspective?

De Kooning knew paints. He knew how to keep the paint on the canvas alive until the last possible moment, ready for its eradication and substitution with another colour, another shape. For every vision there was a revision. And revisions of the revisions. The cumulative visual effect is of time and space suspended in a moment, congealed into one representation. If this leads us to think of Freud's mystic writing-pad as a metaphor of the unconscious, realised in these paintings as layer upon layer of the many strokes of the brush, it also suggests Freud's metaphor of life itself, the self as the city of Rome in all its stages – Etruscan, Empire, Medieval, Renaissance – visible in the same gaze and superimposed on one another. Such is the story of any self. In the works of de Kooning one gazes upon an object that in its revisional intensity reflects the dense overdetermination of psychic life. We witness it, indeed for some we are bewilderingly moved by it, guided less by Western conventions of narrative and figuration, than by objectification of us, not as body or social being, but as unconscious movement or intelligent emotion.

'Art is a method of opening up areas of feeling rather than merely an illustration of an object', writes Francis Bacon (1953: 620). Our words – feelings, affects, moods – are not adequate signifiers, as Bacon means much more through 'feeling' than is conjured by this word. He adds, 'A picture should be a re-creation of an event rather than an illustration of an object; but there is no tension in the picture unless there is struggle with the object'. Emotion (from 'movere'), or moving experience is an inner event and may get us closer to what we try to signify by affect or feeling. We seem to be set in motion either by internal stimuli (such as a memory or a wish or a mysterious idea) or external stimuli (such as meeting someone, or reading a book).

Complex states of mind, emotions arise out of the vagaries of life, thick meetings between inner interests and circumstance. 'The way I work', said Bacon, 'is accidental...How can I re-create an accident? [Another accident] would never be quite the same' (622). So too with an emotional experience. Bacon continues: 'This is the thing that can only probably happen in oil paint, because it is so subtle that one tone, one piece of paint, that moves one thing into another completely changes the implications of the image'. Many would agree that no two emotional states are alike, that each emotion changes the contents on the internal canvas.

It is possible to see, therefore, how some painters – following the surrealists – managed to identify (consciously or not) with the project that was Freud's. Indeed, it is more than possible that abstract expressionism actually has succeeded where surrealism failed, extending our understanding of the creative process that was tapped by free association, presenting us with a different type of Rome: a history of the differing emotional experiences of the painter, congealed into one single image, one that materialises psychic life in the form world of painting.

Dream theory, which includes the dream day, the dream event, its breakdown into other scenes upon association, and the discovery and interpretation of tissues of thought, is a particular theory of creativity. Examining this may enable us to see how – if at all – what takes place in analysis shadows some of the more radical representational expressions in the worlds of poetry, painting and music.

Freud however was stubbornly opposed to consideration of the dream work as art-like. Wary of over-enthusiastic adoption by aestheticians, whom he feared would appropriate psychoanalysis, he openly ridiculed any vestige of the aesthetic in the dream. He worried that the transcendental aims of the aesthete would bypass the body's raw urges – the instincts – which held no aesthetic ambitions of their own, eviscerating the drive from the gestalt. Indeed, he thought that the aim of all instincts was to extinguish excitation, though he could find few examples to support this view. Stravinsky might have agreed with him. 'All music', he wrote, 'is nothing more than a succession of impulses that converge towards a definite point of repose' (1942: 35).

Perhaps if Freud had constructed his theory of the dream after Kandinsky, Pound, Stravinsky and Schoenberg, he would have thought differently, for their works have a lyrical raw passion, asserting the pleasure of the aesthetic that gives rise to new expressive forms. Perhaps he would have seen that the total dream process is very likely the cornerstone of the creative, a movement of the 'to be represented' towards the fulfilment of this desire.

Those psychic intensities that are the ordinary inspirational events of everyday life are largely accidental, so what is their psychic status before they are dreamed? They would be, I suggest, internal mental structures – the little Rome of the day being designed but not yet dreamed – energised over-determinations moving towards some form of elaboration. In *Being a Character* I used the term 'psychic genera' to identify an unconscious complex that uses its own gravity to draw to it previously unrelated mental phenomena. The gathering of these psychic gravities would be unconscious, but perhaps sensed as a mood arising out of a previous experience. The continuous presence of these psychic phenomena in the self often provides us with the feeling of being guided by a shaping spirit. What Wordsworth wrote in 'Tintern Abbey' – 'in the mind of man – / a motion and a spirit that impels / All thinking things, all objects of all thought, / And rolls through all things' – is strikingly similar to the way artists describe the creative process.

Stravinsky believed emotion that passes as inspiration is a sign of the presence of something being worked upon by the artist in the moment. 'Is it not clear', he writes, 'that this emotion is merely a reaction on the part of the creator grappling with that unknown entity which is still only the object of his creating and which is to become a work of art?' (1942: 50). The inspired state of mind in the artist, he suggests, is a sign of an internal generative object emerging toward consciousness: 'This foretaste of the creative act accompanies the intuitive grasp of an unknown entity already possessed but not yet intelligible, an entity that will not take definite shape except by the action of a constantly vigilant technique' (51).

The dreamer-to-be carries around unthought known foretastes of their dream during the day, not only elaborating disseminations from past dreams but seeking objects that will move them further along the paths of dream life.

For the most part Freud ignored the daily role of unconscious observation – the collecting, scrutinising, and selecting of psychical objects – an imbalance that Anton Ehrenzweig redressed in his theory of 'unconscious scanning'. We might also say that each person will of course have a long and exceedingly complex history of dream experiences, which over time will establish a kind of inner unconscious network that scans the world, collecting, scrutinising and separating out those elements that are of interest. The dreamt looks for its dream objects in subsequent lived experience.

The dream is a puzzling illumination of one's unconscious interests, a manifestation of intangible interests seeking presentation. This transformation of the unthought known into consciousness becomes a kind of sphinx – a compound object – wrought from the intercourse of the self's psychic life and the aleatory movement of evocative objects. It is the moment when the collective impact of the day, bound into complexes of memory and desire, presents itself.

Freud's dictate that the dreamer should free associate to the dream, meant that whatever integrity the dream seemed to have as an event in its own right was illusory, as associations fragmented it into shards, eventually disclosing tissues of thought that could be knitted into an interpretation. The unconscious latent thought of a dream could be found after free association created enough material to reveal the connecting links.

Depending on one's point of view this is where Freud either limited or empowered psychoanalysis. For some, including many artists, Freud's reduction of this extraordinary process to a single latent idea, was anti-climactic. Just as he declined to credit the work of the unconscious ego in the assimilation of psychically significant moments during the day, now he played down the fecund power of free associations. Freud was not interested in the dream as a paradigm of the creative. His more restricted aim was to gain access to the unconscious meanings of the patient's symptoms through free association to dreams. He did, however, allude to the impossibility of fully interpreting any dream, even though the extraordinary range of his own dream associations seems a pleasure in itself, equal to the delight of interpretation. Furthermore, it seems likely he would have agreed that, once set in motion, free associations not only reveal hidden tissues of thought but become a network of thought that will continue into the next day, and, together with other surviving networks, will collect, sort, dream and disseminate future emotional moments.

It may be a measure of Freud's genius that this discovery, which would have been sufficient for many people, was only the first of many. For me, however, this is his greatest accomplishment. In a few years of work with his patients – affected by their rejections of his techniques – he settles on free association, and in that moment Western culture is changed forever. Many artists, like Joyce, were wary of affiliating themselves with Freud, yet grasped the psychoanalytic revolution, arguably more immediately and perhaps more extensively than did those in the psychoanalytical movement.

And what was so radical?

To find the truth determining one's peculiar, inevitably conflicted states of mind, one discards the energy to know how and why and instead simply reports what happens to be on one's mind in the presence of the analyst. Of course there would be resistances to this request – although paradoxically enough a resistance often pointed directly to the ideas that were being held back – but we would have to say that an entire civilisation would find itself in resistance to something so up-ending.

Yet it is alluring, even when it brings up unwanted ideas. It is speech as true self, the verbal equivalent of Winnicott's 'squiggle' or the moment when, according to Lacan, the subject discovers his own voice, revealed through slips of the tongue and curious wordings.

'It is through the unhampered play of its functions', writes Stravinsky, 'that a work is revealed and justified', and in the pure state he adds, 'music is free speculation' (1942: 49). Free association is also a speculation, a visionary moment in which the self derives from the prior day a hint of its future.

What does psychoanalysis bring to creativity? Freud unconsciously comprehended the process that was not simply at the heart of the creative, but was the creative process – a process involving two people where only one in privacy had been before. Narrating their day, their dream, their associations, analysands create themselves in the presence of the analyst. They may try to 'figure' themselves, but the associative eventually breaks down these figures, and from the broken lines, discordant harmonies, and *caesurae* the psychic creations assert themselves.

The dream materialises the day's psychic reality through a transformation of form. It takes psychic intensities, held inside and sensed, and puts them into the form of a dream. This may be partly why people are not simply puzzled by their dreams, but curiously rather proud of them. We are not only impressed by their content, but because they are transubstantiations – intangible psychic reality is briefly visualised – we are slightly in awe of the process. 'The basis of musical creation', writes Stravinsky, 'is a preliminary feeling out, a will moving first in an abstract realm with the object of giving shape to something concrete' (1942: 27). But the musical idea moving about in Stravinsky's mind will change upon moving into 'sound and time', the material of music.

This brings us to the oddity of creativity. When the painter paints, or the musician composes, or the writer writes, they transfer psychic reality to another realm. They transubstantiate that reality, the object no longer simply expressing self, but re-forming it. This might be considered a type of projection – a putting of the self into an object – but it is also a transubstantial change, where psychic reality leaves its home in the mind and moves into a different intelligence. Commenting on a recent work, Gerhard Richter said: 'that was an expression of my personal state of mind, and it hints at a method of translating my changed way of thinking into reality' (1995: 60).

The term 'transubstantial object' allows me to think of the intrinsic integrity of the form into which one moves one's sensibility in order to create: into musical thinking, prose thinking, painting thinking. These processes could be viewed in part as transformational objects in that each procedure will alter one's internal life according to the laws of its own form. But a transubstantial object also emphasises the 'body' of the transforming object that receives, alters, and represents the sensibility of the subject who enters its terms and now lives within it.

An artist does not go easily into this altered state of unconsciousness. They feel the boundary between ordinary psychic life and the artistic workspace, as one that is always difficult to cross and sometimes unbearably so. Even as they become accustomed to entering this other realm they are acutely aware of leaving themselves behind, thrown into a different form of life.

This challenge is not without precedent as at least once we have been presented with the challenge of language, whether to enter it and to be transformed by it, or to refuse speech. For Lacan, to enter language is to accept a deep change in the human sense of form, from the sensorial imagined order (of an apparently unified self) to wording the self in a new form of being. Art forms offer further challenges to the self and as with language, what emerges from one seems not to be of one's own making, but guided by the form of an other.

Writers, painters and composers often comment on the unknown yet felt inner structure gathering a specific work and its outcome.

'Often when I sit...and turn on my computer or my typewriter and write the first sentence, I don't know what I'm going to write about because it has not yet made the trip from the belly to the mind', writes Isabel Allende (in Epel 1994: 7–24).

> It is somewhere hidden in a very sombre and secret place where I don't have any access yet. It is something that I've been feeling but which has no shape, no name, no tone, and no voice. So I write the first sentence – which usually is the first sentence of the book.... By the time I've finished the first draft I know what the book is about. But not before.
>
> (8)

Art not only embodies this shapeless something, it transforms it into a different realm altogether. 'A thing is brought forth which we didn't know we had in us', writes Milosz (in Gibbons 1979: 3). Wallace Stevens writes:

> While there is nothing automatic about [a] poem, nevertheless it has an automatic aspect in the sense that it is what I wanted it to be without knowing before it was written what I wanted it to be, even though I knew before it was written what I wanted to do.
>
> (50–51)

'If each of us is a biological mechanism, each poet is a poetic mechanism', he continues, to which we might add that the mechanism of transformation from the unthought known object that is the poem to be to the poetic object is derived from the aesthetic process that goes under the name of poetry. In the same way, that order of thinking that is painting, or composing, is the structure of transformation that transubstantiates internal objects from the deep solitude of an internal world into altered external actuality. 'The poet at work is an expectation', writes Valéry in 'A Poet's Notebook'. 'He is a transition within a man'.

This transition is not representational. It is presentational. What the poet writes or the painter paints or the composer composes has not existed before.

Something of this same transubstantiation occurs in an analysis. The patient has in mind a dream, or an event of the previous day, or a thought about the analyst, and as they speak their thoughts they experience its alteration through speech. Thinking something and speaking it are differing forms of representation. But speaking in a freely associative manner inaugurates a transubstantial shift, as the self senses a move from what has heretofore been the common ground of self experience – thinking and talking – to a new form for being. As with the paints splashing on the canvas, or the musical ideas forming notes on the page, the free associating analysand not only creates himself in another place, but instantiates himself in the logic of an aesthetic that differs from purely internal experience or conversation.

Is it possible that this ending of a person's idiom as a self, and new beginning as a different form, is part of the pleasure of creativity? Of course the leap into a different skin may be in order to evacuate the self into the object rather than elaborate inner life. Often enough the new form articulates psychic reality in ways not possible through customary modes of expression.

This raises a further question. What do the differing artistic realms offer as transubstantial objects? If I paint my ideas rather than put them to musical sound I not only select a different form, I also find a different unconscious aesthetic. My ideas will materialise, transformed according to the characteristics of the representational form's unconscious structure. Perhaps we are all evolving towards some day in the far future when each of us will have developed sufficient skills as a poet, artist, musician and mathematician – amongst others – to live in different forms, each of which must of necessity process us very differently, and of course reflect us in aesthetically distinguished manners. Creativity, then, could be viewed as a development in civilisation, not necessarily in terms of the evolution of art or poetry, for example, but as multiple expressions of psychic reality, which in time would be more intelligently served by crafting it in music, paint, poetry.

Works of artistic imagination are form objects, samples of individual idiom made available to the other. Each form object demonstrates the compositional intelligence of its creator and its aesthetic structure suggests to its subsequent appreciators a peculiarly evocative integrity. Although the reader, listener, or viewer will always receive a form object according to the idiom of the self's receptive intelligence, each form object evokes a formal response.

This helps me understand the reassurance I experience on seeing the works of an artist whom I admire. If I travel to a new museum and find a de Kooning I feel delight and reassurance. These are works I feel I know.

But what do I know? The transubstantial object certainly allows for the possibility that my aesthetic grasp of the other is linked with the aesthetic category of the object. That is, these works evoke the experiencing me that exists in and through the medium of paint. It brings something out in me, or to put it in the vernacular: it 'speaks to me'. I could not, however, put what it 'says' or what I 'hear' into words. Some individuals are irked by the critical examination of their work, not only because they may be distressed with the judgement, but also, it seems to me, because they have entered a different realm which is not the written word, even if their realm is prose fiction or poetry which uses the word as its medium.

In a psychically literal sense we are moved by the work of art, processed by its form. And even if we only glance at one painting, hear a few bars of music, or read a few lines of a poem, we shall have been gathered by the aesthetic of the other, remarkably preserved in the after-effects of their life, forms of their idiom left behind.

'If I alter any reader's consciousness, it will be because I have constructed a consciousness of which others may wish to become aware, or even, for a short time, share', writes William Gass (1996: 47). But as Gass knows only too well the consciousness constructed by the novel is not the same as ordinary consciousness, although each writer uses that medium to express aspects of his own idiom.

Is it accurate to say that the artistic object only reflects the self, even if we qualify this by assuming that the artist also expresses contemporary culture and artistic tradition? As the transubstantial object differs in form from the self, it bears the self yet becomes a new body for that being. 'The music of prose', writes Gass, 'elementary as it is, limited as it is in its effects, is nonetheless far from frivolous decoration; it embodies Being; consequently, it is essential that the body be in eloquent shape' (326). The 'object' through which we create – painting, prose, music – has its own processional integrity, its own laws, and when we enter it to express our idea within its terms, we shall be altered by the object. 'For the last two years I have been making a series of paintings with "je t'aime" written across them', writes Robert Motherwell. 'I never thought much about it, but I am sure in part it is some kind of emphasis or *existing in* what is thought' (in Caws 1996: 18). Existing in a thrown thought, projected into a different aesthetic realm, and objectified in a different and challenging way. Transubstantial projective objectification.

The same principle operates when the analysand enters analysis. There are familiar elements – a vestige of social life, ordinary talk, a unit of time etc. – but the free associative medium, although borrowing its integrity from inner speech and inner association, becomes a new medium for self expression. Entering analysis a person will never be the same again. He will have found a new object for self transformation and there is nothing like it, just as there is nothing like painting, nothing like poetry and nothing like music.

'Art belongs to the *unconscious!*' wrote Kandinsky to Schoenberg.

One must express *oneself*! Express oneself *directly*! Not one's taste, or one's upbringing, or one's intelligence, knowledge or skill. Not all these *acquired* characteristics, but that which is *inborn, instinctive*. And all form-making, all *conscious* form-making, is connected with some kind of mathematics, or geometry.... But only unconscious form-making, which sets up the equation 'form = outward shape', really creates forms.

(Schoenberg and Kandinsky 1984: 23)

Perhaps that inner object that is the work to be finds its most direct expression in the geometry or mathematics – i.e. the specific intelligence – of the medium of the creativity rather than in the object. The work that Allende says is 'in her belly' only emerges through writing, and one of the features of any person's creativity is the selection of the particular form through which to express the creative idea.

'In one way only can form be discussed in an objective sense', writes Ernst Bloch in *Essays on the Philosophy of Music*. 'This is where the formal, constructional, objectifying element is not a medium but itself an objective component', he adds, 'as is especially the case with stage effects, with rhythm and especially with the different types of counterpoint that determine the shaping subjects as categories of their innate being' (1985: 87). This determination of the shaping subject – the logic of form – is an expression of the innate being of the subject, now moved from inner experience to the property of musical expression. He continues: 'here the shaping subject has truly entered into a "form" as its deeper aggregate condition, a "form" accordingly representing the lower, quasi-epistemological, metaphysically skeletonic part of the object arrangement itself' (87–8). Musical form, we may add, is not simply a medium, it is an objectification of that intelligence that is shaping its idea, and the structure of inspiration reveals itself in the object arrangement, that is, in musical form.

Creative life usually involves a drawing in of the self perhaps because all the self's inner resources are devoted to the creative act. Freud also recognised this need in the formation of psychoanalysis, as patient and analyst retreat from stimuli of the world. A withdrawal in order to crystallise the work harks back to the age before social responsiveness, predating even the primary mediating presence of language. Each of us has been part of this drawing in of being, first when we are inside the mother's body and then held by her concentration for many weeks after our birth, what Winnicott termed primary maternal preoccupation. In psychoanalysis the recumbent position, the absence of visual socialisation, the presence of an auditory intimate, and the absence of an agenda recreate the mood of the earliest states of consciousness. Free associative thinking may begin as a type of chat, just as the artist's sketch is a way of beginning, but eventually analysand and artist respond to what is being called for. For the patient it means a deepening of the associations, in the artist/analyst as well, a generative loosing of self into the work.

In our beginnings, held inside the mother's body, then immersed in her psychic and somatic textures, we are enfolded beings. Wilfred Bion believed that analysis allowed for an alteration in the analyst's being, as he dreamt the patient's material, transforming the patient's communications into his dream objects. This craft certainly derives from a maternal process and gives birth to inspired ideas and interpretations. In the composer, writer, or creative artist, a similar reverie is established although after years of practising this retreat, creative people enter it alone, manage it by themselves, and take the object-to-be as a type of other.

Retreat into this realm taps and develops the skill of unconscious creativity, driven by the core of one's being. Psychoanalysis transforms unconscious complexes – symptomatic, pathologic, transferential – into consciousness, but it also enhances the self's unconscious capability. Bion reckoned that psychoanalytic training was an education in intuition.

The kind of thinking required in psychoanalytic work evokes those objects of conflict that are a part of our existence. No one represented conflicts with early objects as well as Melanie Klein. In her mind, each self is engaged in a ceaseless remembering of the earliest encounter with the object, enacting them in all subsequent relations. The type of thinking evoked by psychoanalysis or the concentration of the creative artist calls forth the passions of love and hate, the objects of each, and the self's violent evasions of the consequence of being. Thus free association may intend to be objective and dispassionate, but as the associations move deeper into the self, they will convey the self's experience of its objects, a burden that saturates the freely associated thought with meaning. For these ideas not only bear their symbolic structure as Lacan emphasised, they are also like independent characters in a developing opera of sorts. The classical way of listening allows the logic that is sequence to arise out of the material, taking into account those ruptures or shallows that indicate resistance, those emphases created by parapraxal moments, and those disseminations occasioned by polysemous words. The object-relational way of listening to the same material transforms the sequence of ideas into characters – treated as parts of the self or parts of the object – who constitute the theatre of transference. Each way of listening finds a different type of conflict operating in a different realm. In literature, it may be the difference between the conflict revealed in the idiom of the writing and the conflict demonstrated in the enactments between characters. In painting it may be the difference between the logic of the developing ideas – thought constituting itself in the intelligence of the step-by-step move of the brush – and the theatre of established figures of the painter's world once again engaging themselves on the canvas.

In 'The Use of an Object', Winnicott argued that spontaneity could only develop out of a principle of ruthlessness. In order to use an object, the self must be free to destroy it. It is the mother who sanctions this in the first place; indeed, she is to be the initial object of such destruction. After a period of relating in which the infant's love and hate are mingled through a sense of concern for her, the infant gradually feels more secure in his or her ability to use the mother, not confusing such wear and tear with damage.

Perhaps something of the same principle underlies Freud's injunction to the dreamer to break up the body of the dream through free association. The feelings and self states brought into the dream as an experience are stored as is; breaking them up through free association will not erase memory of the dream experience. Indeed, the security of the dream as a thing in itself allows for its destruction, and use as an object of inspiration.

Whether one considers the dream or the mother as object, both the Freudian principle and Winnicott's idea amount to a breaking-up of the figure. Freud breaks up the figures of the dream and Winnicott breaks up the mother, and from each emerges a dynamically fragmented universe of potential meanings. These psychological theories were developing over a period of sixty years when something of the very same principle was being celebrated in fine art, music and prose. Following the impressionist breaking of representational figuration, we find in cubism, surrealism, abstract expressionism a moment in the artist's development when the figure breaks up. It may shatter into the cubist, futurist, surrealist, or abstract. Furthermore, this dissemination of the object was often signified by the figure of a woman, painted again and again, who begins to break up.

Many critics, looking at Picasso's or de Kooning's paintings of a woman, argue that she is being destroyed in a misogynist attack on the female. These criticisms miss the context of this breaking-up. It usually occurs just before the fragmentation of the sublime other into a bizarre refiguration or a shattered object, often abstracted into a thick movement of colour and shape. I suggest that what we see here mirrors what Freud and Winnicott wrote about the breaking-up of the figurative. Breaking the woman becomes the breaking of the mother's body, momentarily losing the need for figuration but employing her as a project for the realisation of self. She is now the process of painting, an immanent presence, de-objectified and re-formed as the guardian intelligence of the form of painting.

Certain abstract works of art, like certain modern novels (of Joyce, Faulkner) disfigure customary representation in order to present the work of creativity within the form itself, playing with the elements of form, implicitly recognising the desire in the recipient to see something of the magic of form at work.

179

Psychoanalysis can show a similar lack of respect for the sanctity of the figurative. In the struggle to engage the invisible, the analyst (like the artist) breaks the figure: not to find out what is inside but to realise the immaterial intelligence of form that is authorised in the name of the mother. If the infant is to come into true self relating, says Winnicott, then he or she must be free to invent the mother and self. For patients to use analysis, they must be free to invent many an analyst in the transference and to destroy the integrity of the person of the analyst in order to express themselves. The analyst up to a point accepts this use.

Painters, composers and writers who take liberty in destroying the figures of our life, nonetheless rely upon the integrity of the figure even as they destroy it. Like psychoanalysts, they recognise the paradox of this freedom. It could not occur without a sense of privilege deriving from the figure – the mother who gives birth – but who shall be 'destroyed' as she is used. Taking liberties, as it were, is not sublime. As a self creates many an other out of the primary figure, what is gained in freedom of expression is lost in terms of personal security. In time the waves of representation suggest too many possible figures and eventually the primary mother is beyond reach. Abstract expressionists may well have pined for the simplicity of the figure, just as the self, beset by creation of so many multiple representations of the primary object, grieves the mother lost to us all.

A Picasso or de Kooning may well return in mind to the woman, armed with the ambivalence that comes from the freedom to destroy. How, it might be posed, can the mother allow us to destroy her? Refinding her, even in altered form, then, may be a relief in the midst of what will be renewed efforts of destruction.

We are separated from the mother, the father, the family, and arguably from our culture, by the fecund complexity of psychic life. No figure shall survive intact. Our thoughts – in visions and revisions – will revise all figures so frequently that only the principle of figure shall remain. Free association releases this complexity in a bound space further narrowed by the reluctance of the patient to fully embrace it, and by the analyst who seeks his interpretations. Creative work in dance, poetry, drama, prose fiction, music, painting, sculpture, also involves tacit devolutions of the figure as revisioning creates multiple figures, overlying one another.

If we cannot have singular objects to embrace for consolation's sake, we do have the body of separate forms, into which and through which we alter and articulate our being. This is the great promise of any art form. It is often enough the reality of the psychoanalytical method.

16

THE MYSTERY OF THINGS

Theories of mental life and human behaviour will come and go much as they have since the beginning of psychoanalysis. Only the passing of time will determine the value of any particular theory and some models which seemed assured of perpetuity, such as the structural theory, will be abandoned, even by their most avid supporters. What will not change is the deeply evocative effect of the psychoanalytical situation and its method.

In this book I have reviewed the method from differing perspectives: as a type of autobiography, as a realisation of our place in the mystery of an embracing intelligence, as a new form for the self's habitation, as a new form for thinking, and as a new type of relationship. In *Shadow of the Object* I suggested that while Freud's theory of the self's psychic structure took the father as the primary object, the setting and process lived silently with the mother. Freud only partly understood what he invented and each of the schools that operates around the name of one profound thinker – Klein, Lacan, Kohut, Bion, Winnicott etc. – takes a particular perspective to its extreme, inevitably pushing aside what cannot be included in the limited vision of a theory gone too far.

To indicate further how the differing theories offer essential, although different, perspectives I shall look again at the Freudian and then the Kleinian technique, my hidden agenda being to conclude this study with further consideration of the ways in which Freud's method is more profound, and mysterious, than we appreciate. I also hope to indicate how Klein's method differs completely from Freud's, even though, in the politics of psychoanalysis, the Kleinians repeatedly assert her derivation from Freud's thinking. Although this is true in relation to the generation of theories such as mourning, castration anxiety, and the search for knowledge, the Freudian and Kleinian ways of listening are completely different, though each is an important theory of hearing and each merits a place in the overall practice of psychoanalysis.

Let us return once again to Freud.

Freud made the dream the cornerstone of the psychoanalytic moment. In *Being a Character* I argued that the dream is the median point in a psychic journey we could call the total dream process, beginning during the dream day with psychic intensities that need to be slept on and which then compete with one another to be dreamed. Psychic intensities of the day are highly over-determined unconscious emotional moments. The dream is a way – perhaps the best way – of thinking further about such emotional experiences. Ironically enough, its very primitive character, thinking in pictures, allows for many ideas to be bound in a few images, that economically allow for further elaboration of the day's intensities. A dream is both highly self-involving and iconically vivid and therefore hard to forget upon waking. Remembering the dream will itself spring new ideas and guide us toward potential realisations about life.

By situating psychoanalysis in the wake of the dream, on the day of associations, Freud introduced a newly formed human relation into a hitherto solitary episode. 'Do you recall your dream?' puts all analysands in a new place, as now for the first time the human other arrives to listen to our associations, giving them new strength and purpose. Prior to this, each dreamer was more or less left to the occasional flash of the associative, before it was buried in oblivion.

We are still processing the after-effects of this request in psychoanalysis.

Freud understood that in sleep we return to a foetal and infantile posture and when dreaming we return to an infant-like state of hallucinatory thought. As Pontalis and Khan amongst others have suggested, the body of the dream is like the mother's body. Each night we rendezvous with mother, returning like clockwork to her order, once again thinking in visual terms and living amongst the hallucinated.

When reporting a dream analysands feel they are presenting an oracle. They will initially resist the call to association, not simply because they may fear disclosure of repressed ideas, but more importantly, because they wish to remain within the maternal spell. It is as if the dreamer, hearing Freud's invitation to the infant and the mother, replies, 'At last there is some place for me to bring the infantile and the maternal'. The call for association is resisted because no one wants to be separated from this moment. 'Why should I associate? I have told you the dream. Just tell me what it means', analysands reply.

Having constructed a space for the materialisation of the infant-with-mother Freud introduces the unwanted father who insists upon the obligation to associate. In his dream book Freud relishes this moment, stressing that associations 'destroy' the manifest content of the dream, something I shall discuss in more detail shortly. By asking for associations – introducing the father's law – Freud's method resulted in a movement of ideas which separated the analysand from the integrity of the text and from the very mother evoked by dreaming. The breaking-up of the manifest text constitutes a small breaking-up of the self's prior habitation in the maternal order.

Free association, however, is an ingenious means of separation.

Although instituted in the name of the father, an obligation expected of the analysand, the method of simply speaking what occurs in the moment, in an unfocused and momentarily unscrutinised manner, without fear of consequence, and held by the analyst's supportive silence and unjudgemental attitude, is a form of discourse borrowed from the maternal order. Free association is thus a bridge from one order to another, a compromise that suits the needs of both object relations, now joined through the act of association.

Each analytical hour, then, results in a continuous oscillation between the bringing of the dream (maternal order), separation from it through application of the method (paternal order), joined in the medium of free association. From maternal to paternal, back to maternal, returned again to paternal. In one session alone the patient will bring a dream, eliciting the infantile, then subjecting it to the destruction of free association, only to recollect another dream with the entire process repeating itself. These relationships will be repeated hundreds and thousands of times, month after month, year after year. An intrinsic part of the method, though not explicit, psychoanalysis enlists the maternal and paternal orders in a working partnership.

Both the evocation of the maternal in this context and the separation from the dream-as-mother are unique to psychoanalysis. The father who enters this scene differs from the fathers of ordinary family life, and this mother is a new figure coming into existence after the Oedipal period, when the law of the father is assumed to be part of one's psychic structure. The mother and the father who emerge and join in a psychoanalysis are new elaborations of the maternal and the paternal. Rather than simply a matter of negotiating new internal objects associated with these names, the method uses the function of these early figures to elaborate new forms of parenting, sustained over years by patient and analyst.

An important feature of this new marriage of the maternal and the paternal is the oscillating transformation between the visual and the verbal order, or between the imaginary and the symbolic. To remember the dream is to recall a visual experience. The work of association, however, transforms this picture not only into other scenes – memories not included in the dream experience – but also into an increasingly verbal order. Working on a dream in psychoanalysis moves the self from the pre-verbal to the verbal, or, from the maternal to the paternal order. At the same time, however, as I shall discuss, the associative process also sets the self into subsequent deep internal imaginings, that is, back into the visual-sensorial-affective orders, more characteristic of life in the maternal order. Emerging from such reveries into speech the analysand renews language with unconscious depth.

In the state of 'evenly suspended attentiveness' the analyst is 'to surrender himself to his own unconscious mental activity', giving up 'reflection', 'conscious expectation' and 'memory, and by these means to catch the drift of the patient's unconscious with his own unconscious' (1923a: 238). Patients new to analysis find the transition to this new relation somewhat jolting, even if they unconsciously sense its aptness. Ordinarily when people talk there is conversational mutuality: one speaker pauses, allowing the other to say something in turn. When the new analysand pauses they will not find the analyst replying. Instead there will be silence. The effect is transformative. The analysand will hear their words echo in the quiet that follows. If discomforted by this silence they soon discover that the absence of a predictable reply is a new writ for freedom of expression.

Now and then the patient will say something and the analyst will repeat a single word, which if well timed, will elicit further material. This analytical echo must be sincere and without guile. If the analyst is leading the patient toward some interpretation-in-waiting it is an abuse of the function of their evenly suspended attentiveness, of their own surrender to their unconscious life. While listening to the patient a particular word or image will have a more intense effect than other phrases or images and in such moments they will repeat the word or the image without knowing what it means. If unconsciously engaged with their patient, their repetition will have the effect of engaging the patient's more psychically intense wordings. Without ever mentioning feelings or affects, this is a Freudian means of releasing affectively significant words or images that drive the meaning of an hour.

We can see how this type of listening slows matters down. Realising that their analyst will not reply to their mental meandering in an ordinarily conversational mode, the patient usually slows down, their speech less urgently seeking reassurance. It ceases its sign function of 'Is what I've said "okay"? Say so and I'll tell you when it's my turn that what you've said is "okay" '. Instead it becomes open speech, a discourse driven by the unconscious speaking in the presence of an other newly arrived on the scene. Fifteen or twenty minutes may pass before the analyst says anything. He may allow the entire session to go by without comment, although it would be unusual were he not to echo certain words or images. With the Freudian technique there can be no hurry. Freudian time realises aspects of unconscious time, limited only by the end of the hour, as the patient loses the time-keeping function of conversational mutuality and gains the temporality of the timeless. In this speech, the analysand interrupts himself as new thoughts arise to displace narrative hegemony, customarily moving with the flow of more sentient ideas that seem to arise out of nowhere. Analysands have to learn how to do this, but when they do, they find this new relation affords them the opportunity to live in past, present and future tenses, mixing the objects and psychic realities of all times in one continuous stream of consciousness.

Freud made it very clear that the core of his technique was to be centred around unconscious communication, and while the integrity of this position was sustained in classical continental European psychoanalysis, it was largely abandoned in the Anglo-American classicism which founded ego psychology. 'Evenly suspended attentiveness' seemed to suffer a witless dismantling of its meaning: 'evenly' became 'even', as in equanimous or calm; 'suspended' became 'removed' or 'detached'; 'attentiveness' became 'attentive'. Removed from Freud's original context these words now meant that the analyst was to be even-minded, suspended from his patient and very attentive. Psychoanalysts supervised in ego psychology were asked to describe the patient's ego state from moment to moment especially in relation to the id and the superego; and, when making interpretations, they were asked to identify exactly how they understood the ego's requirement at this point in time and why they made the comment they did. What had once been a technique formed around the analyst's suspension of consciousness now became a technique centred on the analyst's consciousness. In clinical discussions analysts did not discuss thoughts arising while in the state of evenly suspended attentiveness; if they had, there would have been no need for subsequent generations to move with desperation toward countertransference theory in order to recuperate the evisceration of the analyst's unconscious contribution to the analysis. Freud's theory of the partnership between the analysand's free associations and the analyst's evenly hovering attentiveness was a theory of the countertransference well before the term meant much at all.

Freudian clinical time allowed the analyst to lose himself in the patient's discourse, to be moved by the flow of imagery, the arrivals and departures of the patient's friends, family and enemies; to be left with the curiously lasting impressions of the ordinary detail. Freud said that those free associations which the patient regarded as 'irrelevant to what is being looked for' would prove to be 'of particular value', but these ordinary objects would also prove to be unusually significant to the analyst. Within weeks of beginning my life as a psychoanalyst I was struck by something I had never anticipated. Even though patients would often describe an important event in their lives, or tell me something about their character that was richly insightful, certain images or words would become lasting impressions on my mind. Sometimes it would be a fragment of a dream, sometimes a perfectly ordinary word that in that context seemed memorable, sometimes it would be a feeling out of which I constructed an abstract image. In time, scores of such mental objects became memorable, even though I did not comprehend their meaning. I believe these objects were conscious manifestations of unconscious lines of thought, but we cannot cheat when discussing the unconscious. As they were not fully in consciousness, except in these derived fragments, I was not to know what they meant, and, with very few exceptions, these fragments never were to be comprehended by me.

Such impressions are part of the psychic furniture of the Freudian space. In evenly suspended attentiveness, just as an atemporality is momentarily accomplished, so a new mental space is also constructed, one in which many objects – sensible and insensible – sit in unobjectionable juxtaposition to one another. This can only be accomplished with the suspension of customs of consciousness, a core of the Freudian method. But as we see, free association and evenly suspended attention foster unconscious communication, which in turn changes the function of speaking and listening.

In time the analyst will suddenly see a chain of ideas in the material. Freud loved this moment. He became a detective on the scene, trying to piece together the evidence. But even a detective such as Columbo must be lost in his thought before he sees through the evidence to discover the trail of intention. The suspects in Columbo's television dramas are always somewhat irritated by how slowly he proceeds, or amused by how far off from finding the truth he appears to be. In a process not too dissimilar from the psychoanalytical one, the detective must allow the evidence to influence him but without forming a premature idea of what is taking place before his eyes.

In Freudian listening, when the analyst or patient sees the tissue of thought that constitutes the latent content resting amidst the logic of connection between the differing passing ideas, he will speak up for it. The evidence will be available for each participant. It is a matter of pointing to the recent past – perhaps in the last fifteen minutes of the hour – to the connection of certain ideas. The analyst need not be heavy-footed; indeed, the best comments are simple repetitions of a few words which evoke the patient's immediate realisation.

Freudian reflection is deeply respectful of the specific contents of the patient's mind, their own unique logic of thought, and their precise words. In commenting on these specifics an analyst may say something like, 'I find it interesting what you have been saying', or 'You have said you do not know what you mean, but actually you have revealed an interesting line of thought', or, 'I think what you are teaching me is...' and then proceed to speak the links. If the analysand agrees but reveals in subsequent associations unconscious disagreement, the analyst can point out the correction. Of course, these detecting reflections can only be achieved after the creation of Freudian time and space, and they usually only come to the analyst as sudden realisations. Often they arrive in the analyst's and the patient's mind at the same time. Sometimes after a long silence the patient will reflect on what they have been saying and speak from inspired recognition of their own unconscious meaning.

These understandings, however, do not distinguish the psychoanalytical session. Valued though they are, most of the time both participants are too deeply involved in the method to know the meaning of arriving thoughts, images, words, feelings and so forth. This way of listening takes time, lots and lots of time. It takes time for the logic of sequence to be comprehended, it takes time for the evocative movement of the patient's discourse to affect the analyst's unconscious life. This aspect of an analysis leads to a greater appreciation of unconscious time and unconscious thought; indeed, it gives its participants a new appreciation of time itself. It is the most sophisticated method we have developed in Western culture for unconscious life to matriculate into consciousness, and long after the analysis is over the analysand will bear within themselves a toleration for the temporal and spatial worlds of their unconscious life, that will serve them well as the occasional recipient of inspired reflections derived from the mystery of their being.

Melanie Klein's way of listening to the patient was very different from this. It must be remembered that even when working with adults she took the model of the analyst at work with the small child as her paradigm. The child does not free associate, but does play with toys. Observing this play, Klein narrated the child's unconscious meanings as they occurred in the here and the now. She voiced over the child's play with interpretation and, as she almost always interpreted the child's actions as directed towards the inside of the mother's body, where one was to find a cornucopia of body parts of mother, self, father and siblings, it was a very rich commentary.

In her work with adults Klein viewed the people and events narrated by the patient as objects that served to represent differing parts of the patient's self engaged with one another in that moment. If the patient talked about a friend who was irresponsible the patient was projectively identifying an irresponsible part of the self into this internal object. The Kleinian way of listening discovered a rich theatre. It was a visual order *par excellence*, as the people or events in the narrative were personifications of mental qualities, a medieval psycho-machia for the twentieth century. The genius of this way of listening is that work with patients who were rather sparse in their communications, or for whom Freudian time would have been a seeming descent into chaos, were immediately comprehensible, if one simply translated the objects talked about into parts of the self.

Klein's students extended her theory of projective identification to indicate how the patient's narrative about another person was a splitting-off of something felt about the analyst in the here and the now. The degree of splitting could seemingly be calculated in terms of the temporality of the split. If the patient talked about someone in the waiting area who seemed to disapprove of the way the patient dressed this might be considered a less severe split than if the patient talked about a similar criticism from a person in the distant past (i.e. more split-off from the present time). There was also a spatial dimension. If the patient talked about someone they met at a party who they thought was sneaky, this could be a less severe split than if they talked about how dishonest they thought Saddam Hussein was. Usually Kleinian analysts skilfully sought to interpret these split-off parts of the analysand in the here and now, linking the contents to the imagined person of the analyst in the transference.

Early Kleinian writings stressed that the analyst must not wait for the patient's material to unfold. Candidates in supervision would invariably be asked why they had remained quiet while the patient was talking, since this colluded with the patient's projective identification. The patient, they were told, would assume the analyst was silent for innumerable wrong reasons: they were in agreement with putting a part of the self into another, they were afraid of confronting their patient, they were too disgusted to speak up, they were furious and harbouring a grudge, they were excited by the patient's narrative and wanted more of the same to go forward, they were damaged and depressed and unable to speak. The analyst, it was argued, must interpret not only the parts of the self presented in the narrative, but also the function of these objects as manifestations of feelings about the analyst in the present tense.

Since the Kleinian analyst's task is to interpret a projective identification before patients lose further contact with themselves, this necessitates a type of listening in which the analyst immediately translates to himself or herself the dynamic meaning of the play of the parts. To allow the patient to continue talking, which is seen as a form of splitting and projective identification, without intervening to analyse the aggression intrinsic to this frame of mind, is to abandon the patient to his pathology, so the analyst continuously intervenes with an interpretation – or voice over – of the material.

More than any other analytical theoretician Klein worked with and extended Freud's ideas of human motivation and conflict. Her theories of the death instinct, mourning, manic defence, early Oedipal conflict, splitting of the ego, are profound elaborations of his thinking, even if in all respects she creatively changes them and makes them her own. She and her followers could rightly point to the many ways in which they derived their theories from Freud, but in her way of working and especially the technique of Kleinians who followed, there was a complete change in the psychoanalytic method.

Freud's technique, where the analyst remains silent, gives the patient plenty of time to talk, allowing for the gradual unfolding of many differing unconscious interests. Klein's technique insists that the analyst intervene to interpret the patients' projection of parts of themselves into the people they were talking about. Freud's technique suggests that the analyst suspend reflection, memory and concentration in order to become unconsciously present. Klein's technique demands an alert conscious presence in the analyst who will as soon as is humanly possible translate the projections into their self parts. Freud's technique invites the pictorial world of the dream into its vivid telling, but then breaks the visual order down into its thousand words, each moving in differing realms of psychic logic. Klein keeps the visual order intact; indeed, she enters it with the patient only to transfer it to another visual place: so if a child is moving a toy car into a toy bus they are moving a penis into the womb, or, an adult who is talking about a depressed boss reproaching his negligent employee is the exasperated part of the analyst talking to the skiving-off patient.

Klein does not alter the fundamental terms of the visual order. Her patient describes their inner world which Klein substitutes with the visual world of the mother's body, or, with the later Kleinians, the visual world of a part of the patient talking to an imagined part of the analyst. Indeed the genius of this technique is precisely that the Kleinian does not attempt to alter the fundamental medium of self presentation, but actually enters into it with the patient, achieving an immediate intimacy and exceptionally direct expression of feeling. Further, the evidence is not the stitched together logic of Freudian sequence, taking long periods of time to gather, but is immediately present. If the patient has just talked about their friend Cindy who likes to steal clothing from the store and the patient is afraid that their friend risks being caught one day, the analyst can immediately say 'perhaps the Cindy you is afraid that I will catch you stealing some of my possessions', which may immediately lead the patient to discuss fears of the analyst's judgement and the impulse to steal certain comments from the analyst without properly acknowledging their source; i.e., paying for them.

What are we to make of these fundamental differences? They differ in the type of mentality that invites the patient's unconscious participation. They differ in the fate of the patient's unconscious participation in the session. They differ in their orientations to the visual and the verbal orders, or the imaginary and the symbolic. They differ in their conceptions of analytical time and space. They differ in the after-effects of an analysis.

It would be a sad misconception indeed to see these differences as incompatible in the conduct of an analysis. In their own separate ways they are invaluable to the full course of a psychoanalysis. Each way of listening speaks to a changed function in the analysand's discourse and transference. If the core of the psychoanalytical enterprise rests in the Freudian way of listening, in which the analyst conceives of himself as a medium of the patient's unconscious thought, there will be innumerable occasions when the patient will change this function, and use narrative objects to contain aspects of the self. I believe that the psychoanalyst can sense this change of function. If I am just listening to the patient at the start of an hour, lost in the course of his associations, I can feel the moment when the people and places he is describing are fundamentally changing from lines of thinking to receptacles for the deposition of parts of the self. As Klein emphasises in her early works, there is something aggressive in the deposition of a part of the self into the internal object, and before long psychoanalysts can feel this force. If not interpreted, often the material of the hour will go flat with the subsequent associations rather lifeless, repetitive or rationalised.

The Freudian and Kleinian ways of listening are fundamentally different ways of inviting, receiving, processing and interpreting the analysand's unconscious. It is an unfortunate feature of the psychoanalytical movement that these different functions are largely separated by the political agendas of the classical and the Kleinian groups, for each form of working is vital to the psychic transformation of the analysand.

It may very well be, however, that Wilfred Bion's mentality, and his theories, offer transformation to both groups, in which both can change by moving towards the other without political cost. For when Bion writes that the analyst must do without memory or desire, he recommends a technique that is contrary to the Kleinian way of working. Yet as a Kleinian making the statement – albeit without ever linking this comment to Freud's own theory of technique – he makes it possible for Kleinians to become Freudians without loss of face. Indeed, if my argument is correct, part of Bion's enormous popularity is because he functions as a transformational object for the Kleinians, meeting their unconscious need to be delivered from the limiting dogmas of their own technique. At the same time, open-minded classical analysts, such as Roy Schafer, are now able to write about the valuable contributions of Kleinian analysts to analytical work. For the other side of the coin is that Freud's technique is limited. It always needed the emendations made by Klein and her followers. And the more actively interpretive engagement offered by Kleinian technique will only enrich classical techniques.

Bion and Winnicott also constructed different ways of receiving the patient's unconscious life. Like many Kleinians of the 1950s Bion believed that the analyst was a container to the patient's introduction of mental contents, as if the patient were posing a question: 'How do *you* live with these contents and what will you do to find them survivable?' In time Bion developed a subtle theory of the elements of being passed from the patient to the analyst eliciting differing functions of the analyst's mind. This is not the place to discuss a profound rethinking of the analytical process, but Bion's mentality is undeniably new: it receives the patient differently than Freud or Klein; it permits a differing type of unconscious object usage, and it results in a different type of analytical intervention.

Winnicott, like Bion, was deeply influenced both by Freud and Klein, yet his technique differed from both. Like Bion he could wait and wait in silence without pouncing on the material as his Kleinian brothers and sisters insisted. Unlike Freud, he was not particularly interested in detecting the latent contents, a practice which he argued was all too often an omnipotent defence against the formlessness of human existence. Neither Bion nor Winnicott had Lacan's interest in language or his passion on behalf of the subject who signifies, and Lacan's emphasis – however poorly followed by his later practice – is itself a profound insistence on following the logic of one aspect of Freud's method. Winnicott, however, believed the analyst should wait for the inevitable arrivals of the true self, often disguised in the thickets of pathology, capable of hiding forever in the pure travail of analytical interpretation of unconscious complexes.

Like Milner, Rycroft, Khan, Klauber and other analysts of the British Independent group, Winnicott was prepared to wait a long time in order to facilitate the stirrings of the true self. If possible, he would suspend standard interpretation and create a holding environment composed of the analyst's silence and unexpectant concentration. He picked certain periods in the patient's analysis to lengthen sessions, scheduling a patient to have two to three hours 'open'. (Freud argued much the same when he wrote that 'occasionally...one comes across patients to whom one must give more than the average time of one hour a day, because the best part of an hour is gone before they begin to open up and to become communicative at all', 1913: 127–8). Winnicott believed that given enough time and the absence of interpretive organisation a patient would experience a 'formless', often rather desultory state. One point was to create the right environment for the opportunity of a pathologic structure to dominate an hour. He knew that many patients loved to present and re-present their illness to the analyst, evoking the same rather monotonous interpretations. What if the analyst did not respond to type? What if the span of time defeated or lessened the omnipotence of illness? What would the patient do or say?

He found that after certain lamentations and expressions of anxiety, a restful quiet arrived, the patient felt himself drifting, lost in reverie. Work like this could, and very often did, go on for months, repeated stirrings and imaginings not organised into themes and the patient who arrived out of this frame of mind would often look back, at the end of analysis, to say (somewhat mystified) that this era had been deeply transformative.

To use Bion, we might say that Winnicott found a technique for the patient's unconscious creation of alpha.

Repeated efforts to interpret a patient's pathology in the here and now transference may ironically shadow the structure of pathology itself. Psychoanalysts maintain that through repeated interpretations of a pathological communication they seek to de-toxify pathology through voice, and this works much of the time. But some patients seek this procedure, indeed they thrive on it. Speech (as narrative communication or performative action) seeks its transformation as an end-in-itself, creating a new virus derived only from psychoanalysis: the interaction of communication–interpretation as illness.

Winnicott and Khan and others decided not to cultivate this illness, and, while empathically supporting the patient, waited to see if anything would emerge from elsewhere. They occasionally took the unusual step of telling the patient to stop talking, to see what would arise in that sort of time not determined by militant reporting of inner states of mind. Although momentarily refusing the patient's wish to present himself only as a pathology seeking its transferential realisations, these analysts were nonetheless 'affectionate', as they expressed their feelings, concentrated, and tempered their rejection with an invitation to the patient to speak from the parts of the self eliminated by the ever-present priority of pathology. Feeling 'in' the voice is immanent communication; very different from expressing feelings to the patient about the patient or about oneself.

Perhaps these analysts were unbinding psychoanalysis, working for periods of time along the lines of an 'anti hermeneutic', as Laplanche argues one must do. Or perhaps they were dismantling the known-predictable structure of psychoanalysis, moving the patient toward 'O', Bion's sign for infinity.

In the formless, the analysand gradually speaks their idiom through multiple uses of the analyst's personality. And even though their illness will restrict them, and concentrate the analyst's attention on interpretation of the pathological complex, on an entirely different plane of self presentation they will present their aesthetic of being.

Shaping the psychoanalyst through idiosyncracies of voice, wording, mood, gesture, silence and the other languages of character, into a subjective field that will have registered the effect, it is as if the human personality, once it suspends itself in the interests of 'evenly suspended attentiveness', becomes a unique organ for the analysand's instrumental presentation of its style. Paradoxically, it is precisely because the psychoanalyst allows himself a deeply subjective response to the patient, wandering off through his own associations, that the patient's effect creates an astonishing amount of information. The psychic material exceeds the analyst's conscious sense of what it all means, displacing his own known subjective response, yet such deep work yields its own strangely objective quality. Objective if we appreciate that the method creates abundance of mental objects, realising the paradox of deep subjectivity, that it *objectifies* the self through subjective productivity and therefore has its own unique claim to a form of objectivity in the study of the self.

Unguided by any known psychic interests of the analyst – including sharings of their own personal past – deep subjectivity strikes the analyst, upon reflection, as mysterious.

Although such deep subjectivity will contribute to the network of the unconscious, thoughts arising will soon link with related mental phenomena to weave further areas of unconscious perception, as patient and analyst build unconscious matrices for work with one another. Neither may consciously grasp their formal effect on each other, but each will know something about the other, although this will have been deeply unconscious and procedurally conveyed. Remembering that our argument is that form is the work of the ego, the patient will have worked their analyst into experiencing them even if they cannot consciously think them.

It is not difficult to see how the Freudian project evokes far more than it can solve and it is understandable that psychoanalysts tend to write about what they know and how they can work with their patients. In this book we have isolated at least eight differing forms of unconscious presentation: the logic revealed through the sequence of freely associated thoughts; the sprung latent material released by the psychoanalyst's evocative request for association that displaces any material into a future with no boundary; the conjuring of lost memories evoked by cracking open single images or words that reveal hidden preoccupations; the masked ball of the self's inner object relations dramatised in narrative objects; the transference of parts of the self or its early environment into the psychoanalyst who unconsciously takes on their characteristics; the language of emotion born in body and voice announcing the self state; the creation of intermediate objects in the potential space between analyst and patient; and finally the movement of the patient's idiom expressed through the activation of elements of the analyst's personality: the work of form.

Given that each of these orders of presentation and representation are ever-present, the mental density of any single psychoanalytical hour is beyond integrative thinking. In their reverie the analyst submits to the total movement of these differing orders, now and then arriving at some point of insight as the logic of free associations reveals a line of thought broken up by new associations arriving out of a different past, suggesting new, future meanings not yet realised. The theatre of the objects reveals allegoric personifications, strangely intense figurations of ideation and affect shaping the analyst's inner sense. The compelling organisation of emotions sets the mentality of an hour, and objects created by patient and analyst (for example, certain metaphors or interpretations) become part of the bricolage of this local culture.

Even though the analysand's use of their analyst is the deepest of unconscious communications, the transmission of one's idiom conveyed through orchestration of the other's subjectivity, shall remain a mystery. The people, places, events, legends and emotions reported by the analysand take on a new life in an analysis; uprooted from their origins, like those objects in the paintings of de Kooning, these objects are 'dissociated from their sources in nature', and like 'organic shapes carry emotional charges of the same order as numbers, mathematical signs, letters of the alphabet' (1982: 115). Each of these objects springs small constellations of emotion, memory, ideation wrapped in the fabric of association, and as Rosenberg says of de Kooning: 'the memory of a friend may be aroused by a pair of gloves or a telephone number, an erotic sensation by a curved line or an initial' (115) – the objects conveyed by the analysand in the compositional world termed psychoanalysis become a world unto themselves.

One finds in Rosenberg's description of de Kooning a metaphor fitting for psychoanalysis. De Kooning

> frees the shape that is a sign, from the stasis of both free-standing objects and symbolic systems into a new kind of psychodynamic composition...each of his forms enters as a separate integer of suggestion into complex interaction, at once formal and subjective.
>
> (116)

To this 'continuous effect' de Kooning gave the term 'slipping glimpses'. This description also makes sense in the different realm of psychoanalysis, as the analyst – recipient of the analysand's 'continuous effect' – glimpses the patient's unconscious. The work of psychoanalysis is a composition, both participants producing material for the analysis, each re-working it, giving it new shape and meaning.

I think of Robert Duncan's use of the salmon's quest as a metaphor for the work of poetry in 'Poetry, a Natural Thing'. 'The poem / feeds upon thought, feeling, impulse, / to breed itself/a spiritual urgency at the dark ladders leaping'. So too does the work of analysis derive nourishment from the movement of a self's form drive, which constitutes its spiritual urgency.

And what of this work? What does it accomplish?

It relieves suffering. The analysand knows almost immediately that this is the place in which a self is permitted its illness, and fortunately, a structure is presented that is analysable and available for working through.

But it does more than this.

It provides a new form of pleasure and a new skill, which we might call the playing of the unconscious. Patient and analyst repeatedly abandon themselves to unconscious forms of perception, reception, creativity and communication. After a year, an analysis may deepen in ways that are striking to both participants. Well into a fictional world every bit as dense as a Dostoevsky novel, they are partly-aware beneficiaries of a radical new human skill: intentionally arranged for unconscious communication. Whatever their doubts about such possibilities to begin with, in time both are humbled by the waves of realisation that this work, though mediated by conscious deliberative thought, originates in a place out of sight and out of mind, but forever streaming into consciousness.

'What we can absolutely demand of an analyst is a knowledge of what speaking means', writes Serge Leclaire, 'what decisive shadows words can hide, and how they can show the subject crossing their web' (1996: 52). To see this crossing the analyst must listen to the analysand from a 'gap through which speaking and desiring are constantly reborn', and it is here in this very particular space, that the analyst can envision the 'particular mode of' the analysand's 'hold in the order of words, the singular ordering of his connection with the silences of the first object'. The analyst must remain within this gap, keeping it 'open', keeping it 'alive, like a desire' (53). 'The analyst's attention, floating like a spirit above the waters', he adds, 'is first of all openness to the transparency of words, their shadowy roots as well as their fruits of light' (62).

Helen Vendler, the literary critic, argues the fundamental difference between self and soul and the novel and the lyric. A self bears its history, lives in social space, and thrives as a personage in the novel which presents selves in social relationship. Soul lives in the form of the lyric poem, a 'congeries of forces', each word saturated with a 'long history, each word appears as a "character" heavy with motivation, desire, and import'. When these 'characters' are bound by the 'force of syntax, sound, and rhythm' they are 'subjected to what, in a novel or play, we would call "fate" ' , although interestingly, she then writes of the 'destiny' of the words in the lyric being as 'complex as the destinies of human beings in life' (1995: 6). The novel works from the perspective of the social self and mirrors itself in a discourse which we recognise as the form of convention, in being a self and in being a relater. What does the lyric mirror?

The characteristics of lyric, argues Vendler, namely compression, apparent spontaneity, vivid and compelling rhythm, the 'binding of sense by sound', 'a structure which enacts the experience represented, an abstraction from the heterogeneity of life, a dynamic play of semiotic and rhythmic', give 'a voice to the "soul" ', the moment when the self is suspended from its social order and by itself, when 'its socially constructed characteristics' are 'in abeyance' (6–7). In the poets she admires there is 'idiosyncrasy rather than typicality', or what she calls 'the compelling aesthetic signature of each' (7).

What Rosenberg says of de Kooning, Leclaire of the psychoanalyst, and Vendler of the lyric poet, is evocative description, a conjuring of the nominated. Confronted with the impossible task of describing the mystery of things unconscious, these authors defy this fact and write anyway.

What things?

The things that live as effects, in the subjects who cultivate them, in the objects presumed to contain them, in the receivers assumed to know them not for what they are, but the familiar movement of the 'are not'. Not the themes of life, the plots of the novel, the urgent reports of the analysand, but the forms of life.

What mystery?

An unanswerable, perhaps presiding question. What is the intelligence that moves through the mind to create its objects, to shape its inscapes, to word itself, to gather moods, to effect the other's arriving ideas, to...to...to?

If there is a God this is where it lives, a mystery working itself through the materials of life, giving us shape and passing us on to others.

NOTES

3 THE NECESSARY DESTRUCTIONS OF PSYCHOANALYSIS

1 By 'psychic genera' I mean a form of unconscious organisation of daily life that generates human creativity. For a discussion of this rather odd phrase, please see my essay 'Psychic Genera' in *Being a Character*.

4 FIGURES AND THEIR FUNCTIONS

1 Arguably no one in the psychoanalytic movement is truly outside tribal thought and this author is certainly aware of the part he has played in intellectual territorialism.

2 Although I suppose we shall never know, I would not be surprised if detailed sessional reports of the way of working of these two remarkable psychoanalytical thinkers and clinicians would reveal each of them 'crossing over' and working in the manner of the presumed opposite.

3 Masud Khan would term this 'the experiencing of one's being' (see 'Vicissitudes of being, knowing, and experiencing in the therapeutic situation' in *The Privacy of the Self*, 1974: 203–18). Such inner evolutions, in which the patient feels the unconscious logic of his own existence – even if he cannot grasp it in consciousness – constitute an important part of the deep work of an analysis and such silences are not to be confused with resistance when the patient is remaining silent in order to stop the flow of association or to conceal a particular mental content.

4 Of course this is what Lacan meant by the symbolic order which as a self experience opens any person out into an infinite chain of signifiers that immediately link the subject to networks of meaning well beyond the nuclear moment that sponsored the utterance in the first place. Psychoanalysis has quite rightly looked back to find the link between the networks of signifiers and the originating moment – as this is the more immediately meaningful search for a patient – but at the same time, birth of the subject through his utterance means that speech also delivers the subject into other worlds to which he ultimately may travel. This is less a sublimation – of the original contents – than it is a directional force: each utterance points to future utterances and interests that emerge out of it.

5 Readers will at some point rightly ask 'how does any of this apply to the borderline patient?', or to the schizophrenic, or to the...and one could add many another patient. Any book of this kind cannot address the many different

variations on the above, although the family of authors described above all have a place in the analysis of any patient regardless of diagnostic type.

6 See Roy Schafer, 'The analytic attitude: an introduction' in *The Analytic Attitude*, 1983: 3–13.

7 By vivid ideas I mean those inner associations – which might very well be evoked by actual objects in ordinary everyday life – that arise saturated with feeling, memory potential, and porous to instinctual derivatives.

8 When an analyst makes an inspired interpretation – collecting together disparate elements for the first time – they actually bear psychic change in their comment. If the patient tolerates the interpretation and proceeds to work on it, such a working through constitutes the patient's introjection of a truth that will in itself be the catalyst of change. Inspired interpretations are usually the outcome of unconscious collaboration between patient and analyst and announce the arrival of the nascent psychic structure that is addressed in the content (see Bollas, 'Psychic genera' in *Being a Character*, 1992: 66–100).

9 These orders do not in fact reflect the patient's mother or father so much as they express a part of the subject who has come to use these orders to constitute important forms of experiencing and knowing.

6 THE GOALS OF PSYCHOANALYSIS?

1 However, this is very likely the character of the course of ideas in any field of thought. Nonetheless, as this is a violent course it should be of some interest to psychoanalysis, which aims to make irrational mental processes available to consciousness and potential change.

2 It will be appreciated that when the analysand puts 'himself in the position' to free associate he enters a new form for thinking and speaking, as discussed in Chapter 12.

3 For many reasons many differing patients seem deficient in the ability to free associate, but it is unlikely that these difficulties are total. All persons who talk in an unstructured situation will eventually find their narratives breaking up under the force of unconscious ideas.

8 MENTAL INTERFERENCE

1 The ego can symbolise a need by using an object as if it were another object, in this case using me in a sense as if I were the mother. Ego symbolisations such as this take place frequently in any person's life and express the symbolic through use of the object rather than substitution of the object. A thing does not stand in the place of another thing: the use of the thing changes the meaning of the thing.

2 See Clifford Scott, 'Self-envy and envy of dreams and dreaming', *The International Review of Psycho-Analysis* 2 (3): 333–7, 1975.

9 DEAD MOTHER, DEAD CHILD

1 Please see 'The structure of evil' in *Being a Character*, Bollas (1992).

10 BORDERLINE DESIRE

1 See Steiner (1993) *Psychic Retreats*.

2 Kristeva (1987) argues that the depressive's affect is the evocation less of an object, than of *the thing*, a conjuring of the real.

BIBLIOGRAPHY

Abrams, M.H. (1971) *Natural Supernaturalism*. New York: W W Norton & Company.

Arendt, Hannah (1958) *The Life of the Mind*. Chicago: University of Chicago Press.

Bacon, Francis (1953) 'Catalogue'. London: Tate Gallery.

Bacon, Francis 'Statements, 1952–1955', in Herschel B. Chipp, *Theories of Modern Art* (1968). Berkeley: University of California Press, 620.

—— (1963) 'Interview', in Chipp 622.

Balint, Michael (1968) *The Basic Fault*. London: Tavistock, 1968.

Barratt, Barnaby (1993) *Psychoanalysis and the Postmodern Impulse*. Baltimore: Johns Hopkins University Press.

Blanchot, Maurice (1969) *The Infinite Conversation*. Minneapolis: University of Minnesota Press, 1993.

Bloch, Ernst (1974) *Essays on the Philosophy of Music*. London and New York, 1985.

Bollas, Christopher (1987) *Shadow of the Object*. New York: Columbia University Press.

—— (1992) *Being a Character*. London: Routledge.

—— (1996) 'Figures and their functions: on the Oedipal structure of a psychoanalysis'. *The Psychoanalytic Quarterly* 65, 1–20.

Breton, André (1934) 'What is Surrealism?', in Chipp 410–17.

Caws, Mary Ann (1996) *What Art Holds*. New York: Columbia University Press.

Corrigan, Edward and Gordon, Pearl-Ellen (1995) *The Mind Object*. New York: Jason Aronson.

Dali, Salvador (1934). In André Breton. 'What is Surrealism?', in Herschel B. Chipp, Theories of Modern Art (1968). Berkeley: University of California Press, 410–17.

Dante (1292–94) *La Vita Nuova*. Bloomington: Indiana University Press, 1962.

Ehrenzweig, Anton (1967) *The Hidden Order of Art*. Berkeley: University of California Press, 1971.

Ellman, Richard and O'Clair, Robert (1973) *The Norton Anthology of Modern Poetry*. New York: W W Norton & Company.

Epel, Naomi (ed.) (1994) *Writers Dreaming*. New York: Vintage Books.

Erikson, Erik (1968) *Identity*. London: Faber.

Ferenczi, Sandor and Rank, Otto (1923) *The Development of Psycho-Analysis*. Madison: International Universities Press, 1986.

Freud, Sigmund (1905d) 'Fragment of an analysis of a case of hysteria' (also known as 'Dora'). *Standard Edition* 7, 3–122.

—— (1909d) 'Notes upon a case of obsessional neurosis'. *Standard Edition* 10, 3–149.

—— (1911b) 'Formulation on the two principles of mental functioning'. *Standard Edition* 12, 215–26.

—— (1913c) 'On beginning the treatment'. *Standard Edition* 12, 123–44.

—— (1920g) 'Beyond The Pleasure Principle'. *Standard Edition* 18, 3–64.

—— (1923a) 'Two Encyclopaedia Articles'. *Standard Edition* 18, 235–59.

—— (1924f) 'A short account of psycho-analysis'. *Standard Edition* 19, 191–209.

—— (1927c) 'The Future of an Illusion'. *Standard Edition* 21, 3–56.

—— (1930a) 'Civilisation and its Discontents'. *Standard Edition* 21, 59–145.

—— (1933b) 'Why War?' *Standard Edition* 22, 197–215.

—— (1940a) 'An outline of psycho-analysis'. *Standard Edition* 23, 141–207.

—— (1985) *The Complete Letters of Sigmund Freud to Wilhelm Fliess 1887–1904*. Jeffrey Masson (ed.), Cambridge and London: Harvard University Press.

Gass, William (1996) *Finding a Form*. New York: Knopf.

Gibbons, Reginald (ed.) (1979) *The Poet's Work*. Chicago: University of Chicago Press.

Giovacchini, Peter (1979) *Treatment of Primitive Mental States*. New York and London: Jason Aronson.

Green, Andre (1977) 'Conceptions of affect'. In *On Private Madness*. London: Hogarth Press, 1986, 174–213.

—— (1983) 'The dead mother'. In *On Private Madness*. London, 1986, 142–73.

—— (1993) *Le Travail du Negatif*. Paris: Editions de Minuit.

—— (1997) 'What kind of research for psychoanalysis?' *International Journal of Psychoanalysis* 5(1), 10–14.

Heimann, Paula (1956) 'Dynamics of transference interpretation'. In *About Children and Children-No-Longer*. London: Routledge, 108–21.

Irigaray, Luce (1987) *Sexes and Genealogies*. New York: Columbia University Press, 1993.

Kahane, Clare (1995) *Passions of the Voice*. Baltimore: Johns Hopkins University Press.

Khan, M. Masud (1974) *The Privacy of the Self*. London: Hogarth Press.

—— (1988) *When Spring Comes*. London: Chatto and Windus.

Klauber, John (1987) 'The role of illusion in the psychoanalytic cure'. In *Illusion and spontaneity in psychoanalysis*. London: Free Association Books, 1–12.

Klein, Melanie (1961) *Narrative of a Child Analysis*. London: Delacorte Press, 1975.

—— (1975) *The Psycho-Analysis of Children*. London: Free Press.

Kohut, Heinz (1984) *How Does Analysis Cure?*. Chicago: University of Chicago Press.

Kooning, Willem de (1982) 'Painting is a way'. In Harold Rosenberg, *The Anxious Object*. Chicago: Chicago University Press.

Kris, Anton (1982) *Free Association*. New Haven: Analytic Press.

Kristeva, Julia (1987) *Black Sun*. New York: Columbia University Press, 1989.

Laplanche, Jean (1986) 'Psychoanalysis as anti-hermeneutics'. *Radical Philosophy* 79, September/October, 7–12.

—— (1992) *Seduction, Translation, Drives*. London: The Institute of Contemporary Arts.

Leclaire, Serge (1995–6) 'Sygne, or transference love'. *Journal of European Psychoanalysis* 2, Fall–Winter, 51–62.

Lichtenstein, Heinz (1961) 'Identity and sexuality'. In *The Dilemma of Human Identity*. New York: Jason Aronson, 1977, 49–122.

Marcel, Gabriel (1968) *Tragic Wisdom and Beyond*. Evanston: Northwestern University Press, 1973.

Melville, Herman (1851) *Moby Dick*. New York, 1967.

Milner, Marion (1952) 'The role of illusion in symbol formation'. In *The Suppressed Madness of Sane Men*. London: Routledge, 1987, 83–113.

—— (1969) *The Hands of the Living God*. London: Hogarth Press.

—— (1977) 'Winnicott and overlapping circles'. In *The Suppressed Madness of Sane Men*. London: Routledge, 1987, 279–286.

Milosz, C. (1979) 'Ars poetica?' In Reginald Gibbons, *The Poet's Work*. Chicago: Chicago University Press, 3–4.

Olney, James (ed.) (1980) *Autobiography*. Princeton: University Press.

Olson, Charles (1997) *The Collected Poems*. Berkeley: University of California Press.

Pontalis, J.-B. (1981) *Frontiers in Psychoanalysis*. London: Hogarth Press.

Richter, Gerhard (1995) *The Daily Practice of Painting*. Cambridge: MIT Press.

Rickman, John (1950) 'The factors of numbers in individual and group dynamics'. In *Selected Contributions to Psycho-Analysis*. London: Hogarth Press, 1957.

Rosenberg, Harold (1982) *The Anxious Object*. Chicago: Chicago University Press.

Rycroft, Charles (1986) *Imagination and Reality*. New York: H. Karnac.

Sandler, Joseph and Dreher, Ursula (1996) *What Do Psychoanalysts Want?*. London: Routledge.

Schafer, Roy (1983) *The Analytic Attitude*. London: Basic Books.

Scott, Clifford (1975) 'Self-envy and envy of dreams and dreaming'. *The International Review of Psycho-Analysis* 2, part three, 333–7.

Schoenberg, Arnold and Kandinsky, Wassily (1984) *Arnold Schoenberg, Wassily Kandinsky: Letters, Pictures, Documents*. London and Boston: Faber and Faber.

Searles, Harold (1979) *Countertransference*. New York.

—— (1986) *My Work With Borderline Patients*. Northvale and London: Jason Aronson.

Steiner, John (1993) *Psychic Retreats*. London: Routledge.

Stevens, W. (1979) 'The irrational element in poetry'. In Reginald Gibbons, *The Poet's Work*. Chicago: Chicago University Press, 48–58.

Stravinsky, Igor (1942) *Poetics of Music*. Cambridge: Harvard University Press.

Valéry, P. (1979) 'A Poet's Notebook'. In Reginald Gibbons, *The Poet's Work*. Chicago: Chicago University Press, 170–83.

Vendler, Helen (1995) *Soul Says*. New York: Belknap Press.

Winnicott, D.W. (1958) 'The observation of children in a set situation'. In *Through Pediatrics To Psycho-Analysis*. London: Hogarth Press, 52–69.

—— (1971) 'The Use of an Object and Relating through Identification'. In *Playing and Reality*. Harmondsworht: Penguin, 1974.

Wordsworth, William (1959) 'The Prelude'. In Ernest de Selincourt (ed.) *Wordsworth's Prelude*. Oxford and London: Oxford University Press.

Wright, Ken (1991) *Vision and Separation*. London: Free Association Books.

INDEX